AZTEC THOUGHT AND CULTURE
A Study of the Ancient Nahuatl Mind

THE CIVILIZATION OF THE AMERICAN INDIAN SERIES

AZTEC THOUGHT AND CULTURE

A Study of
the Ancient Nahuatl Mind

By Miguel León-Portilla

Translated from the Spanish
by Jack Emory Davis

UNIVERSITY OF OKLAHOMA PRESS : NORMAN

By Miguel León-Portilla

La Filosofía Náhuatl (Mexico City, 1956, 1959)

Ritos, Sacerdotes y Atavíos de los Dioses (Mexico City, 1958)

Siete Ensayos sobre Cultura Náhuatl (Mexico City, 1958)

Visión de los Vencidos, Relaciones Indígenas de la Conquista (Mexico City, 1959)

Aztec Thought and Culture: A Study of the Ancient Nahuatl Mind, translated by Jack Emory Davis (Norman, 1963)

Pre-Columbian Literatures of Mexico, translated by Grace Lobanov and the author (Norman, 1969)

LIBRARY OF CONGRESS CATALOG CARD NUMBER: 63–11019
ISBN: 0–8061–0569–0 (cloth)
ISBN: 0–8061–2295–1 (pbk.)

Aztec Thought and Culture: A Study of the Ancient Nahuatl Mind is Volume 67 in The Civilization of the American Indian Series.

10   11   12   13   14   15   16   17

Contents

Illustrations

Preface
to the
Paperback Edition

T HE conception and writing of this book on the world view and thought of the ancient Mexicans was based on the assumption of the existence of reliable indigenous sources. Some recent writers questioned the validity of some, if not all, of the native sources on which I, as well as other colleagues, have drawn in our respective researches. It is argued that the available testimonies in Nahuatl are at best late-alphabetical renditions of texts composed to be chanted or solemnly pronounced, or in some circumstances recited, following the contents of the ancient pictoglyphic books. Those texts, deprived of their original form of transmission, are felt to lose much of their meaning. Further, the fact that many of the texts were collected by the Spanish missionaries or their catechized native assistants makes them even more suspicious, as these collectors were likely subject to various kinds of Euro-Christian influence.[1]

---

[1] See Serge Gruzinski, *La Colonization de l'imaginaire, Societés indigenes et occidentalization dans le Mexique espagnol XVIe–XVIIIe siècles* (Paris: Gallimard, 1988), 51–76; and Louise M. Burkhart, *The Slippery Earth, Nahua-Christian Moral Dialogue in Sixteenth-Century Mexico* (Tucson: The University of Arizona Press, 1989), 5.

In view of these and similar objections, I deem it pertinent to devote this preface to a sort of *apologia fontium,* a critical defense of the questioned sources. I will not enter into an analysis of each one of the indigenous sources on which this book has been structured. An evaluation of them is provided by the book itself. Rather, I will consider the major themes discussed in the book, essential to the ancient Nahuatl world view and thought. Besides the nature and origin of the sources, I will discuss their parallels with testimonies of various kinds from other Nahuatl or Mesoamerican regions, including some cases of contemporary survival. Such external evidence is sought in order to detect whether the adduced sources are or are not threads belonging to one and the same complex indigenous weaving.

Let us consider first the appearance of questions discussed in chapter 1, those addressed to one's own heart (*ninoyolnonotza,* "I address myself to my heart"), concerning human destiny on earth and in the beyond; the fugacity of life; the possibility of pronouncing true words and performing rightful actions. Most of the Nahuatl texts that convey such anguished doubt and moral concern derive from the "Collection of Mexican Songs," preserved in Nahuatl in linear alphabetical script, dating from the second half of the sixteenth century (now housed in the National Library of Mexico). Can we say that these expressions of moral concern and recurrent anguish about one's destiny on earth and the beyond fit into what is known, through other independent indigenous sources, to be the spiritual preoccupations of the sages, "the elders," the priests?

Examples exist of the *tonalamatl,* "books of the destinies" (the pre-Hispanic codices *Borgia, Vaticanus B, Cospi, Fejérváry-Mayer,* and *Laud,* as well as several others of the early colonial period), which give testimony to a constant preoccupation with one's own destiny. Also, some "readings" of the contents of such pictoglyphic books of the destinies are available in the compilations of Bernardino de Sahagún (*Madrid* and *Florentine* codices) and of other friars such as Diego Durán in his *History of the Indians of New Spain.* In them, one can perceive a continuous, anxious searching to unveil the destiny in the life of individuals and the community.

And there are other texts in Nahuatl, also in alphabetical writing, that can shed light on this matter. One is the manuscript curiously entitled "Romances de los Señores de la Nueva España," preserved at the Latin American Collection of the University of Texas Library in Austin. In it, several compositions correspond, with slight variations, to those in the "Collection of Mexican Songs." In both manuscripts a few composers are introduced by their names, like the famous Nezahualcóyotl of Tezcoco, Cuacuauhtzin of Tepechpan, and Aquiauhtzin of Ayapanco. We know about them and their reputations as composers of songs from other independent indigenous sources as the *Annals of Cuauhtitlán*, the pictoglyphic books *Codex Xolotl* and *Mapa de Tepechpan*, the *Relaciones* by the chronicler Chimalpahin, and the *Historia* of Alva Ixtlilxóchitl.

As to the ideas about the fugacity of life and other moral concerns expressed in those compositions, it can also be asserted that they have parallels in several *huehuehtlahtolli,* testimonies of "The Ancient Word," which have been independently collected and transcribed.[2]

The temporal and spatial image of the universe discussed in chapter 2 of this book is another theme essential to the Nahuatl world view. The relatively large number of written Nahuatl sources on this subject can be contrasted with the contents of several "pages" of some extant pre-Hispanic pictoglyphic books. The concept of the horizontal universe has two extraordinary delineations (accompanied by glyphs) in *Codex Fejérváry-Mayer* (page 1) and in the Maya *Tro-Cortesiano* (pages 75–76). Concerning vertical space, the Nahuatl text of the *Florentine Codex*

[2]Olmos, as his contemporary Alonso de Zorita declares, knew how "the principal Indians preserve them [those texts] in their painted books . . . ," and adds that, "he asked them to commit them to writing . . . and that they did it so, without his being present, and took the texts from their paintings which are like their own script, and they understand themselves very well by means of them, and that nothing was changed but a division of paragraphs was introduced . . ." See Alonso de Zorita, *Breve y Sumaria Relación* (Mexico: National University, 1948), 112–13.

(book III, fol. 25 r.-v) appears as a "reading" of page 1-v. of the early colonial *Codex Vaticanus A*. Images in two Mixtec codices, the *Selden Roll* and *Gómez de Orozco*, represent with slight variations the same conception of the upper strata above the surface of the earth.

Concerning the conception of time and the cosmic ages, besides the many texts in Nahuatl, Yucatec Maya, and Quiché, one has the corpus of pre-Hispanic testimonies related to the Mesoamerican calendar. The cosmic and daily cycles were computed and man's and the world's fates investigated in terms of this calendar. In regards to the cosmic cycles or "solar ages," there is one text in particular included in *Codex Chimalpopoca*, the so-called "Legend of the Suns," that merits special attention. Comparing it with the delineations of the cosmic ages that appear in pages 4–7 of *Codex Vaticanus A* and with an early text transcribed in Spanish around 1536, "History of the Mexicans through their Paintings," one can perceive that such Nahuatl text is a "reading" of a pictoglyphic book.[3] Evidence for this is provided by the many instances in which expressions such as "here is," "here one sees . . . ," introduce parts of the text. Such comparison permits an evaluation of the close relationship between the pictoglyphic productions and their "readings," later converted to alphabetical writing. This also can be achieved in the case of several historical texts in Nahuatl that are derived from "readings" performed by native sages of pictoglyphic manuscripts.[4]

Further support of the authenticity of the Nahuatl texts that describe the spatial-temporal image of the universe is provided by other narratives proceeding from faraway Mesoamerican re-

[3] Mercedes de la Garza, "Análisis comparativo de la *Historia de los mexicanos por sus pinturas* y la *Leyenda de los Soles*," in *Estudios de Cultura Náhuatl* (Mexico: National University, 1983), vol. 16, 123–34.

[4] Edward E. Calnek, "The Analysis of pre-Hispanic Central Mexican Historical Texts," in *Estudios de Cultura Náhuatl* (Mexico: National University, 1978), vol. 13, 239–66.

gions: texts in Yucatec Maya in several *Chilam Balam* books, *The Ritual of the Bacabs,* and the renowned *Popol Vuh* of the Quiché. It can certainly be stated that the adduced Nahuatl texts "fit in" as variant threads of a more ample and rich weaving, that of Mesoamerican culture.

The conception of the divine as a dual reality, discussed in chapter 3, is also an essential part of the ancient world view and thought of the Nahuas. The supreme Dual God, *Ometéotl,* manifests him/herself through his/her "children," the other gods. Here also the contents of the adduced texts present striking coincidences with a variety of other independent Mesoamerican sources.

Several *huehuehtlahtolli* of at least three different original provenances (preserved in Florence and Mexico, as well as in Austin, Texas, Washington, D.C., and Berkeley, California) are replete with allusions to the supreme Dual God and his/her attributes. Pictographic delineations related to him/her are found in codices of pre-Hispanic origin, such as the *Borgia, Vaticanus B,* and *Fejérváry-Mayer,* and of early colonial fabrication, such as the *Vaticanus A,* or the pre-Hispanic Mixtec *Vindobonensis,* in addition to the *Selden Roll* and *Gómez de Orozco.* In some Nahuatl sacred hymns (in the *Florentine Codex*), other songs (Collection of Mexican Songs), and the *Historia Tolteca Chichimeca* (a manuscript that is a mixture of alphabetical and pictoglyphic renditions from the area of Cuauhtinchan, Puebla), invocations are found that shed light on the attributes and other titles of the same supreme Dual God. Parallel references can be identified in the *Popol Vuh* and the *Chilam Balam* books.

As to conceptions related more directly to humans and their origin, destiny, and sustenance on earth, which are discussed in chapters 4 and 5 of this book, I will restrict my comments to two points. One is the concept of "face, heart" (*ixtli, yollotl*), understood as parallel to that of "person." The relative abundance of texts in which these two words are expressed permits a glimpse of at least something of the complexity of their connotations.

Another source of evidence concerning the richness of connotations of "face, heart," is provided by the Nahuatl vocabulary itself, in which hundreds of compound words are found, including the *ix(tli)* and *yol(lotl)* roots.

One last theme—the rediscovery of human sustenance on earth—although briefly discussed in this book, calls for attention, as it is documented with variants surviving to the present among different Nahua groups. The human body, according to several Nahuatl and Maya texts, was formed of maize. This cereal, among its many names, had that of *tonacayotl*, a linguistically absolutized form of *to-nacayo*, "our flesh." In some of the texts that describe the cosmic ages, references are made to a sort of evolutionary process that ended in the appearance of maize as we know it today.

Maize, as well as the "precious bones" (*chalchiuhomitl*) of people who existed in a previous cosmic age, had to be rescued by the gods, whose mission was to restore life on the earth. As stated in several other Nahua and Maya texts, the gods were in need of humans in order to be nourished by the precious, vital water that is blood. The ancient narrative of Quetzalcóatl's two trips to the Land of the Dead and the Mountain of Our Sustenance, in search of the precious bones and of the grains of maize, has survived with slight changes among a rather large number of Mesoamerican people. Transcriptions of the contemporary narrative in different Mesoamerican languages (Maya, Tzeltal, Tzotzil, Nahua-Pipil) have been published.[5] Such contemporary survivals, variant renderings of the ancient word, are another evidence of the authenticity of those texts that in the sixteenth century became "converted" to linear alphabetical writing.

These survivals, and the many parallels in other sources derived from the ancient oral tradition and/or pictoglyphic books, the convergent testimonies from other Mesoamerican regions demonstrate that—notwithstanding possible, and at times real

---

[5] Several texts in those languages concerning this and other themes closely related to the Nahuatl world view have been included in *Tlalocan* (eleven volumes up to 1989), currently published by the National University of Mexico.

and detectable, influences of Euro-Christian origin—there exist sources in Nahuatl for the world view and thought of the ancient Mexicans. To give two further instances, compositions like the twenty hymns to the gods in the *Madrid* and *Florentine* codices and several *huehuehtlahtolli,* such as those impetrative orations addressed to Tezcatlipoca and Tlaloc or the admonitory discourses to the young boys and girls, can be safely taken as faithful testimonies of the ancient culture.

The Nahuatl language itself, in which most of these songs and narratives are transmitted, is indicative of their origin. It is rich in complex reverential forms and other unmistakable stylistic features, such as its *difrasisms,* or parallel sentences, and its recurrent metaphors, some of them with couples of words—kinds of kennings—oblique conveyors of subtle meanings.[6] The polysemous nature of many of the expressions, esoteric, sacred, or magic, at times of very difficult comprehension, allow one to perceive through their obscure connotations their distinct origin, the threads of weaving centuries in the making. Sacred orality, "professional orality," was closely linked to the pictoglyphic contents of the ancient books. Those who, after the Spanish conquest, worked to rescue the memory of the indigenous past—friars and Indians—knew this fact. They recorded all they could of the distinct language of the elders, keeping an eye, whenever it was possible, on the contents of the pictoglyphic books.

Reversing the process, we can contrast today the extant sources alphabetically rendered in Nahuatl with what is discernible in the paintings and the glyphs of the few remaining pre-Hispanic codices, in some stone carvings and inscriptions, and in the more abundant codices that continued to be produced after the Conquest. Besides the comparison of independently made transcriptions of the same or parallel texts, these tangible testimonies—the codices and other inscriptions—make feasible a most valuable hermeneutic procedure to detect which of the

[6]On the stylistics of the Nahuatl expression, see Miguel León-Portilla, "Cuicatl y Tlahtolli, las Formas de Expresión en Náhuatl," in *Estudios de Cultura Náhuatl* (Mexico: National University, 1983), vol. 16, 13–108.

alphabetically transcribed Nahuatl texts can be accepted as threads belonging to the Mesoamerican cultural weaving, and to what degree. This is the procedure I have followed in this book, which now leads me to reassert the existence of reliable indigenous sources for the study of the ancient Nahuatl thought and world view.

MIGUEL LEÓN-PORTILLA

Paris, France
Mexican Delegation to Unesco

Preface
to the
First Edition

FOR at least two millennia, and possibly more, before the advent of the Spaniards in 1519, Mexico supported a flourishing civilization that produced institutions of an exceedingly high order. During this long period of alternating creative activity and stagnation typical of maturing civilizations, a cultural evolution took place which saw the development of ceramics, sculpture, architecture, mural painting, writing and chronology, complex religious doctrines, systems of education, and diverse political, religious, and social organizations.

There is no better way to discover the essence of these institutions than through the history of ideas. What constituted the intellectual evolution? What were the principal ideas that the wise men conceived regarding man, the world, and God?

The answers to these questions, fundamental to the comprehension of any culture, are to be found in the rich documentation that exists concerning the people who inhabited the central region of Mexico in pre-Hispanic times. In addition to a small number of codices, or books of pictures, written before the Conquest and now preserved in a number of European libraries, there are thousands of folios in the Nahuatl or Aztec language written by natives after the Conquest. Adapting the Latin alphabet, which they had been taught by the missionary friars, to their native tongue, they recorded the poems, songs, chronicles, and traditions that they or their fathers had learned by rote before Spanish domination.

It is true that some of the humanistic friars had a hand in editing these documents—Fray Bernardino de Sahagún, for example, who employed a battery of scribes to record all that elderly Indian informants could tell him of what they remembered or had been told about their civilization. And while some of the information is probably inaccurate or incomplete—certain subjects not covered at all—because many of the native scholars had fled or been killed during the Conquest, the fact remains that from the thousands of folios extant the fundamental concepts of ancient Mexico can be derived.

The concepts presented and examined in this book are based on the literal translation of more than ninety native documents. They include conjectures on the origin of the universe and of life, the mystery of God, the possibility of comprehending what is beyond the realm of experience, free will, life after death, and the meaning of education, history, and art. The philosophy of the Nahuatl wise men, which probably stemmed from the ancient doctrines and traditions of the Teotihuacáns and Toltecs, quite often reveals profound intuition and in some instances is remarkably "modern." Nahuatl philosophy offers the present-day philosopher a unique opportunity to observe man—removed from all contact with the ancient civilizations of Africa, Asia, and Europe—in the role of creator of a way of thinking and of living.

Originally published in 1956, *La Filosofía Náhuatl* was revised in 1959 when a second edition was issued by the National University of Mexico. From the latter the Section of Foreign Publications of Moscow prepared a Russian translation in 1961 without the knowledge of the author. The present English edition is not a direct translation of the second edition in Spanish, but rather an adaptation and rewriting of the text.

Preface to the First Edition

A number of organizations and people have been concerned with this undertaking, which, for one reason or another, has stretched over more than three years. To the staff of the University of Oklahoma Press; Professor Jack Emory Davis, of the University of Arizona, who prepared the first and more literal translation of the book; Eliud Martínez, of the University of Texas; and Professor Fernando Horcasitas, Thelma Sullivan, and Grace Lobanov, I should like to express my deep appreciation for their invaluable co-operation.

MIGUEL LEÓN-PORTILLA

National University of Mexico

Pronunciation Note

THE AZTEC LANGUAGE, which is also known as Nahuatl or Mexican, has been spoken in Central Mexico, as well as in various parts of Central America, from Toltec times to the present.

Written Nahuatl, using the Latin alphabet, was introduced by the Spanish missionaries immediately after the Conquest. All the letters have the same phonetic value as in Spanish with the following exceptions:

(1) the *h* is pronounced with a soft aspiration as in English;

(2) the *tl* and *tz* represent a single sound and therefore should not be divided;

(3) the *x* has the sound of the English *sh*.

Practically all Nahuatl words are accented on the next to the last syllable. This is often indicated today by accents used according to rules of Spanish accentuation.

Introduction

Philosophy and Culture
in Ancient Mexico

AT the beginning of the sixteenth century, the ancient Mexicans—Aztecs, Texcocans, Cholulans, Chalcans, and Tlaxcaltecs—were people of diverse cultural interests and activities. Although they settled in the great Valley of Mexico and its environs at different periods, they were linked by a common language, Nahuatl, and inherited not only many of the traditions and ideas of the ancient Toltecs, but also something of their extraordinary creative spirit.

It must be borne in mind that the Aztecs, who, because of their military and economic splendor, tend to overshadow other Nahuatl groups, were not the only representatives of the Nahuatl-speaking world during the fifteenth and sixteenth centuries. For although the Aztecs had conquered many inhabitants of the area extending from the coast of the Gulf of Mexico to the Pacific Ocean and as far south as Chiapas and Guatemala, other Nahuatl peoples lived side by side with them and maintained varying degrees of independence. Some, like the Tlacopans and the Texcocans, the latter famous for the great poet-king Nezahualcóyotl, were allies of the Aztecs; others, like the Tlaxcaltecs and Huexotzincans, were enemies.

THE VALLEY OF MEXICO

Despite their differences, these ancient Mexicans shared the same cultural heritage, bequeathed them by the founders of Teotihuacán and Tula. Because of their cultural similarities and their common linguistic bond, Nahuatl—the lingua franca of Middle America—these groups will hereafter be referred to generically as the Nahuas, and their culture, as it flourished in the principal centers of the fifteenth- and sixteenth-century pre-Hispanic world, as the Nahuatl culture.

The expressions of art and culture in the great centers of the Nahuatl renaissance, Texcoco and Tenochtitlan, dazzled even the Spanish conquerors, who were, for the most part, a rough lot not usually impressed by aesthetic endeavor. The accounts of Hernán Cortés and Bernal Díaz testify to the amazement and admiration evoked by the marvelous stone buildings and great plaza of the city of Mexico. And the Spaniards were no less astonished by the rigorous religious, social, and military organization of the Nahuas.

Other less obvious aspects of the cultural life of the Nahuas escaped the attention of the conquerors and were discovered only by the first missionary friars. Impelled by their eagerness to know more about Nahuatl culture, Olmos, Motolinía, Sahagún, Durán, and Mendieta, principally, delved deeper and deeper until they uncovered that masterpiece of native genius, Nahuatl chronology. With its aid, they were able to interpret the great cosmological myths which formed the basis of Nahuatl philosophy and religion. By questioning the old people, they also brought to light—and recorded—songs with which the Nahuas honored their gods, discourses and orations, verdicts given by judges, and sayings and proverbs learned in their schools, the *Calmécac* and *Telpochcalli*. That enterprising cleric Fray Bernardino de Sahagún, devising a new method of historical investigation and utilizing the rich information gathered by Olmos and the first twelve friars who arrived in New Spain, ultimately was able to assemble hundreds of folios containing an enormous amount of material in the Nahuatl language. These folios he used as the documentary basis for his encyclopedic work on the Nahuas, the *Historia General de las Cosas de Nueva España*.

Later investigations added to the picture of the Nahuatl world presented by Sahagún. Juan de Torquemada, a Spanish friar and chronicler, managed to augment Sahagún's account in spite of his tedious digressions, while Juan Bautista Pomar and mestizo Fernando de Alva Ixtlilxóchitl described in detail the greatness of Texcoco. Diego Muñoz Camargo wrote a history of Tlaxcala, and Hernando Alvarado Tezozómoc traced, in his *Crónica Mexicana* and the *Crónica Mexicáyotl*, the glories of Mexico-Tenochtitlán. Alonso de Zurita, *oidor* of the royal *audiencia* of New Spain, gathered additonal data about the extraordinary system of justice and law which prevailed among the Nahuas. Don Francisco Hernández, physician to Philip II, supplemented Sahagún's work on ancient botany and medicine, while Father José de Acosta gathered interesting information on some of the characteristics and natural resources of the land inhabited by the Nahuas.[1]

While much that has been written about the Nahuas is based on what these early chroniclers and scholars have left us, modern archaeological investigations have added significant facts. As a result, we know that the Nahuas possessed a superb architecture, sculptural art, and pictograph manuscripts (usually called codices), an exact science of time (expressed in their two calendars), a complex religion, just but severe laws, organized commerce, an educational system, a knowledge of herbal medicine, and a powerful warrior class. Indeed, theirs was one of the few cultures of which, as Jacques Soustelle has expressed it, "mankind can be proud."[2] There remain, however, two aspects of Nahuatl culture which have been neglected all too long—literature and philosophy.

Primarily through the patient efforts of the distinguished Nahuatl scholar, Angel María Garibay K., we now have access to true literary works in the Nahuatl language. The manner by which these works have come to us in their own language and original form is described in detail in Garibay's book, *Historia de la Literatura Náhuatl*, a basic work and point of departure for all investigation of the subject.

There remains the matter of philosophical thought. Did the

[1] The Bibliography lists the complete titles of the works of the chroniclers and historians mentioned.

[2] Jacques Soustelle, *La Vie Quotidienne des Aztèques à la Veille de la Conquête Espagnole*, 275.

Nahuas concern themselves with the traditional problems of philosophy? Did they experience, in addition to a religious-mythical *Weltanschauung,* that human restlessness resulting from doubt and a sense of awe which gives rise to rational inquiry into the origin, essence, and destiny of man and the world?

Studies of the origin of Greek philosophy show that its history is but "the process of progressive conceptualization of the religious image of the world implicit in myths."[3] This does not mean that myth must disappear as philosophy develops, for, as Werner Jaeger writes, "authentic mythogony is still found at the core of the philosophy of Plato and in the Aristotelian concept of motion as the love of the world for the Unmoved Mover."[4]

Putting the question, then, in Jaeger's terms: Can the Nahuas be said to have begun, just prior to the Conquest, the process of progressive conceptualization of their mythical-religious image of the world? Had that restlessness of spirit, stemming from a sense of wonder and doubt, manifested itself in the rational inquiry into the nature of things which we call philosophy?

In the Nahuatl hymns and songs quoted by Garibay in his discussion of lyric and religious poetry, we can detect questions and ideas that profoundly concern man. As Irwin Edman has succinctly stated, "The poet is a commentator on life and existence; in his immediate and imaginative way, he is a philosopher."[5] Among the Nahuas, then, as among the Greeks, it was the lyric poets who first became aware of and enunciated the great problems of human existence.

If certain of the Nahuas were indeed aware of such problems as those related to the nature of the ultimate reality, then one might say that they had come upon the path of philosophical knowledge. To attribute to them a clear perception of the differences between the formal objectives of philosophy and other varieties of religious and scientific knowledge or artistic intuition would be an anachronism. Such a separation of fields of investi-

---

[3] Werner Jaeger, *Paideia,* los ideales de la cultura griega, I, 173.

[4] *Ibid.,* I, 172–73.

[5] Irwin Edman, *Arts and the Man,* 133.

gation is, in a strict sense, the work of modern Western thought. Neither the Ionian philosophers nor the Hindu wise men perceived it, nor did the medieval men of learning to whom philosophical, scientific, and even theological knowledge were parts of one whole.

Without expecting to find any radical differentiation in the various forms of Nahuatl knowledge, but prompted by the evidences of rational inquiry and intellectual restlessness found in the lyric as well as the religious poetry of the Nahuas, the author decided to search for more precise manifestations of what can rightly be called Nahuatl philosophical knowledge—on the same basis as that on which Aldous Huxley designated as authentic philosophy those writings expressing the most penetrating perceptions of the human mind.

> In Vedanta and Hebrew prophecy, in the Tao Teh King and the Platonic dialogues, in the Gospel according to St. John and Mahayana theology, in Plotinus and the Areopagite, among the Persian Sufis and the Christian mystics of the Middle Ages and the Renaissance—the Perennial Philosophy has spoken almost all the languages of Asia and Europe and has made use of the terminology and traditions of every one of the higher religions. But under all this confusion of tongues and myths, of local histories and particularist doctrines, there remains a Highest Common Factor, which is the Perennial Philosophy in what may be called its chemically pure state.[6]

If, in reality, that type of profoundly human philosophizing of which Huxley speaks existed also among the ancient Mexicans, their ideas undoubtedly will not be reconstructed on the basis of either pure hypothesis or pure fantasy. In such an intricate field as philosophy, although there is an abundance of texts, obscure interpretations are common. Therefore it would be puerile to launch an investigation without taking into consideration those original sources having genuine historical value. Search and research have proved that sources for the study of

---

[6] Aldous Huxley, *Introduction to the Song of God, Bhagavad-Gita*, 11–12.

Nahuatl thought do exist, and in the original language; they have provided rich material for this book.

In order to avoid any possible misunderstanding, it is necessary to emphasize the fact that these sources deal principally with the thinking of the Nahuas immediately prior to the Conquest. They reflect the various doctrines taught in the centers of higher education (the *Calmécac*) during the fifteenth and beginning of the sixteenth centuries. Any attempt to study the evolution of Nahuatl thought beginning with the Teotihuacán or Toltec periods would therefore be impeded by the limitations of the texts. If the annals and the archaeological monuments reveal more about their religion and history, with respect to purely abstract ideas and concerns they can do so only partially. Consequently, although many ideas and traditions from earlier periods are found in the texts consulted, a sound critical approach requires that definite assertions be made only where no doubt remains that the sources reflect the philosophical thinking current for at least forty or fifty years before the Conquest.

A treatment of the various Nahuatl sources for this study, with some discussion of their antiquity and value, and a historical presentation of the most important investigators of Nahuatl thought will be found in the appendices following the text.

AZTEC THOUGHT AND CULTURE
A Study of the Ancient Nahuatl Mind

I

The Birth of Philosophy among the Nahuas

THE religious world view of the Nahuas at the beginning of the sixteenth century is known today because of the work of such investigators as Eduard Seler, Alfonso Caso, Angel María Garibay K., and Justino Fernández. These scholars have reconstructed the Nahuatl *Weltanschauung* from direct sources, but with different points of view. Alfonso Caso, in particular, has recreated the essence of the Aztec concept of the universe, demonstrating that the various cosmic beliefs of the Nahuas revolved around the great solar myth which enthroned the Aztecs specifically as "the people of the Sun."

If the Nahuatl wise men had done nothing more than create and preserve a rich mythology, their thought could not be discussed as philosophy. For although myths and beliefs constitute the primary attempts to solve the mysteries of the universe, true philosophic development requires conscious and formal inquiry.

To establish a universally acceptable definition of philosophy would be a formidable task. Genuine philosophizing arises from the explicit perception that problems are innately involved in the essence of things. A sense of wonder and a mistrust of the solutions derived from tradition or custom are requisite to the formulation of rational questions about the origin, the true nature, and the destiny of man and the universe. The philosopher must experience the need to explain to himself why things happen as they do. He directs himself to the meaning and true value of things, seeking the *truth* about life and life after death, even speculating on the possibility of knowing anything at all of that afterlife where myths and beliefs find their final answers.

Is there, then, proof that such an attitude actually existed among the Nahuas? Were there men who began to look skeptically upon the myths and to try to rationalize them by formulating questions in abstract and universal terms about man and the world? The Nahuatl documents discussed in Appendix I give an affirmative answer. These documents speak for themselves, but, in spite of every attempt at accuracy and fidelity to the original texts, the translations can hardly express the conciseness and subtle shades of meaning characteristic of Nahuatl. An analysis of various compound words for which only the roots are given in the Nahuatl dictionaries of Molina and Rémi Simeón illustrates this elusive quality. Nahuatl, like Greek or German, is replete with long compound forms juxtaposing various roots, prefixes, suffixes, and infixes. Since a complex conceptual relation can thus be expressed in one word, the Nahuatl idiom often becomes a marvel of "linguistic engineering."[1] Nahuatl is, therefore, adequate for the expression of philosophical thought.

The Nahuas first expressed their doubts in the form of short poems. These poems, along with religious songs and epic and erotic poetry, are among the documents in the pre-Columbian collection of Mexican songs of the National Library of Mexico and in certain other collections.

A poem attributed to the famous Nezahualcóyotl questions the possibility of finding satisfaction in earthly things:

What does your mind seek?

---

[1] For further discussion of the philosophical implications embodied in the Nahuatl language, see Agustín de la Rosa, *Estudio de la Filosofía y Riqueza de la Lengua Mexicana*. The most interesting part of this study was also published in a supplement to the journal *Et Caetera*, No. 1, March, 1950, pp. 1–15.

Where is your heart?
If you give your heart to each and every thing,
you lead it nowhere: you destroy your heart.
Can anything be found on earth?[2]

Three philosophical attitudes expressed in this poem reveal the depth of thought of the Nahuas. The poet first asks himself what the mind and heart can discover of real value here on earth. The mention of the heart in line two alludes to the person considered in a dynamic sense—the being who seeks and desires something. In Nahuatl, *yóllotl* (heart) is derived from the same root as *ollin* (movement), which may be defined as the dynamic quality inherent in the human being.

The second important idea is contained in the third and fourth lines. Man, a restless being, gives his heart to anything (*timóyol cecenmana*), and proceeding without a definite destination or goal (*ahuicpa*), he loses his heart, again in the sense of his dynamic being.

Of urgent importance is the question in the last line, "Can anything be found on earth?" *In tlaltícpac can mach ti itlatiuh?* The poet questions the possibility of finding anything on earth (*in tlaltícpac*) capable of satisfying the heart (the whole dynamic being) of man. This last expression is frequently opposed to the idiomatic complex *topan, mictlan,* "that which is above us" (the world of the gods) and "that which is below us" (the region of the dead)—that is, the unknown. *Tlaltícpac* (that which is on earth) is consequently what is here, what changes, what is visible, what is manifest to the senses. The Nahuas, then, were aware of the problems involved in an attempt to establish values in a changing world.

Other Nahuatl texts in the National Library collection deal more explicitly with the urgency and difficulty of the search. The ambiguity of the final purpose of human action is thus expressed:

Where are we going?

---

[2] *Colección de Cantares Mexicanos* (ed. by Antonio Peñafiel), fol. 2,v. The original manuscript of this work is found in the National Library of Mexico.

We came only to be born.
Our home is beyond:
In the realm of the defleshed ones.[3]
I suffer:
Happiness, good fortune never comes my way.
Have I come here to struggle in vain?
This is not the place to accomplish things.
Certainly nothing grows green here:
Misfortune opens its blossoms.[4]

The Nahuas sought with equal anxiety an explanation of life
and of man's work, for both were threatened with extermination
by the prophesied end of the Fifth Sun, the present age. According to their cosmogonic myth, there had been four historical
ages, called Suns—those of earth, wind, fire, and water—and
each had been destroyed; the present epoch was that of the Sun
of Movement, *Ollintonatiuh*. During this Sun, their elders said,
there would be earthquakes and famine, and finally mankind
would vanish forever. To the conviction that all things must
perish was added a profound doubt about what exists after
death:

Do flowers go to the region of the dead?
In the Beyond, are we dead or do we still live?[5]
Where is the source of light, since that which gives life hides itself?[6]

These questions clearly imply a distrust of the myths concerning the hereafter. Those who questioned themselves in this way
were not content with the answers provided by religious and
traditional thought. They doubted; they admitted that much had
not been adequately explained. They longed to see with greater
clarity the real outcome of our lives, and, through this, to learn
what importance there might be in this struggle. For if nothing

---

[3] *Ibid.*, fol. 3,r. The term *Ximoayan,* "the abode of the defleshed ones," was
one of the Nahuatl expressions for the hereafter.

[4] *Ibid.*, fol. 4,v.

[5] *Ibid.*, fol. 61,r.

[6] *Ibid.*, fol. 62,r.

except misfortune "grows green" on earth, and if the beyond is inscrutable, it is appropriate to question the meaning of human life, in which things exist for the moment, only to disappear forever:

> Truly do we live on earth?
> Not forever on earth; only a little while here.
> Although it be jade, it will be broken,
> Although it be gold, it is crushed,
> Although it be quetzal feather, it is torn asunder.
> Not forever on earth; only a little while here.[7]

Life in *tlaltícpac* is transitory. In the end everything must vanish; even rocks and precious metals will be destroyed. Is there anything, then, that is really stable or true in this world? Such is the question the Nahuatl poet asks of Ipalnemohuani, the supreme god, the Giver of Life:

> Do we speak the truth here, oh Giver of Life?
> We merely dream, we only rise from a dream.
> All is like a dream . . .
> No one speaks here of truth . . . .[8]

The recurrent idea that life is a dream appears not only in these songs, but also in the moral exhortations of the *Huehuetlatolli*, the "discourses of the elders." With the denial of all stability and permanence in *tlaltícpac*, there arises the profound and anguished question: Has man any hope for escape from the unreality of dreams—from this evanescent world?

> Does man possess any truth?
> If not, our song is no longer true.
> Is anything stable and lasting?
> What reaches its aim?[9]

---

[7] *Ibid.*, fol. 17,r. The compiler attributes this passage to King Nezahualcóyotl (1402–72).

[8] *Ibid.*, fol. 5,v.; fol. 13,r.

[9] *Ibid.*, fol. 10,v.

The word "truth" in Nahuatl, *neltiliztli*, is derived from the same radical as "root," *tla-nél-huatl*, from which, in turn, comes *nel-huáyotl*, "base" or "foundation." The stem syllable *nel* has the original connotation of solid firmness or deeply rooted. With this etymology "truth," for the Nahuas, was to be identified with well-grounded stability. The question, "Does man possess any truth?" should be construed as, "Does he have firm roots?" This idea is amplified by the next question: "Is anything stable and lasting?" which in turn acquires a much fuller meaning when related to the Nahuatl conception of a transitory temporal existence. Thus the Nahuatl concern about whether anything "is true" or "is stable and lasting" actually questioned the possibility of escaping the elusive present and finding something more certain than the emptiness of earthly things. One may speculate on the relationship of this attitude to Western European philosophical thought concerning the substantiality of what exists or appears to exist. The Scholastic philosophers believed that being was sustained by a transcendental principle. Other thinkers have associated reality with a universal immanent substance, as in Hegelian pantheism. Existentialists see reality as "existing," without any foundation at all. In any case, what is of most interest here is the fact that the Nahuas, facing the unequivocally transitory nature of earthly things, became deeply involved in an attempt to discover a foundation—a true basic principle—for man and the universe. How else to interpret their questions: "What is there that is stable and lasting?" and "Does man possess any truth?"

To appreciate the intellectual progress indicated by such an acute self-questioning about the truth of man, we need merely recall that this same problem, stated in a similar way, did not emerge in Greek philosophy until the time of Socrates and the Sophists, approximately two centuries after Thales of Miletus. They were the first to apply philosophical modes of thought to the subject of man. The Nahuatl enunciation of such questions is sufficient evidence that they were not satisfied by myths or religious doctrines. Their writings evince a vigorous mental development, an interest in the value, stability, or evanescence of things, and a rational vision of man himself as a problem.

That such texts as these—chosen from many which touch upon similar themes—exist does not in itself prove that there were men dedicated to the intellectual formulation of metaphysical questions, or, above all, that there were men who attempted to answer them. Such speculations could easily have had a more or less spontaneous origin independent of the activities of professional wise men or philosophers. So the problem remains: Is there historical evidence that such scholars did exist among the Nahuas? The answer provided by Fray Bernardino de Sahagún and his native informants will next be considered.

References to the existence of Nahuatl wise men or philosophers occur often in Sahagún's *General History*. In the introduction to Book I, Sahagún writes: "The knowledge or science of these people has great fame, as will be observed in Book X, Chapter XXIX. It is stated that the first settlers of this land had perfect philosophers and astrologers."[10] And in the prologue to Book VI, which contains his treatment of "the Rhetoric, Moral Philosophy, and Theology of the Mexican People" and is a treasure trove of Nahuatl beliefs and doctrines, Sahagún stresses the authenticity of his data.

> In this book it will be seen very clearly that the claims of some rivals that everything written in this *History* represents lies and inventions are themselves intolerant lies. It would not be within the power of the human mind to invent what is written here, nor could any living man counterfeit the language set forth herein. If we were to question all the prudent and enlightened Indians, they would confirm that this language is indeed that of their ancestors and that it describes their activities and work.[11]

The original Nahuatl texts, it must be stressed, are not the work of Sahagún, but of his elderly native informants from Tepepulco and Tlatelolco. They are describing what they saw and learned

[10] Bernardino de Sahagún, *Historia General de las Cosas de Nueva Espana*, I, 13. All references are to the Acosta Saignes edition.
[11] *Ibid.*, I, 445–56.

as young men in the *Calmécac,* the institutions of higher learning, before the arrival of the Spaniards, and they speak with authority on these matters.

In the text now to be considered there appears the marginal notation "*Sabios o Philosophos* [wise men or philosophers]," written in a hand unquestionably that of Fray Bernardino de Sahagún. This is a clear indication that he firmly believed that these lines described the functions and activities of men who deserved to be called philosophers.

1. The wise man: a light, a torch, a stout torch that does not smoke.

2. A perforated mirror, a mirror pierced on both sides.

3. His are the black and red ink, his are the illustrated manuscripts, he studies the illustrated manuscripts.

4. He himself is writing and wisdom.

5. He is the path, the true way for others.

6. He directs people and things; he is a guide in human affairs.

7. The wise man is careful (like a physician) and preserves tradition.

8. His is the handed-down wisdom; he teaches it; he follows the path of truth.

9. Teacher of the truth, he never ceases to admonish.

10. He makes wise the countenances of others; to them he gives a face (a personality); he leads them to develop it.

11. He opens their ears; he enlightens them.

12. He is the teacher of guides; he shows them their path.

13. One depends upon him.

14. He puts a mirror before others; he makes them prudent, cautious; he causes a face (a personality) to appear in them.

15. He attends to things; he regulates their path, he arranges and commands.

16. He applies his light to the world.

17. He knows what is above us (and) in the region of the dead.

18. He is a serious man.

19. Everyone is comforted by him, corrected, taught.

20. Thanks to him people humanize their will and receive a strict education.

21. He comforts the heart, he comforts the people, he helps, gives remedies, heals everyone.[12]

COMMENTARY:

LINE 1: *The wise man: a light, a torch, a stout torch that does not smoke.*

The wise man: this is the usual translation of the Nahuatl word *tlamatini*.[13] The word is derived from the verb *mati*, "to know." The suffix *ni* gives it the substantive function, "he who knows" (Latin *sapiens*). The prefix *tla* before the verb form indicates that "things" or "something" is the direct object. So, etymologically considered, *tla-mati-ni* means "he who knows things" or "he who knows something." The character of the *tlamatini* is here conveyed metaphorically by describing him as the light of a stout torch which illumines but does not smoke.

LINE 2: *A perforated mirror, a mirror pierced on both sides.*

A mirror pierced on both sides: tézcatl nécuc xapo. The allusion here is to the *tlachialoni*, a type of scepter with a pierced mirror at one end. This object was part of the equipment of certain gods, who used it to scrutinize the earth and human affairs. Literally, as Sahagún notes, *tlachialoni* "means a lookout or observatory . . . because one observed or looked through it by means of a hole in the middle."[14] Applied to the wise man, it conveys the idea that he is himself a medium of contemplation, "a concentrated or focused view of the world and things human."

LINE 3: *His are the black and red ink, his are the illustrated manuscripts . . . .*

Here the wise man is described as the possessor of the codices and of the *Amoxtli*, the ancient Nahuatl books of paper made from the bark of the amate (wild fig tree) folded like a screen or

---

[12] *Códice Matritense de la Real Academia de la Historia*, VIII, the last lines of fol. 118,r. and the first half of fol. 118,v. (All references to Vol. VIII are to the Francisco del Paso y Troncoso facsimile edition.)

[13] Alonso de Molina, *Vocabulario en lengua castellana y mexicana*, fol. 126,r.

[14] Sahagún, *op. cit.*, I, 40.

an accordion. Only relatively few of these priceless manuscripts escaped destruction at the time of the Conquest. The fact that important philosophical concepts were preserved in these codices is proved by the *Codex Vaticanus A 3738*, the first "pages" of which contain stylized drawings of the Aztec conception of the supreme principle, the directions of the universe, and so on.

LINE 4: *He himself is writing and wisdom.*
The Nahuatl expression used here, *Tlilli Tlapalli*, means, literally, that the wise man is black and red ink. But since these colors symbolize throughout Nahuatl mythology the presentation of and knowledge about things difficult to understand and about the hereafter, the obvious metaphorical implication is that the wise man possesses "writing and wisdom."

LINE 8: *His is the handed-down wisdom; he teaches it; he follows the path of truth.*
His is the handed-down knowledge or wisdom: This thought is expressed in Nahuatl by a single word, *machize,* derived from *machiztli,* with the suffix *e* indicating possession; thus "to him belongs . . . ." The compound loses the ending *tli* and becomes *machiz-e. Machize* is derived from the passive form of *mati,* "to know," which is *macho,* "to be known"; accordingly, it may be called "a passive substantive," wisdom known, handed down from person to person by tradition. Its correlative form is *(tla)-matiliztli,* wisdom or knowledge in an active sense; that is, acquired knowledge. This gives some indication of the subtlety of Nahuatl thought and of the flexibility of the language which can concisely express such fine shades of meaning.

LINE 10: *He makes wise the countenances of others; to them he gives a face (a personality); he leads them to develop it.*
Three Nahuatl nouns of unsuspected depth enrich the meaning of this line: *teixtlamachtiani, teixcuitiani, teixtomani.* The word *tlamachtiani* means "he who teaches or communicates something to someone else." The particle *ix* is an indefinite personal prefix indicating the receiver of the action of the verb or noun

to which it is attached, "to the others." Consequently, *te-ix-tla-machtiani* denotes "he who teaches or communicates something to the countenances of others." The context shows that the "something" is wisdom, since the wise man has been described as "teacher of the truth," "the one who teaches truth."

The other two words, *te-ix-cuitiani*, "the one who makes others to take a face," and *te-ix-tomani*, "the one who makes others to develop a face," are even more interesting, for they reveal that the *tlamatini* functioned as a teacher and psychologist. In this passage, as well as in lines 11 and 12, the word *ixtli*, "face," whose root *ix* occurs in all three compound terms, carries a meaning strikingly similar to that of the Greek word *prosopon*, "face," not only in the anatomical sense but also in the metaphorical significance of personality. This figurative meaning of *ixtli* appears very often in the discussions and speeches of Sahagún's Indian informants and in many other Nahuatl documents.

> LINE 14: *He puts a mirror before others; he makes them prudent, cautious; he causes a face (a personality) to appear in them.*

Here the *tlamatini* takes on the role of moralist. In the word *tetezcaviani*, "he puts a mirror before others," the basic element is *tézcatl*, "mirror made of carved and polished stone," which, in Sahagún's words, "faithfully reproduced the face."[15] From *tézcatl* is derived the verb *tezcavia*, which with the prefix *te* means "to place a mirror before others." The ending *ni* gives the term *te-tezca-via-ni* the substantive character, "he who places a mirror before others." The purpose of this action is then clarified: "to make them prudent and careful." Again there is a similarity to the ethical thought of Greece and India: man needs to have knowledge of himself, the *gnóthi seautón* or "Know thyself" of Socrates.

---

[15] Andrés de Olmos, *Arte para aprender la lengua mexicana*, 247; see also Angel María Garibay K. (tr.), *"Huehuetlatolli, Documento A," Tlalocan*, Vol. I, No. 1 (1943–44), 45.

LINE 16: *He applies his light to the world.*

The Nahuatl conception of the world was designated by the term *cemanáhuac,* whose component parts are *cem,* "entirely," "completely," and *a-náhuac,* "that which is surrounded by water [like a ring]." The world was, then, "that which is entirely surrounded by water." This idea had a certain geographical confirmation in that the so-called Aztec Empire was bounded on the west by the Pacific and on the east by the Gulf of Mexico, the latter being a veritable *Mare Ignotum* beyond which remained only the mythological "place of Knowing," *Tlilantlapalan.* From the word *cemanáhuac* and the verb *tlavia,* "to illumine," "to apply a light," comes the composite "to apply a light to the world." This attributes to the *tlamatini* the nature of an investigator of the physical world.

LINE 17: *He knows what is above us (and) in the region of the dead.*

Here is another traditional aspect of the wise man: "he knows about that [which is] above us," *topan,* and below us, *mictlan,* "the region of the dead," that is, the hereafter.

The idiomatic complex *topan, mictlan* carries the meaning, "what is beyond our knowledge, what is in itself beyond experience." The Nahuatl mind formulated what we today would call a metaphysical order or noumenal world. Its counterpart is the world itself, *cemanáhuac,* "that which is entirely surrounded by water."

At other times, as has been noted, a contrast is made between what is "above us, the beyond," and "what is on the surface of the earth [*tlaltícpac*]." The distinctness of this contrast and its frequent occurrence suggest strongly that, in their own way, the Nahuas had divined the duality or ambivalence of the world —a theme which has so deeply concerned Western European thought since pre-Socratic times. On the one hand, there is that which is visible, immanent, manifold, phenomenal, which for the Nahuas was "that which is upon the earth," *tlaltícpac;* on the other, there is that which is permanent, metaphysical, transcendental, expressed in Nahuatl as *topan, mictlan,* "what is above us and below us, in the region of the dead."

LINE 20: *Thanks to him the people humanize their will and receive a strict education.*

Itech netlacaneco, "thanks to him, the people humanize their will"; such is the translation of the Nahuatl word *ne-tlaca-neco. Neco* is the passive voice of *nequi,* "he desires," "he is desired"; *tlaca* is the root of *tlácatl,* "man," "human being"; *ne* is an indefinite personal prefix. The combination of these elements therefore means "the people are loved as human beings," *itech,* "thanks to him [the wise man]."

Another function of the *tlamatini,* then, is to teach the moral quality existing in "that which is human." In a sense the text points to the existence of a "humanistic" thought among the Nahuas, for it seems to indicate that this "humanizing of the will" was one of the basic tenets of a Nahuatl education.

Summarizing what has been said concerning the whole text, it might be noted that the Nahuatl philosopher was symbolically described putting together the most meaningful aspects of his intrinsic nature: he throws light upon reality; he is a concentrated vision of the world; "his are the illustrated manuscripts"; "he himself is writing and wisdom." He also appears in his relationship with other men. He is a teacher (*temachtiani*), "the road"; "his is the handed-down wisdom"; "he is the teacher of the truth and he does not cease to admonish." Moreover, he performs the duties of a psychologist (*teixcuitiani*), through whom "the faces of others look wise"; "he opens their ears . . . and is a master of teachers." That he also functions as a moralist (*tetezcahuiani*) becomes evident in these words: "He puts a mirror before others, he makes them prudent, cautious." Immediately after this, his interest in examining the physical world is discussed: "*cemanahuactlahuiani,*" "he attends to things, he applies his light to the world." One single sentence shows him to be a metaphysician, for he studies that which escapes our finite comprehension—"the region of the dead," the hereafter. Finally, as though in summation of his qualities and in explanation of his principal goal, we are told that "thanks to him people humanize their will and receive a strict education."

Thus it seems quite proper to attribute to the wise man—anachronously and by analogy, to be sure—the qualities of those men we designate today as teachers, psychologists, moralists, cosmologists, metaphysicians, and humanists.

A valuable corroboration for this may be found in the prologue to Ixtlilxóchitl's *History of the Chichimec Nation,* which contains a résumé of the various types of wise men found in Texcoco. After referring to those who put "in order the events that happened each year," those "in charge of genealogies" and "of the maps concerning the boundaries and limits of the cities . . . and the distribution of land," those men familiar with the laws, and the various types of priests, Ixtlilxóchitl writes:

> And finally, the philosophers and wise men had charge of recording all the sciences of which they had knowledge and of which they had achieved understanding, and of teaching from memory all the songs that preserved their sciences and histories. All of this was changed with the downfall of the Kings and Lords and with the suffering and persecutions of their descendants.[16]

The *tlamatinime* were specifically responsible for composing, painting, knowing, and teaching the songs and poems in which they preserved their scientific knowledge. For the Nahuas, like many other ancient peoples, found in the rhythm of poetry an easy and accurate way of retaining in their memories what was inscribed in their books of paintings.

Proof of the existence of philosophers among the Nahuas is also available in negative form. For, while the Sahagún informants told of the true wise men, they also mentioned the charlatans, who might indeed be called the sophists—in the pejorative sense—of their time. Here is a Nahuatl depiction of the pseudo wise man:

[16] Fernando de Alva Ixtlilxóchitl, *Obras Históricas,* II, 18.

The false wise man, like an ignorant physician,
a man without understanding, claims to
know about God.
He has his own traditions and keeps them secretly.
He is a boaster, vanity is his.
He makes things complicated; he brags and exaggerates.
He is a river, a rocky hill (a dangerous man).
A lover of darkness and corners,
a mysterious wizard, a magician, a witch doctor,
a public thief, he takes things.
A sorcerer, a destroyer of faces.[17]
He leads the people astray;
he causes others to lose their faces.
He hides things, he makes them difficult.
He entangles them with difficulties; he destroys them;
he causes the people to perish; he mysteriously puts an
end to everything.[18]

In this description of the *amo qualli tlamatini*, "the not good
wise man," the contrast between his characteristics and those of
the authentic Nahuatl wise man is clear and unmistakable. One,
the good wise man, "to the others he causes to take a face
[*teixcuitiani*]"; the other, the charlatan, "to the others he causes
to lose their faces [*teixpoloa*]." And while the genuine wise man
"attends to things, regulates their path, arranges and puts in
order," the Nahuatl "sophist" "mysteriously destroys everything
[*tlanahualpoloa*]."

They both actively aspire to influence the people: one teaches
the truth and thereby "makes wise the countenances of others";
the other, like a witch doctor, distorts truth by "concealing
things" and by "causing the people to perish and [by] mysteriously destroying everything." Such is the testimony of Sahagún's

[17] *Teixcuepani*, "he makes the others turn their faces," which, as the following words of the text indicate, means "he leads astray the people, he con-
fuses them."

[18] *Códice Matritense de la Real Academia*, VIII, fol. 188,v. This entire passage follows directly the lines about the wise men or *philosophos*.

Indian informants. It shows conclusively that they clearly understood that boastful and vainglorious imposters existed among them—men who contrasted sharply with the real *tlamatinime*.

The problems of truth and "roots" formulated by the Nahuatl sages were the fruit of rational meditation and embodied doubt concerning the meaning of life and the infinite. This element of doubt attests to a divergence from religious thought. The priest, as such, believes. While he can systematize and study his beliefs, he cannot accept the existence of problems which conflict with the precepts of his religion. Therefore, although the *tlamatinime* might have belonged originally to the priestly class, as scholars they must have been something more than priests.

To demonstrate the range of their thought, I am quoting below an excerpt from the *Colloquies of the Twelve*, the origin and historic value of which are more fully discussed in Appendix I. It is sufficient to say here that the particular importance of this document lies in the fact that the Nahuatl wise men are openly and freely discussing and defending their concepts in opposition to the Spanish friars.

Apparently the discussion was provoked by the Spaniards' missionary activity, when the friars were attempting to indoctrinate a group of the leading figures or lords of recently conquered Tenochtitlan and included condemnation of their ancient indigenous beliefs in the program. It is related that the Indians listened in silence. Only after the friars had finished the lesson did the unexpected occur. One of the principal lords rose and "with every courtesy and civility" cautiously voiced his displeasure at the attack upon customs and beliefs "so highly esteemed by his ancestors." Confessing that he himself was not a learned man, he nevertheless claimed to have competent teachers—and he enumerated the various categories of priests, astronomers, and wise men—who could refute the arguments of the friars:

1. But, our lords,
2. there are those who guide us;
3. they govern us, they carry us on their backs

4. and instruct us how our gods must be worshiped;
5. whose servants we are, like the tail and the wing;
6. who make offerings, who burn incense,
7. those who receive the title of *Quetzalcóatl.*
8. The experts, the knowers of speeches and orations,
9. it is their obligation;
10. they busy themselves day and night
11. with the placing of the incense,
12. with their offering,
13. with the thorns to draw their blood.
14. Those who see, those who dedicate themselves to observing
15. the movements and the orderly operations of the heavens,
16. how the night is divided.
17. Those who observe [read] the codices, those who recite [tell what they read].
18. Those who noisily turn the pages of the illustrated manuscripts.
19. Those who have possession of the black and red ink [wisdom] and of that which is pictured;
20. they lead us, they guide us, they tell us the way.
21. Those who arrange how a year falls,
22. how the counting of destinies, and days, and each of the twenty-day months all follow their courses.
23. With this they busy themselves, to them it falls to speak of the gods.[19]

COMMENTARY:

LINES 2–7: *There are those who guide us; they govern us, they carry us on their backs, and instruct us how our gods must be worshiped; whose servants we are, like the tail and the wing; who make offerings, who burn incense—those who receive the title of Quetzalcóatl.*

The *Códice Matritense de la Academia* (folio 119, r. ff.) mentions more than thirty distinct classes of priests. This text from the *Colloquies* lists briefly the various types and concludes with a reference to the high priests who received the title of *Quetzal-cóatl*. Sahagún also points out more than once that the title of *Quetzalcóatl* was reserved for high priests or pontiffs. Speaking of a high priest who had addressed a speech to the new king, he says: "The orator who gave this oration was one of the very learned priests and a great rhetorician, one of the three high priests who, as has been said elsewhere, were called *Quetzal-cóatl*."[20]

LINE 8: *The experts, the knowers of speeches and orations.*
Tlatolmatinime, whose literal meaning is "wise men of the word." The reference here is also to other priests, for in the following lines a number of the principal tasks of these "knowers of orations" are listed.

LINES 14–15: *Those who see, those who dedicate themselves to observing the movements and the orderly operations of the heavens....*

"The movements and the orderly operations of the heavens": *in iohtlatoquíliz in inematacachóliz in ilhuícatl.* Because of the rich ideological meaning of these terms, a brief analysis is in order. *I-oh-tlatoquíliz* is composed of the prefix *i* ("its"), which refers to *ilhuícatl,* the sky; *oh,* the root of *ohtli,* "road" or "path"; and finally *tlatoquiliztli,* meaning the act of running. The literal interpretation of *i-oh-tlatoquíliz,* then, is "the running along the path of the sky," that is, the courses of the stars in their proper paths. The other term, *inematacachóliz,* is formed by the same prefix *i,* which again refers to the sky; *ne,* another indefinite personal prefix meaning "some"; *ma,* the root of *maitl,* "hand"; *taca,* "to put," "to place"; and *chóliz-(tli),* a noun derived from the verb *choloa,* "to flee." Assembling these elements, the word *i-ne-ma-taca-chóliz* may be translated as "he places his hand upon the flight of the sky," or "he measures with his hand the flight or the crossing of the stars." That the Nahuatl astronomers not only observed but also measured the stars and plotted their

[20] Sahagún, *op. cit.,* I, 498.

courses is proved by the exact mathematical calculations involved in the calendar and by the even more obvious fact that the *maitl* or hand was a Nahuatl unit of measurement.

> LINES 17–19: *Those who observe [read] the codices, those who recite [tell what they read]. Those who noisily turn the pages of the illustrated manuscripts. Those who have possession of the black and red ink [wisdom] and of that which is pictured . . . .*

Here is an allusion to one of the chief tasks of the *tlamatinime*: to read and make doctrinal commentaries on the codices. With striking vividness and realism, these men are described as "noisily turning the pages of the manuscripts." Since the long strips of amate paper on which the codices were painted were dry and hard, unfolding them produced a characteristic sound which inevitably became associated with the figure of the wise man.

> LINES 21–22: *Those who arrange how a year falls, how the counting of destinies, and days, and each of the twenty-day months all follow their courses.*

This reference is to the priests in charge of the two calendars, the *tonalpohualli* and the *xiuhpohualli*. The former was the sacred almanac or divination calendar. It was used in casting horoscopes and interpreting the influences that affected men's lives from birth to death; it also dealt with the historical events of the world. The *xiuhpohualli* was the solar or year-count calendar. The Nahuatl year was made up of eighteen 20-day months, to which were added 5 additional days—the ominous and unlucky *nemontemi,* or "days left over"—in order to complete the solar year of 365 days. Since these calendars demanded complicated, minutely precise mathematical calculations, it may reasonably be held that the knowledge and calculations of these men came very close to true science.

This description of the *tlamatinime,* like the one given by Sahagún's Indian informants, portrays the wise men as the possessors and interpreters of the illustrated manuscripts, as the guardians of the black and red ink—*in tlilli in tlapalli,* "writing and wisdom." In both documents the wise man appears as a guide, a person who points out the path to others.

Moreover, the sharp distinction made between priests (lines 2 to 13) and wise men (astronomers, guardians of the codices and knowledge, experts in the calendars and in chronology— lines 14 to 23) corroborates the conclusion that both Sahagún's informants and the Indians who responded to the twelve friars possessed something more than mere traditional knowledge of the gods and the rituals.

There were Nahuatl men capable of perceiving problems in the "a-little-while-here" nature of all that exists, in the ephemeral quality of this life, in man's very being, about whose essence so little is known. They recognized problems related to the mysteries of the hereafter—where there may or may not be a new life, with songs and flowers. These men who were given to inner questioning were the same ones who composed the songs where the answers are found. To them belonged the black and red ink—writing and wisdom. They read and wrote the manuscripts. They were the teachers of truth; they "placed mirrors" before their fellow-men to make them prudent and cautious. And, above all, they investigated with insatiable curiosity; they applied their light to the world, to the conditions of *tlalticpac.* They boldly inquired into "what is above us, and what is below us, the region of the dead."

This is not all. Reflecting upon their own status as wise men and perceiving within themselves an irresistible desire to probe and fathom the unknown, they came to an understanding of what a contemporary Spanish thinker has called "being born condemned to philosophize." According to Indian tradition:

It is said that prior to his [the *tlamatini's*] being born, four times from the womb of his mother he disappeared, as if she were no longer pregnant, and then he would reappear. When the child had grown up and had become a youth, his profession and way of acting evidenced themselves. It is said that he would be concerned with the region of the dead [*Mictlan-matini*], and with that which is above us [*Ilhuícac-matini*].[21]

With this mental image of the *tlamatini* or Nahuatl philosopher, we may proceed to a study of his thought and his doctrines based on the texts. With the exception of Nezahualcóyotl and a few other wise kings and poets, there is little to be said about the names and biographical details of the men whose ideas are represented. There are two reasons for this. First, the men who handed down Nahuatl philosophical doctrines were generally not the wise men themselves, but rather former students of the various *Calmécac*. Although they had been taught the ideas prevalent in their time, they did not usually mention the names of their teachers. More significantly, the elaboration of Nahuatl philosophy, as in the case of Hindu philosophy contained in the *Upanishads*, cannot be attributed to isolated thinkers but to ancient schools directed by the wise men. It would therefore be a mistake to apply the criteria of the cult of the individual, which prevails in modern Western European culture, to the more socialized efforts of the philosophers of other times and places.

The development of Nahuatl philosophy from Toltec times must be credited to whole generations of wise men, known by ancient tradition as:

Those who
carried with them
the black and red ink,
the manuscripts and the pictures,
wisdom [*tlamatiliztli*].
They brought everything with them:
the song books and the music of the flutes.[22]

And perhaps they were the men who conceived in that distant

[21] *Códice Matritense del Real Palacio*, VI, fol. 126; see also Angel María Garibay K., "Paralipómenos de Sahagún," *Tlalocan*, Vol. II, No. 2 (1946), 167—the source of this quotation.
[22] *Códice Matritense de la Real Academia*, VIII, fol. 192,r.

past the legendary symbol of Nahuatl knowledge—the great figure of Quetzalcóatl.

The paucity of biographical data does not mean that the *tlamatinime* were indifferent to the value of the individual. Many texts indicate that their attitude was quite the opposite. The passage quoted above, for example, describing the mission of the Nahuatl sage or *philosopho* as teaching men "to have and develop in themselves *a face*," voices their interest in eliminating human anonymity, graphically expressed as man's "lack of face." The wise men also put "a mirror before their fellow-men," so that self-knowledge might cause each individual to be prudent and careful.

II

The Pre-Columbian
Concept of the Universe

THE Nahuas' first attempts to understand the origin of the universe, its essence, and natural phenomena took the form of a great body of myths, generally thought to be part of their Toltec heritage. While the majority of the people unquestioningly accepted the myths as valid cosmogonic explanations, the *tlamatinime* eventually began to analyze the ancient concepts inherent in them, not for the purpose of denying their validity, but in order to delve deeper into the meaning of their symbols. Inevitably, they came upon certain problems in the traditional accounts of the origin, immutability and change, and ultimate fate of the world. In expressing their doubts and formulating their new ideas, however, they continued to use the language of myth.

In his discussion of the beginnings of Greek philosophy, Werner Jaeger comments that "rational thought, in its first stages, uses the language of myth to express its observations in such symbols" in order to capture attention.[1] Rational elaboration later becomes a means of further penetration into these ideas, but even then myths must provide the elucidating sym-

[1] Jaeger, *op. cit.*, I, 173.

bols. As Jaeger points out, genuine mythogony appears in the philosophies of Plato and Aristotle, and even the accepted scientific truths of today utilize an astonishing amount of myth, symbolism, and metaphor.

The cosmology of the Nahuas is expressed in numerous myths which, like the eternal fire of Heraclitus and the Unmoved Mover of Aristotle, embody observations of universal validity. Attempting to explain the temporal origin of the universe and the nature of its spatial structure, the *tlamatinime* clothed their thoughts in the rich symbolism of the very myths which they were in the process of modifying in accordance with their rational discoveries.

As the texts show clearly, the Nahuas had arrived at the distinction between concepts based on observation and experience and those based on magic and superstition. The former they considered as *true*, the latter as *false*. The following passage distinguishes sharply between true physicians, healers who acquire their knowledge through experimentation and use it properly in the application of medicine, and false ones, those who use witchcraft and sorcery:

The true doctor.
He is a wise man (tlamatini);
he imparts life.
A tried specialist,
he has worked with herbs, stones, trees, and roots.
His remedies have been tested;
he examines, he experiments,
he alleviates sickness.
He massages aches and sets broken bones.
He administers purges and potions;
he bleeds his patients;
he cuts and he sews the wound;
he brings about reactions;
he stanches the bleeding with ashes.
The false physician.
He ridicules and deceives the people;

he brings on indigestion;
he makes illness worse;
his medicines are fatal.
He has dark secrets he will not reveal;
he is a sorcerer and a witch;
he is familiar with the noxious herbs and possesses their seeds,
he practices divination with knotted ropes.
He makes sickness worse;
his herbs and seeds poison and his cures kill.[2]

This passage reveals the true physician to be a *tlamatini,* or wise man, who has learned his profession by practicing it— *tlaiximatini,* which means literally, "he who has firsthand knowledge [*imatini*] of the character or nature [*ix*] of things [*tla*],"— that is, he understands the nature of the herbs, rocks, roots, and the other things he uses in his cures. He proceeds by a "scientific" method, studying the effects of his medicines and testing their curative powers before applying them. Finally, he restores health by setting broken bones, massaging, administering purges, bleeding, performing surgery, and inducing beneficial reactions in his patients. The standards which the good Nahuatl physician had to meet were not very different from our own.

The false physician is a sorcerer (*nahualli*) and a charlatan, given to brewing questionable potions from noxious herbs and telling fortunes with the aid of ropes.[3] The difference between the good physician and the quack is the difference between a practice based on knowledge and method and one based on magic and witchcraft. This picture of the "true" healer refers precisely to the kind of knowledge that the Nahuatl wise men were seeking.

In mathematics and astronomy, the Nahuas' wise men found direct observation of phenomena necessary to their calculations. It is said that the astronomers used their hands in the

---

[2] *Códice Matritense de la Real Academia,* VIII, fol. 119,r.

[3] Motolinía describes the practice of divining with ropes in his *Memoriales,* 126.

manner of sextants to measure the movements of the stars.[4] They could calculate with precision the exact time the sun would rise and set each day. They had an accurate calendar of years and months (*xiuhpohualli*) and an astrology based on a complex of days and hours (*tonalpohualli*) which they used for casting horoscopes. It is logical therefore that the Nahuas, trained in the observation of phenomena and advanced in their knowledge of mathematics, astronomy, and chronology, should have developed an extraordinary cosmology, constructing a complex mythological system for symbolic explanation.

Pre-Columbian thinkers were convinced that if man lacked a solid foundation, even his most profound thoughts and accomplishments could not possibly convey truth—they could not have any real significance and they would not endure. In the same way, the problem of the nature and truth of the universe loomed over them:

Is anything stable and lasting?
What reaches its aim?[5]

Convinced that the physical world, in which even "gold and jade are broken" and which appears to be only a dream, could not reveal to them the fundamental principle or foundation which they sought, the *tlamatinime* moved to the metaphysical level: *topan*, "the world above and beyond us."

This metaphysical approach, however, was modified by a certain religiosity, not unlike that which appeared among the early Greeks. Thales, for example, had declared that "everything is replete with gods," and even Aristotle maintained that the Unmoved Mover of the universe was the Divine itself. Werner Jaeger's statement that the development of philosophy is "the progressive rationalization of the religious conception of the world implicit in myths"[6] perhaps applies to the *tlamatinime*'s approach.

[4] Lehmann (ed.), *Colloquies and Christian Doctrine*, 97 (fol. 3,r.).
[5] MSS *Cantares Mexicanos*, fol. 10,v.
[6] Jaeger, *op. cit.*, I, 172–73.

Many of the texts which contain the first references to inquiries into the origin and foundation of the universe are those collected by the early missionaries. These documents attempt to answer questions, presupposing that they had been asked. Perhaps in no other place is the answer so clearly expressed as in an ancient manuscript contained in the *Annals of Cuauhtitlán*. The truth, wrapped in the vestments of myth and considered to be the product of wisdom, is symbolically attributed to Quetzalcóatl, the personification of wisdom:

1. And it is told, it is said
2. that Quetzalcóatl would invoke, deifying something in the innermost of heaven:
3. she of the starry skirt, he whose radiance envelops things;
4. Lady of our flesh, Lord of our flesh;
5. she who is clothed in black, he who is clothed in red;
6. she who endows the earth with solidity, he who covers the earth with cotton.
7. And thus it was known, that toward the heavens was his plea directed,
8. toward the place of duality, above the nine levels of Heaven.[7]

COMMENTARY:

LINE 1: *And it is told, it is said.*
These words are clearly indicative of traditional knowedge and probably refer to what "was told and said" in the *Calmécac*, where the method of teaching was "to explain" (*pohua*) what was painted in the manuscripts.

LINE 2: *that Quetzalcóatl would invoke, deifying something in the innermost of heaven.*
The Nahuatl word used here, *mo-teo-tiaya*, means literally, "he deified someone for himself," or, in other words, he "sought for himself that god who lived in the innermost [part] of heaven."

LINE 3: *she of the starry skirt, he whose radiance envelops things.*
It should be pointed out, although the Nahuatl concept of the

---

[7] *Annals of Cuauhtitlán*, fol. 4.

Divine is discussed later, that this double title is frequently used in reference to the double role of Ometéotl, the god of duality, who inhabits *Omeyocan,* "the place of duality." The first two names by which the god is designated—Citlalinicue, "she of the starry skirt," and Citlallatónac, "celestial body which illumines things"—describe the double action of Ometéotl. He makes the stars shine by night, and is identified with the sun during the day as the celestial body which gives life to all things that share its radiance.

LINE 4: *Lady of our flesh, Lord of our flesh.*
The twofold nature of Ometéotl is even more apparent in this line; he is simultaneously "Lord" and "Lady" of our flesh (of our sustenance)—Tonacatecuhtli, Tonacacíhuatl.

LINE 5: *she who is clothed in black, he who is clothed in red.*
The double aspect of the god of duality is reiterated; he is both night and day. He is *tecolliquenqui,* "she who is clothed in black," and he is *yeztlaquenqui,* "he who is clothed in red." The latter term actually means "clothed in the color of blood." The juxtaposition of these two colors also evokes the idea of wisdom, as did the metaphor used to describe the *tlamatini*: "His are the black and red ink . . . ."

LINE 6: *she who endows the earth with solidity, he who covers the earth with cotton.*
The answer to the *tlamatinime*'s inquiry into the nature and "truth of the universe" appears in this line. In his lengthy meditation, Quetzalcóatl discovered that it is the dual divinity who maintains and gives order to the universe. Ometéotl, the god of duality, in his simultaneous feminine and masculine role "endows the earth with solidity," *tlallamánac,* and "covers the earth with cotton," *tlallíchcatl.* As will later be demonstrated by a more elaborate study of the principal attributes of Ometéotl, this supreme Nahuatl deity was both a masculine and feminine personification, in spite of being one entity, and was considered to be the generative nucleus and universal cosmic energy from

which all life gained sustenance. Ometéotl supported the earth's foundation and furnished the power which produced changes in the sky and in the clouds. The latter function is vividly described in the phrase, "he who covers the earth with cotton."

LINE 7: *And thus it was known, that toward the heavens was his plea directed, toward the place of duality, above the nine levels of Heaven.*

Here the place of the cosmic origin of all things is explicitly identified as *Omeyocan*, the place of duality above the nine levels of the heavens (this text specifies nine levels, whereas others specify twelve or, more commonly, thirteen).

No one among the Nahuas could symbolize the yearning for a metaphysical investigation of truth more suitably than Quetzalcóatl. Evoker of myths, Quetzalcóatl's name is synonymous with his wisdom and his quest for a beyond, where, unlike the earth, there would be no sin and faces would never age. In Tula, Quetzalcóatl had discovered the existence of sin on earth and the fact that faces must grow old. He had then fled to the East, to the land of the black and red colors, the region of knowledge. While at Tula, however, he had fasted, done penance, prayed, and meditated. And it was finally there that his questions about the one who dwelled in the innermost heaven and the nature and truth of the universe were answered: It is the supreme being who "supports the foundation of the earth and covers it with cotton."

Quetzalcóatl not only discovered that Ometéotl endowed the earth with solidity and foundation, but also observed his red and black attire and thus was able to identify the god with day and night. He discovered in the starry heavens the radiant skirt of the divinity's feminine aspect, while in the sun—the celestial body which illumines all things—he discerned the masculine role, a marvelous symbol of generative power. In short, Ometéotl was the cosmic energy upon which everything depended; the world, the sun, and the stars—everything received its existence and nature from this god. And yet Ometéotl, the

fundamental being—or Huehuetéotl, "the old god," as he is sometimes called—did not stand alone in the universe. He was "mother
and father of the gods" in his primary generative function.[8] As
such, he was the origin of all the natural forces deified by Nahuatl religion:

1. Mother of the gods, father of the gods, the old god
2. spread out on the navel of the earth,
3. within the circle of turquoise.
4. He who dwells in the waters the color of the bluebird, he
who dwells in the clouds.
5. The old god, he who inhabits the shadows of the land of the
dead,
6. the Lord of fire and of time.[9]

COMMENTARY:

LINE 1: *Mother of the gods, father of the gods, the old god.*
This line asserts the dual nature of the cosmic being (the old
god). He is the foundation of the universe, and as father and
mother simultaneously generates and conceives first the gods
and then all existing things.

LINE 2: *spread out on the navel of the earth.*
The expression, *in tlalxicco ónoc,* is derived from *co,* a suffix indicating place (on); the root, *xic,* of the noun *xic-tli* (navel); and
tlal(li) (earth); the meaning is, simply, "on the navel of the
earth." From his position on the navel of the earth, the text implies, Ometéotl sustains the world from its very center, at the
mid-point of the four cardinal directions assigned to the four
sons to whom he gave birth.

LINES 3–5: *Within the circle of turquoise. He who dwells in
the waters the color of the bluebird, he who dwells in the
clouds. The old god, he who inhabits the shadows of the
land of the dead.*

[8] "Mother of the gods, Father of the gods: the old god [*In teteu inan, in
teteu itah, in Huehuetéotl*]"; see *Códice Florentino,* (Sahagún's *History*), Book
VI (unpublished), fol. 34,r. and 71,v. (Hereafter cited as *Códice Florentino,*
Book VI.)
[9] *Códice Florentino,* Book VI, fol. 71,v.

These lines affirm the omnipresence of Ometéotl. He is everywhere—in the navel of the earth, in the circle of turquoise, in the waters, in the clouds, and in the land of the dead.

LINE 6: *the Lord of fire and of time* [*Xiuhtecuhtli*]. This is merely another name for Ometéotl.

Acording to an ancient account in the "*Historia de los Mexicanos por sus Pinturas*," Ometéotl gave birth to four sons:

1. This god and goddess begot four sons:

2. The eldest was named Tlatlauhqui Tezcatlipoca and the people of Huexotzinco and Tlaxcala took him as their principal god and they called him Camaxtli. This one was born red.

3. The second son, Yayauhqui Tezcatlipoca, was the worst and the main one who had more authority and power because he was born between them. He was born black.

4. To the third was given the name Quetzalcóatl, sometimes also known as Yoalli ehécatl.

5. The fourth and smallest was called Omitéotl and also Maquizcóatl, whom the Mexicans called Huitzilopochtli because he was left-handed. And in Mexico, he was the principal deity because he was so regarded in the land from which they [the Mexicans] came . . . .[10]

These four gods constitute the primary forces that activate the history of the world, and the symbolism of their colors—red, black, white, and blue—permits us to trace their identification with the natural elements, the directions of space, and the periods of time allotted to their influence. With the four sons of Ometéotl, space and time enter fully into the world. Both space and time are conceived not as empty stage settings, but as factors that combine to regulate the occurrence of cosmic events.

The early activities of the four gods are described in the "*Historia de los Mexicanos*"; they created fire, the sun, the land of the dead, the place of the waters, and the regions beyond the heavens. They were also responsible for the earth and man, the

[10] "*Historia de los Mexicanos por sus Pinturas*," in Joaquín García Icazbalceta (ed.), *Nueva Colección de Documentos para la Historia de México*, III, 228–29.

days and months, and time itself. If at first glance this appears to be a contradiction of the previously cited version by Sahagún's informants, which names Ometéotl as the life-giving power and foundation of all these realities, a closer examination reveals that the new data clarify and supplement that story.

In speaking of the existing world, the Indians quoted by Sahagún only said that Ometéotl, located in its navel or center, supported it. Referring to the waters, the clouds, and the land of the dead, they maintained that Ometéotl was present in all of these places, but they did not specify whether the dual being himself produced the world or whether he did so by means of the four cosmic forces (his sons). This ambiguous point is clarified by the *"Historia de los Mexicanos"*:

1. Six hundred years having passed since the birth of the four brother gods, the sons of Tonacatecuhtli, the four assembled and said it would be well to organize what was to be done and to establish the law to be followed.

2. And it was agreed upon that Quetzalcóatl and Huitzilopochtli should be the ones to decide.

3. And these two, through the commission and by consent of the other two, created fire and then the half sun which not being whole gave little light.

4. Later they made a man and a woman; the man was named Oxomoco and the woman, Cipactónal, and they were sent to cultivate the earth. It was ordered that she spin and weave and that they give birth to *macehuales* [people] and that they be not idle but always work.

5. And to her gave the gods certain grains of corn for making cures, for soothsaying and witchcraft, and thus the women use them to this very day.

6. And then they made the days and months, and they gave to each month 20 days; thus eighteen months there were and 360 days in the year, as will be related.

7. Mictlantecuhtli and Mictecacíhuatl were next created, man and wife and gods of hell, to which they were assigned.

8. And then they created the heavens, to the thirteenth level, and caused the waters to be.

9. And from the waters they created an enormous fish known as *Cipactli*, which was like an alligator and from this fish the earth was made, as will be told later . . . .[11]

With the creation of fire and the sun (line 3), man and corn (lines 4 and 5), the days, months, and years (line 6), the land of the dead, the waters, and the earth (lines 7, 8, and 9), the gods began the history of the universe.

The red Tezcatlipoca soon identified himself with the East, *Tlapallan*, the region of the red color; the black Tezcatlipoca, with the night and the region of the dead, located in the North; Quetzalcóatl, night and wind, with the West, region of fecundity and life; and finally, the blue Tezcatlipoca, personified as Huitzilopochtli in Tenochtitlan, associated himself with the South, the area located to the left of the sun. Each then began to act from his own center of action. Huehuetéotl, the supreme being, observed the efforts of the gods from *Omeyocan* and from the navel of the earth.

But the action of these gods, as the Nahuatl texts illustrate, was violent. "The gods battle," says Alfonso Caso, "and their struggle for supremacy is the history of the universe, their alternative triumphs become so many other creations."[12]

A theomorphic struggle for supremacy among the four primary forces, the sons of Ometéotl, explained to the Nahuatl mind the beginning of the universe and the ages through which it passed. In the beginning, immediately after creation, there had been an equilibrium of forces. "The four gods, sons of Tonacatecuhtli [Ometéotl], assembled and said that it would be well to organize what was to be done and to establish the law to be followed."[13]

But the first state of equilibrium was not to last. The gods did not exist of their own will, nor were they the foundation of the universe—for only Ometéotl, root and support of the universe, possessed such powers. The position of the other gods was pre-

[11] *Ibid.*, III, 229–30.
[12] Alfonso Caso, *La Religión de los Aztecas*, 11.
[13] *"Historia de los Mexicanos . . . Pinturas," loc. cit.*, 229.

35

carious and unstable. The state of balance was to be severed by the battle between Quetzalcóatl and the various Tezcatlipocas, for these four sons, the first four gods, were forces held in tension, and because of the perpetual restlessness within them, conflict was inevitable. Fighting avidly for supremacy, each endeavored to identify himself with the sun, so that he could rule the lives of men and direct the destiny of the world. During each age, or Sun, of the earth, one god prevailed over the others, and he symbolized one of the elements—earth, air, fire, or water—as well as one of the four quadrants of the universe. Each god's period of ascendancy constituted one of the ages of the world. But at the end of each age, war broke out and destruction followed. Tezcatlipoca and Quetzalcóatl battled, each subdued the other, then both returned to the field of battle of the universe. The elements of earth, wind, fire, and water then came suddenly upon the scene from the four directions and clashed violently.

With a dialectic rhythm which attempted in vain to harmonize the dynamism of opposing forces, the various Suns appeared and vanished. The Aztecs moved to stop this process: they conceived the ambitious project of impeding or at least postponing the cataclysm which was to put an end to their Sun, the fifth of the series. This idea became an obsession which stimulated and made powerful the inhabitants of Tenochtitlan, ultimately transforming them into:

> . . . a people with a mission. A chosen people who believed their mission was to side with the sun in the cosmic struggle, to side with goodness to ascertain its triumph over evil, and to give to all of humanity the benefits of the victory of the forces of light over the powers of night.
>
> Clearly the Aztec, like anyone who believes himself to have a mission, was more eager to carry it out if in so doing, his conquest of other peoples was brought about. . . .
>
> The idea that the Aztec was a collaborator of the gods, that he was carrying out a transcendent duty and that in his action lay the only possibility for the world to continue its existence, made endurable all of the sufferings of his long pilgrimage. And in addi-

tion, this idea allowed the Aztecs to establish themselves in a place which richer and more cultured peoples had declined, motivated them to impose themselves upon the surrounding peoples, subjugating them and expanding constantly the territories and power of Tenochtitlan until they reached from the Gulf coast to the Pacific. . . .[14]

This powerful motivation soon was transformed into a truly mystical inspiration, and the Aztecs came more and more to unify their personal and social activities with the idea of a collaboration with the Sun. As if hypnotized by "the mystery of blood," they expended all of their efforts and energy to provide the gods with *chalchíhuatl,* the precious liquid drawn from the sacrificed victims, the only suitable nourishment for the Sun.

The collaboration with and intention to preserve the life of the Sun, which no doubt constituted one of the fundamental points of their religion and even of their imperialistic conception of the world, was, it should be remembered, of strictly philosophical origin. If the Aztecs drew such a mystico-religious notion from the very ancient Nahuatl myth of the Suns, the myth in itself, independent of its religious implications, gives the Nahuatl explanation for the nature and the origin of the world.

There are more than ten chronicles and annals in which this myth is related, with some disagreement concerning the number of the Suns. The version given below, contained in the *Leyenda de los Soles* and translated from Nahuatl, appears to be the most complete and most interesting, principally because of its antiquity. Although written in 1558, the form of writing, which consistently juxtaposes such expressions as "here is" to dates, indicates that it was used as a commentary on a native manuscript. It also corresponds in number and order of Suns to the pre-Hispanic monument known as the Calendar Stone and the "*Historia de los Mexicanos por sus Pinturas.*"

The translation of the *Leyenda de los Soles* adheres as closely

[14] Alfonso Caso, "*El Aguila y el Nopal,*" in *Memorias de la Academia Mexicana de la Historia,* Vol. V, No. 2 (1946), p. 103.

as possible to the Nahuatl text and attempts to preserve its character as a description of an ancient Aztec illustrated manuscript:

1. Here is the oral account of what is known of how the earth was founded long ago.

2. One by one, here are its various foundations [ages].

3. How it began, how the first Sun had its beginning 2513 years ago—thus it is known today, the 22 of May, 1558.

4. This Sun, 4-Tiger, lasted 676 years.

5. Those who lived in this first Sun were eaten by ocelots. It was the time of the Sun 4-Tiger.

6. And what they used to eat was our nourishment, and they lived 676 years.

7. And they were eaten in the year 13.

8. Thus they perished and all ended. At this time the Sun was destroyed.

9. It was on the year 1-Reed. They began to be devoured on a day [called] 4-Tiger. And so with this everything ended and all of them perished.

10. This Sun is known as 4-Wind.

11. Those who lived under this second Sun were carried away by the wind. It was under the Sun 4-Wind that they all disappeared.

12. They were carried away by the wind. They became monkeys.

13. Their homes, their trees—everything was taken away by the wind.

14. And this Sun itself was also swept away by the wind.

15. And what they used to eat was our nourishment.

16. [The date was] 12-Serpent. They lived [under this Sun] 364 years.

17. Thus they perished. In a single day they were carried off by the wind. They perished on a day 4-Wind.

18. The year [of this Sun] was 1-Flint.

19. This Sun, 4-Rain, was the third.

20. Those who lived under this third Sun, 4-Rain, also perished. It rained fire upon them. They became turkeys.

21. This Sun was consumed by fire. All their homes burned.

22. They lived under this Sun 312 years.

23. They perished when it rained fire for a whole day.

24. And what they used to eat was our nourishment.

25. [The date was] 7-Flint. The year was 1-Flint and the day 4-Rain.

26. They who perished were those who had become turkeys.

27. The offspring of turkeys are now called *pípil-pípil*.

28. This Sun is called 4-Water; for 52 years the water lasted.

29. And those who lived under this fourth Sun, they existed in the time of the Sun 4-Water.

30. It lasted 676 years.

31. Thus they perished: they were swallowed by the waters and they became fish.

32. The heavens collapsed upon them and in a single day they perished.

33. And what they used to eat was our nourishment.

34. [The date was] 4-Flower. The year was 1-House and the day 4-Water.

35. They perished, all the mountains perished.

36. The water lasted 52 years and with this ended their years.

37. This Sun, called 4-Movement, this is our Sun, the one in which we now live.

38. And here is its sign, how the Sun fell into the fire, into the divine hearth, there at Teotihuacán.

39. It was also the Sun of our Lord Quetzalcóatl in Tula.

40. The fifth Sun, its sign 4-Movement.

41. is called the Sun of Movement because it moves and follows its path.

42. And as the elders continue to say, under this sun there will be earthquakes and hunger, and then our end shall come.[15]

COMMENTARY:

LINE 1: *Here is the oral account of what is known of how the earth was founded long ago.*

"The oral account of what is known"—*Tlamachilliztlatolzazanilli*
—is derived from the word *tlamachiliztli* which, as was noted in

---

[15] Walter Lehmann (ed.), *Annals of Cuauhtitlán and Leyenda de los Soles*, in *Die Geschichte der Königreiche von Colhuacan und Mexico*, 322–27.

the preceding chapter, means "wisdom" in the passive sense, "known wisdom or tradition." This line also reveals the principal source of our information about ancient Mexico: it is that knowledge passed on by word of mouth in the *Calmécac*, where "the oral accounts of what is known" were perpetuated.

LINE 2: *One by one, here are its various foundations* [*ages*]. The word *i-tlamamanca* has been employed in the Nahuatl text to express what may be translated, "foundations." This word is composed of the prefix *i*, "of it, from the earth," and the substantive *tlamamanca*, derived from the verb *mani*, "to endure or to exist permanently." Literally then, the term *tlamamanca* means "the result of actions by which the earth exists permanently."

Walter Lehmann has translated the phrase as "*in einzelnen (Weltaltern) ihre Gründungen (erfolgten)*"—"in each age its foundation took place," which is consistent with the Nahuatl idea of the need "to sustain firmly on its feet," to give roots or foundation to the universe.[16] It should be recalled that the title *Tlallamanac*, "he who gives roots or foundation to the earth," was unequivocally applied to Ometéotl, the god of duality.

LINE 3: *How it began, how the first Sun had its beginning 2513 years ago—thus it is known today, the 22 of May, 1558*. The presence of these dates reflects the Nahuatl desire for exactness—an exactness developed by the constant handling of their two calendars. Not only is the day on which the story is told recorded, May 22, 1558, but the year, believed to be the beginning of the first cosmic age, is also noted.

Dates relating to the *xiuhpohualli*, or "count of the years," appear frequently in this text. The astrological signs of the *tonalpohualli*, corresponding to the various ages and cataclysms, are also included. Thus, even when the dialectic of the evolution of the Suns is wrapped in myth, the tale follows a careful chronology. This presupposes a rational and systematic way of thinking.

16 Lehmann (ed.), *Die Geschichte*, 322.

LINE 4: *This Sun, 4-Tiger, lasted 676 years.*
Each Sun receives the name of the element that brings about its destruction. The date of the destruction of the age corresponds to the day 4 of the calendric sign in which the force was released. Thus, in the first Sun of Tiger, the end took place on the day "4-Tiger." One of the names for tiger used by the Nahuas was *tecuani*, "devourer of people"; he was a monster of the earth. Consequently, he symbolized the action of the first of the elements, earth.

According to the myth of the cosmic struggles in the *"Historia de los Mexicanos,"* when Tezcatlipoca had attained supremacy over the other gods by identifying himself with the Sun and was ruling the world and its inhabitants, Quetzalcóatl struck out against him for the first time, ". . . he struck him with a large club, knocking him into the water and there he became a tiger . . . ."

LINE 6: *And what they used to eat was our nourishment, and they lived 676 years.*
The particular food of each epoch is listed in the *"Historia de los Mexicanos."* At the time of the first Sun, the *macehuales* (men) "used to eat acorns and nothing else."[17] Some scholars have erroneously concluded that the *tonalámatl* date, *7 malinalli* (grass), refers to the type of food consumed during this Sun. That date, however, merely designates a day of the horoscope that came under the influence of Tezcatlipoca, the god who ruled the universe during the First Age.

LINE 10: *This Sun is known as 4-Wind.*
Wind, the second of the elements, is introduced at this point. At the time of the Second Sun, says the *"Historia de los Mexicanos"*: "For 13 times 52, which is 676 years, Quetzalcóatl was the Sun. At the end of this time Tezcatlipoca, wanting to be Sun, turned himself into a tiger, as the others, his brothers, had wanted to do. As a tiger, Tezcatlipoca then kicked Quetzalcóatl, throwing him from his throne, and a great wind arose that car-

[17] *"Historia de los Mexicanos . . . Pinturas,"* loc. cit., III, 233.

ried away Quetzalcóatl and all the *macehuales*. These people became monkeys; the role of the Sun was then assumed by *Tlalocatecli*, god of the underworld."[18]

LINE 15: *And what they used to eat was our nourishment.*
In the Second Age, "nothing was eaten but *acecentli*, a cornlike grain which grows in water."[19] At this time an evolution in the nature of food began to take place; the acorn had been replaced by *acecentli* or water-corn, which culminated in the Fifth Period with *centéotl*, the real corn. This basic American grain food, according to myth, was a gift from the ant to Quetzalcóatl.

LINE 19: *This Sun, 4-Rain, was the third.*
Fire, the third element, dominates this age. Following the narration of the mythical battles of the gods in the *"Historia de los Mexicanos"* is the statement, "These years having passed, Quetzalcóatl sent a rain of fire from heaven. He removed Tláloc and thus ended his role as Sun, and replaced him with his wife Chalchiuhtlicue, who remained Sun six times 52 years, which is 312 years."[20]

LINE 24: *And what they used to eat was our nourishment.*
"At this time men used to eat a seed not unlike corn, which is called *cincocopi*."[21] With each age the food comes closer to what will subsequently be *to-nácatl*, "our subsistence," a synonym for corn.

LINES 26–27: *They who perished were those who had become turkeys. The offspring of turkeys are now called "pípil-pípil."*
Although these two lines may seem irrelevant, they are related to line 20, "They became turkeys." Until the time of the narrator of the myth, the belief was still popular that turkeys were the descendants of the people who had lived in the Third Age. For this reason the Nahuatl word *pípil-pípil* had continued to be used for turkey; it also meant "child" or "prince."

18 *Ibid.*, III, 233.
19 *Ibid.*, III, 233.
20 *Ibid.*, III, 233.
21 *Ibid.*, III, 233.

LINE 28: *This Sun is called 4-Water; for 52 years the water lasted.*

This is the age of the fourth element, water, and the age of the fourth Sun. Its destruction came by water: "In the last year that Chalchiuhtlicue was Sun, so it is said, so hard did it rain and for so long that the heavens fell. All of the *macehuales* were washed away by the rushing water, and from them every variety of fish was made. Thus life ceased, and the heavens no longer were, for they had fallen to the earth."[22]

LINE 36: *The water lasted 52 years and with this ended their years.*

With this event the story of the first four periods of the world comes to a close. The interim between this age and the next is described in the *Leyenda de los Soles*. Included in the account is Quetzalcóatl's trip to *Mictlan*, the land of the dead, to procure human bones to carry out his new creation.

Sahagún's native historians give additional information concerning the creation of the Fifth Sun. They relate that the creation took place at Teotihuacán. Nanahuatzin, "the Pimply One," competing with the arrogant Tecuciztécatl, "Lord of the Snails," courageously hurled himself into a blazing fire to become the Sun. These myths, although of great human and philosophical interest, can only be briefly mentioned. To present them here and to comment on their richness would be to extend this study beyond its limits. It should be pointed out that there is an abundance of information that has yet to be explored.

LINE 37: *This Sun, called 4-Movement, this is our Sun, the one in which we now live.*

This line agrees with the carving on the Calendar Stone in which the central figure within the sign 4-Movement (*Nahui Ollin*) of the *tonalámatl* or horoscopic calendar represents the face of *Tonatiuh*, "the Sun."

This Fifth Sun marks the Nahuas' first conceptual approach

[22] *Ibid.*, III, 233.

to the idea of movement as an important force in the image and destiny of the world.

LINE 38: *And here is its sign, how the Sun fell into the fire, into the divine hearth, there at Teotihuacán.*

The allusion here is to the myth, previously mentioned, telling of the creation of the Fifth Sun at Teotihuacán, where the gods, having arrived at an agreement, decided to recreate the Sun. Nanahuatzin, "The Pimply One," who daringly threw himself into the fire in order to become the Sun, thereby creating a new age, powerfully suggests the hidden roots of future Aztec mysticism. Only by the very act of sacrifice can the Sun and life exist. Only through human sacrifice can life and existence be prolonged. The most dramatic moments, the climax of the creation of the Fifth Sun, have been recorded by Sahagún:

> It was midnight. And the gods all took their places around the *teotexcalli* [divine hearth]. At this place the fire blazed for four days . . . then the gods spoke; they said to Tecuciztécatl, "Now, Tecuciztécatl, enter the fire!" Then he prepared to throw himself into the enormous fire. He felt the great heat and he was afraid. Being afraid, he dared not hurl himself in, but turned back instead . . . . Four times he tried, four times he failed. After these failures, the gods then spoke to Nanahuatzin, and they said to him: "You, Nanahuatzin, you try!" And as the gods had spoken, he braced himself, closed his eyes, stepped forward, and hurled himself into the fire. The sound of roasting was heard, his body crackled noisily. Seeing him burn thus in the blazing fire, Tecuciztécatl also leaped into the fire. When both of them had been consumed by this great fire, the gods sat down to await the reappearance of Nanahuatzin; where, they wondered, would he appear. Their waiting was long. Suddenly the sky turned red; everywhere the light of dawn appeared. It is said that the gods then knelt to await the rising of Nanahuatzin as the Sun. All about them they looked, but they were unable to guess where he would appear. Some thought that he would appear from the north; they stood, they looked to the north. Towards noon, others felt that he might emerge from anywhere; for all about them, everywhere, was the splendor of dawn. Others looked towards the east, convinced that

from there he would rise, and from the east he did. It is said that Quetzalcóatl, also known as Ehécatl, and another [god] called Tótec, had guessed the place from which he would rise. . . . When it appeared, it was flaming red; it faltered from side to side. No one was able to look at it; its light was brilliant and blinding; its rays were magnificently diffused in all directions. . . .[23]

LINES 40–42: *The Fifth Sun, its sign 4-Movement, is called the Sun of Movement because it moves and follows its path. And as the elders continue to say, under this Sun, there will be earthquakes and hunger, and then our end shall come.*

Line 41 alludes to what the informants of Sahagún had disclosed—in the beginning the Fifth Sun was still. "Then the gods demanded, 'How shall we live? The Sun is still!' " The solution was sacrifice; to give the Sun energy, the gods sacrificed themselves and offered their own blood. At last the great wind blew; the Sun was set in motion, and followed its course.

Line 42 announces the end of the present age. Earthquakes will destroy it on the day 4-Movement, in accordance with the date carved on the Calendar Stone.

Such were the beliefs of the Nahuas concerning the various ages through which the earth had evolved. One may abstract from these concepts, leaving aside the purely mythological, what might be called Nahuatl cosmological categories.

An urgent and logical need to conceive of the world as having a solid foundation was the first and most important category. To the Nahuas, only that which was firmly based and permanent could be considered true. And the only entity with a real self-foundation is Ometéotl, the dual deity, origin and foundation of the cosmic forces—his sons. For this reason, although Ometéotl dwells on the summit of *Omeyocan,* the thirteenth heaven, to sustain and to give foundation to the world, he is also in its navel or center.

Another significant category was the cyclical evolution of the foundations of the world. The earth, created by Ometéotl, is not static; it is ever moving. Subjected to the influence of the

[23] Sahagún, *op. cit.,* II, 14–15.

cosmic forces, it becomes the field of action for these forces. When there is an equilibrium of forces, an age or Sun exists. Soon thereafter, within a determined period, the equilibrium is upset and a cataclysm occurs; the only explanation seems to be that Ometéotl has withdrawn his support from the earth. Yet this is not so. Inherent in the various cycles is a latent principle of evolution, proof of his perpetual action. This potentiality for movement, in the particular case of food plants, for example, culminates in the appearance of corn.

Closely related to the theory of cyclical development is the concept of the four elements symbolized in the *"Historia de los Mexicanos"* by the four sons of Ometéotl. By an amazing parallelism, these elements—earth, wind, fire, and water—are the same four hypothesized as the roots (*ritsomata*) of all things by the Greek philosopher Empedocles and transmitted to Western thought through Aristotle. Eduard Seler said of the relationship between the cosmic periods and the four elements: "These four distinct prehistoric or precosmic ages of the Mexicans, each one oriented toward a different direction of the heavens, are astonishingly related to the four elements, water, earth, wind, and fire, known to classical antiquity and which even now constitute the way that the civilized peoples of East Asia look upon nature."[24]

But to the Nahuas, these were not static elements discovered by theoretical analysis or alchemy. Rather, they were identified from the beginning with the cosmic forces which erupt violently from the four corners of the universe.

This approach to the four elements suggests two additional categories of Nahuatl cosmology: the concept of directions in the universe and the idea of struggle. The universe is divided into four well-defined directions which, although coinciding with the cardinal points, encompass much more than mere direction; each includes a whole quadrant of universal space. The directions are: the East, land of the color red and region of light, sym-

[24] Eduard Seler, *"Entstehung der Welt und der Menschen, Geburt von Sonne und Mond,"* in *Gesammelte Abhandlungen,* IV, 38–39.

bolized by the reed, representing fertility and life; the North, black, region of the dead—a cold and desert area symbolized by flint; the West, region of the color white, the land of woman, whose symbol is the house of the sun; and the South, the blue region to the left of the sun, a direction of uncertain character represented by the rabbit, whose next leap, according to the Nahuas, no one can anticipate.

In this quadripartite universe, a seemingly endless struggle unfolds among the four cosmic forces. Each of the elements, the sons of Ometéotl, is eager for supremacy. Their conflicting desires lead to war, so that in each of the Suns a battle is fought from the four directions of the universe. Through the opposition of elements, the history of the cosmos, as conceived by the Nahuas, unfolds cyclically.

In summary, the story of the Suns clearly demonstrates the existence of five cosmological categories: (1) the logical urgency for a universal foundation; (2) the temporalization of the world into ages or cycles; (3) the idea of primordial elements; (4) the division of space in the universe into quadrants or directions; and, (5) the concept of perpetual struggle for supremacy as a framework in which the occurrence of cosmic events can be understood.

The Nahuatl wise men had discovered that the eternal struggle for supremacy among the four original gods caused the cyclical evolution of the various ages of the world. They were also able to attain a coherent vision of universal space. The Nahuas conceived of horizontal space as an enormous disk of lands surrounded by water—with both lands and waters divided into the four quadrants of the universe. Eduard Seler, discussing this point noted that:

> In the manner of other peoples, the earth was conceived by the Mexicans as a large wheel or disc completely surrounded by water. This platform or ring encompassed by water was called *Anáhuatl*, "ring," or *Cem-Anáhuatl*, "the complete circle." Due to an erroneous interpretation, some early historians began to designate the central part of the present Republic of Mexico as the plateau of *Anáhuac*. In reality, to the ancient Mexicans, this term consistently carried the meaning of land situated "at the edge of the water," or all of the land between the two oceans. They called this water surrounding the earth the ocean *téoatl*, "divine water," or *ilhuíca-atl*, "celestial water." The reason for this was that the water merged with the heavens at the horizon.[25]

Seler related these ideas to the Nahuatl theories concerning the sun and the four quadrants of the universe, as well as to the ethnic origins of the Nahuas themselves:

[25] Eduard Seler, *"Das Weltbild der alten Mexicaner,"* in *Gesammelte Abhandlungen,* IV, 3.

From the water that surrounds the world, the morning sun rises from the East; in the evening, it sets in the West. It was the Mexican belief that they had come from the sea, from the region of light (the East) and that their journey's end had finally been at the Atlantic coast. . . . they also believed that on the way to the underworld, the dead had to cross over *Chicunauhapan,* a wide sea "extended nine times" or "waters which stretch out in every direction."[26]

All of these ideas constitute what one might call the Nahuatl concept of horizontal space. Furthermore, the *tlamatinime,* particularly those dedicated to the observation of "the orderly movements and events of the heavens," devised an astronomical explanation for the universe. They believed that the universe consisted of thirteen vertically superimposed divisions, or heavens, above the earth, and nine hells, or inferior levels. The hells were the land of the dead.

The thirteen heavens were separated from one another by what could be called crossbars, which functioned as floor levels or passages between the heavens, allowing the various celestial bodies to move freely from region to region. Their astronomers, said the Indians, were dedicated to the observation of "the movement of the stars through the passages of the heavens (*ilhuícatl i-oh-tlatoquíliz*)."[27]

A synthesis of several surviving native documents, with emphasis on the pictorial representation in the *Vatican Codex A,* yields a description of the various heavens, beginning with the lowest, the one visible to all. It is through this heaven that the moon travels (*ilhuícatl metztli*), and from which the clouds are suspended.

The Nahuatl idea of the moon and its phases was introduced to the students in this way:

When the moon is born anew, it seems like a delicate little arch of wire, no radiance does it emanate; little by little, it begins to grow.

[26] *Ibid.,* IV, 3.
[27] Lehmann (ed.), *Colloquies and Christian Doctrine,* 93 (fol. 3,v.).

Upon the fifteenth day, it becomes full, and when it is so, it appears in the East.

At the setting of the sun, the moon emerges like a large millstone, very round and very red.

And when it is rising, it looks white in its center and radiant; a rabbit it seems to be, and if there are no clouds, it shines like the midday sun.

And after attaining its height of fullness, little by little it begins to wane, ultimately to become what it was in the beginning.

Then they say, "Now the moon is dying, now it is getting sleepy."

It is at this time that the moon appears with the dawn. And at the time of the conjunction, it is said, "The moon now is dead."[28]

The second heaven, beautifully illustrated in the *Vatican Codex A*, was *Citlalco*, the place of the stars.[29] The stars, the luminous skirt wrapped about the feminine aspect of Ometéotl, were divided into two large groups: the four hundred (countless) stars of the North (*Centzon Mimixcoa*) and the four hundred (countless) stars of the South (*Centzon Huitznahua*).

The Nahuatl astronomers also observed constellations; the Big Bear was called the tiger, *Tezcatlipoca*, and the Little Bear was given the name *Citlalxonecuilli*. The latter name, according to Sahagún, was chosen "because of the resemblance of this group of stars to a type of bread which used to be made in the form of an "S" and which was called *Xonecuilli*. . . ."[30] The constellation Scorpio by coincidence received the same name, *Cólotl* (scorpion). The three stars that form the head of Taurus were designated by the word *mamalhuaztli*, which, as Sahagún noted, was the name of the sticks used for lighting the new fire at the beginning of every Nahuatl cycle of fifty-two years. Of great significance to the Nahuas were the movements of this group and the Pleiades, called *tianquiztli*, for the survival of the world depended upon their movements. At midnight of the day ending the fifty-two-year cycle, if the stars followed their courses, the new fire would be lighted as a sign of fifty-two more years

28 Sahagún, *op. cit.*, II, 12.
29 *Codex Vaticanus A*, fol. 1,v. and 2,r.
30 Sahagún, *op. cit.*, II, 18.

of life. Near present-day Mexico City stands the old pyramid of Tenayuca which the Acolhuas, Tecpanecs, and Aztecs elaborated and enlarged by superimposing new levels at the ends of fifty-two-year cycles. This monument is concrete evidence of the profound significance the beginning of every new cycle had for the Nahuas.[31]

The Heaven of the Sun (*Ilhuícatl Tonatiuh*) was the third region of the heavens. *Tonatiuh* (the Sun) traveled over this heaven in his journey from the region of light to his home in the West. Sahagún recorded something of what was taught in the *Calmécac* concerning the sun:

> The Sun, eagle with arrows of fire.
> Lord of time, god.
> He shines, makes things radiant, casts his rays of light upon them.
> His heat is felt, he scorches people, makes them sweat,
> He darkens their faces, blackens them, turns them black as smoke.[32]

Fourth of the heavens was *Ihuícatl huitztlan*. This is where Venus, called *Citlálpol* or *Hueycitlalin*, "the Big Star," is seen. Venus was the planet most carefully observed and studied by the Nahuatl astronomers. Since Teotihuacán times it had been associated with Quetzalcóatl. This association is obvious in the decoration of the temple at Teotihuacán, commonly known as the *Ciudadela* (the Citadel). Among its sculptured ornaments is "the plumed serpent surrounded by sea shells." The association of Venus with Quetzalcóatl can probably be attributed to the fact that when this planet sets upon the moving waters of the Pacific, its reflection seems not unlike a serpent with brilliant scales and plumes.[33]

> The observation . . . of Venus acquired considerable importance in Náhuatl astronomy and chronology. Sixty-five Venusian years were the equivalent of one hundred and four years of the sun, a long period called *huehueliztli* "an old age." At the end of this

---

[31] Ignacio Marquina, "*Estudio arquitectónico de la pirámide*," in *Tenayuca*, an archaeological study of the pyramid of Tenayuca, 101.

[32] *Códice Matritense del Real Palacio*, VI, fol. 177.

[33] Manuel Gamio and others, *La Población del Valle Teotihuacán*, I, p. xlvi.

period the new beginning of the solar and the Venusian cycle coincided on the date of the divinatory calendar. . . .[34]

In the fifth heaven were the comets, the "smoking stars" (*citlalin popoca*).

The sixth and seventh of the celestial levels were two heavens in which only the colors green and blue could be seen; or, according to another version, black (*yayauhco*) and blue (*xoxouhco*), that is, the heavens of night and day.

The eighth heaven appears to have been the place of storms, while the three heavens above the eighth—the white, yellow, and red—were reserved as dwelling places for the gods.

Most important of the thirteen levels were the last two, which constituted *Omeyocan*: the mansion of duality, the source of generation and life, the ultimate or metaphysical region, the primordial dwelling place of Ometéotl.

The originality inherent in this vision of space also endowed the Nahuas with a peculiar and exclusive point of view. This image of the universe affected at least implicitly all of their works, their literature, their painting, and their art. Perhaps there is nothing which verifies this point so conclusively as the total configuration of forms and cosmological relationships in the imposing statue of the goddess Coatlicue, the mother of the Aztec god Huitzilopochtli. Justino Fernández, in his authoritative study of this great work of art, perceived in the sculpture the same meaning revealed in the texts themselves:

> It is not a pre-logical mentality which has conceived Coatlicue; on the contrary, its structural elements are indicative of a clear and logical mentality and its forms attest a vigorous and highly imaginative sensitivity. . . .[35]

Pointing out specifically the fundamental structural elements of the statue—pyramidal, cruciform, and human simultaneously —Fernández discerns in the powerful sculpture the Aztec concept of cosmic space, in all its richness and profundity:

[34] Jacques Soustelle, *La Pensée Cosmologique des anciens mexicains*, 29.
[35] Justino Fernández, *Coatlicue, estética del arte indigena antiguo*, 215.

At the highest level [of Coatlicue], a point to begin or a point on which to end, one arrives at Omeyocan, dwelling place of the divine couple—Ometecuhtli and Omecíhuatl—the supreme creator, origin of begotten gods and men. Even though this bicephalous mass takes the place of the head and appears to emerge from the innermost of the statue's entirety, there is also a feeling of decapitation which suggests *Coyolxauhqui,* the moon, with which the astral system is completed.

As the total cruciform structure suggests, there remain to be added the four cardinal directions; and the fifth direction—upward and downward—in the center of which will be found Xiuhtecuhtli, "the old Lord," the god of fire. And finally, the pyramidal form, descending and ascending, which designates the two extremes from the very depths of the earth, the land of the dead, to the most elevated of the heavens, *Omeyocan* (the place of Duality). Thus the sculptured work is not only conceived from external viewpoint; the bodies of the serpents whose heads emerge from the uppermost level of the statue have their point of departure in its very inner being. And it should be kept in mind that underneath the feet of this statue, the world of the dead extends itself. The total configuration vibrates; an inner and outer life palpitates; it is representative of both life and death. The content of the form encompasses all of the possible directions and is prolonged within them. In summary, Coatlicue is, *in nuce,* the embodiment of the cosmic-dynamic power which bestows life and which thrives on death in the struggle of opposites, a struggle so compulsory and essential, that its fundamental and final meaning is war. . . .[36]

Coatlicue emerges powerfully as the concrete embodiment in stone of the ideas of a supreme cosmic being who generates and sustains the universe. It adumbrates the cruciform orientation of the quadrants of the universe, as well as the dynamic quality of time, which creates and destroys through struggle; this is the central category of Nahuatl cosmological thought. Perhaps of all the symbols of the Nahuatl universe, the most marvelous is the tragically beautiful image of Coatlicue.

Figuring importantly in Nahuatl cosmology is the idea of

[36] *Ibid.,* 265–66.

motion. What was the nature of motion to the Nahuas? How did they conceive it? And what was their position when confronted by this problem? A brief analysis of their attitudes toward the Fifth Sun, or the "age in which we live" will elucidate their approach to the problem which still puzzles Western thinkers.

In each of the four previous ages, one of the four elements had attained supremacy over the others. While each was in power, an age had existed, but the competition for supremacy had led to combat, the harmony of the ages had been destroyed, and the ages had passed, one after another. Once again, say the myths, a certain harmony was established by the gods, who agreed to sacrifice themselves at Teotihuacán. As a result of this harmony, the Fifth Age, the Sun of Movement, had begun; *Nahui ollin* (4-Movement) was its sign. And according to the myths, "the sun moved, it followed its path" as a consequence of the sacrifice of the gods (the cosmic forces).

But to keep the sun in motion, constantly moving, a concession had been necessary. To each of the four fundamental gods, to each of the four directions, a specified period of time within the Fifth Age was allotted for domination and subordination. This division of time gave rise to the years of the East, of the North, of the West, and of the South. In abstract terms, motion appeared as a consequence of the spatialization of time and of the orientation of the years and the days toward the four directions. Such a conclusion can be drawn from the accounts of Sahagún's Indian informants explaining the tabulation of the year-count, in which the years are spatially oriented:

1. One Rabbit, this is the name of the annual sign, the year-count for the region of the South.

2. Thirteen years it carries, guiding, carrying always on its shoulders each of the thirteen years.

3. And it goes along, guiding, beginning; it introduces all of the signs of the years: reed, flint, house.

4. Reed is the name given to the sign of the region of light (East); the same name is given to the annual sign of the region of light, for from there the light appears, the radiance (of each day).

5. The third group of years: flint. It is called the sign of the region of the dead.

6. Because toward that region, as the elders used to say, is the land of the dead.

7. It is said that when one dies, one goes there; one goes directly there, in that direction do the dead set out.

8. And the fourth annual sign, house, was called the sign of the region of women; for so it was said, it is oriented toward the women (West).

9. It is said that there the women always dwell alone, that there are no men.

10. These four annual signs, these series . . . one by one they come along; they become the first days of the various years.

11. When all of the thirteen years had ended, the next thirteen approached; they would also end. Four cycles would they make . . . each group of thirteen would go by, year by year.[37]

A close look at the table of the fifty-two year count preserved by Sahagún shows it to be very similar to the foregoing text, and clearly illustrates that in a Nahuatl century of fifty-two years, each of the four directions was allotted a thirteen-year period of predominant influence. In a similar manner, within each year, the days of the *tonalámatl* (sacred calendar) were divided into sixty-five-day series of five thirteen-day "weeks." In a year of 260 days, there were four of these 65-day groups, and each carried a sign which related it to one of the four cardinal directions. Jacques Soustelle, who has investigated this point carefully noted:

The most important Indian manuscripts demonstrate a clear distribution of twenty day-signs among the four directions:

	East		*North*
Cipactli,	alligator	*Océlotl,*	tiger
Acatl,	reed	*Miquiztli,*	death
Cóatl,	serpent	*Técpatl,*	flint
Ollin,	movement	*Itzcuintli,*	dog
Atl,	water	*Ehécatl,*	wind

[37] *Códice Matritense del Real Palacio,* VII, fol. 269,r.

	West		South
Mázatl,	deer	*Xóchitl,*	flower
Quiáuitl,	rain	*Malinalli,*	herb
Ozomatli,	monkey	*Cuetzpalin,*	lizard
Calli,	house	*Cozcaquauhtli,*	vulture
Quauhtli,	eagle	*Tochtli,*	rabbit.[38]

Thus, not only in each year, but also in each day, the influence of one of the four spatial directions predominated. Space and time, combining and interpenetrating, made possible the harmony among the gods (the four cosmic forces) and, consequently, the movement of the sun and the existence of life. The profound significance of movement to the Nahuas can be deduced from the common Nahuatl root of the words movement, heart, and soul. To the ancient Mexicans, life, symbolized by the heart (*y-óllo-tl*), was inconceivable without the element which explains it, movement (*y-olli*).

The Nahuas, therefore, believed that movement and life resulted from the harmony achieved by the spatial orientation of the years and the days, in other words, by the spatialization of time. So long as this harmony continued, so long as the four directions of the universe were each allotted thirteen years in every century and their supremacy unquestioned during the specified time, the Fifth Sun would continue to exist—it would continue to move. Should this balance some day be disturbed, another cosmic struggle for supremacy would be initiated. There would be one final earthquake—one so powerful that "with this we shall perish."[39]

In the intervening time, as they awaited the arrival of the fatal *Nahui ollin* (day 4-Movement) which would end the cycle of the Fifth Sun, the Aztecs continued to nourish this Sun daily with *chalchíhuatl*, the precious sacrificial liquid. The *tlamatinime*, in turn, observed the world from the original point of view of spatialized time, of which Jacques Soustelle wrote:

The natural phenomena and human activity penetrate each place

[38] Soustelle, *La Pensée Cosmologique*, 46.
[39] Lehmann (ed.), *Annals of Cuauhtitlán, loc. cit.*, 62.

and each moment so that they become impregnated with their own peculiar qualities. Each "place-moment" complex of location and time determines in an irresistible and foreseeable way (by means of the *tonalámatl*), everything existing within it. The world may be compared to a stage screen on which a number of different light filters of various colors are projected by a tireless machine. The color projections follow one another, overlap, and infinitely adhere to an unalterable sequence. In such a world, change is not conceived as a consequence of a "becoming" which gradually develops, but as something abrupt and total. Today the East is dominant; tomorrow the North; today we live in good times, and without a gradual transition, we shall pass into the unfavorable days (*nemontemi*). The law of the universe is the alternation of distinct qualities, radically separated, which dominate, vanish, and reappear eternally.[40]

A retrospective appraisal of the points discussed here provides a synthesis of the various aspects of the Nahuatl cosmological vision.

The surface of the earth (*tlaltícpac*) is a great disk situated in the center of the universe and extending horizontally and vertically. Encircling the earth like a ring is an immense body of water (*téo-atl*), which makes the world *cem-á-nahuac*, "that-which-is-entirely-surrounded-by-water." Neither the land nor the great ring of water is considered to be amorphous or to possess undifferentiated qualities, for the universe is divided into four great quadrants of space whose common point of departure is the navel of the earth. From this point the four quadrants extend all the way out to the meeting place, on the horizon, of the heavens and the surrounding celestial water (*Ilhuíca-atl*). The concept of the four directions of the world is heavy with symbolic meaning. Contemplating the passage of the sun, the Nahuas described the cosmic quadrants from a position facing the West: "There where it sets, there is its home, in the land of the red color. To the left of the sun's path is the South, the direction of the blue color; opposite the region of the sun's house

[40] Soustelle, *La Pensée Cosmologique*, 85.

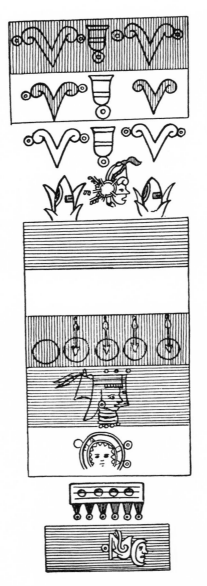

THE ELEVEN LEVELS OF THE HEAVENS
separated by celestial crossbars. From the *Vatican Codex A*, fol. 1.

is the direction of light, fertility and life, symbolized by the color white; and finally, to the right of the sun's route, the black quadrant of the universe, the direction of the land of the dead, is to be seen."

Such was the Nahuatl image of horizontal space. In the vertical division of space, above and below the horizontal world (*cem-a-náhuac*), there were thirteen heavens and nine hells. In the underworlds, each successively deeper than the last, the fleshless (the dead) were to be subjected to a series of trials for four years before complete rest could be attained.

Above *cem-a-náhuac* are the heavens. Resting on an almost metaphysical plane, joining the waters that completely surround the world, these heavens are comparable to a blue dome. Within it, running on different levels and separated by what the Nahuas described as celestial crossbars, are the series of passages in which the heavenly bodies move. On the first five levels are the paths of the moon, the stars, the sun, Venus, and the comets. They are succeeded by the heavens of the different colors; above these is the metaphysical beyond, the region of the gods; and ultimately, above all things, is *Omeyocan* (the place of duality), the dwelling place of the dual supreme deity, generator and founder of the universe.

Anachronously employing a modern Western concept, this vision of the Nahuas might be termed their static cosmology. To complete the total cosmological image of the universe, however, it is well to consider and incorporate the dynamic qualities studied in this chapter. Once again our attention is focused on the center of the world, the navel, as the Nahuas called it. From there the dual deity who dwells on the summit of heaven exercised his sustaining action. Emanating from the navel of the world, Ometéotl "gives foundation to the earth (*tlallamánac*)." Also from there "he covers it with cotton (*tlallíchcatl*)."

Endowing with life and movement all that exists is Ipalnemohuani, "the Giver of life." His presence extends to "the waters the color of the bluebird." From his "enclosure of clouds," he regulates the motion of the moon and the stars, which symbolize the skirt of the feminine aspect of the engendering being. And finally, identified as the celestial body which illumines and gives life to all things, he reveals his principal masculine character as the creator endowed with extraordinary generating power.

Sharing the divine role of perpetual power with the god of duality are the other forces which popular thought designated as the "innumerable gods." These gods, however, from the most abstract point of view of Nahuatl cosmology, are the four powers which Ometéotl had produced. They are his four sons, the four elements: earth, air, fire, and water. Acting from the four directions of the universe, these elements bring into the universe the concepts of struggle, ages, cataclysms, evolution, and spatial orientation of time.

Motivated by the desire for supremacy, each element endeavors to identify itself with the life-giving action of the sun. Consequently, a great cosmic struggle is initiated. Each period of ascendancy represents a Sun, an age; then destruction comes again. Subsequently a new world appears. Corresponding to the evolutionary process of the ages, there appears to be a development of food plants and *macehuales*. The movement is from rudimentary to higher forms of plants and men. In this manner four Suns have ended; ours is the fifth, the Sun of Movement, and for this period a certain harmony—a balance of power among the various cosmic forces—has been achieved. The gods have accepted the alternating distribution of supremacy, orienting it consecutively toward each of the four directions of the universe. From these directions the cosmic forces act and develop. Ours is the age of the spatialized years: years of the direction of light, years of the region of the dead, years of the direction of the house of the sun, and years of the blue zone to the left of the sun. The influence of each direction is felt not only in the physical universe, but also in the life of each mortal. The various influences that endlessly succeed one another can only be revealed by the *tonalámatl*. The succession is part of a mysterious harmony of tensions which the Nahuatl astrologers seek in vain to understand and to control.

The final destiny of our age is to be a cataclysm, the rupture of the established harmony. "There will be earthquakes and hunger, and then our end shall come." But in spite of the pessimistic nature inherent in such a cosmic conclusion, the Nahuas did not lose their vigorous enthusiasm. On the contrary, this conclusion was precisely the powerful impetus that moved them forward in two remarkable ways. The Aztecs oriented themselves toward the path of mystic imperialism. Convinced that in order to avoid the final cataclysm it was necessary to fortify the sun, they undertook for themselves the mission of furnishing it with the vital energy found only in the precious liquid which keeps man alive. Sacrifice and ceremonial warfare, which was the principal manner of obtaining victims for the sacrificial rites, were their central activities and the very core of their personal, social, military, religious, and national life. This mystical vision of the cult of Huitzilopochtli transformed the Aztecs into great warriors, into "the people of the Sun." This was the attitude taken by the Aztecs in the face of the impending final disaster, which was to bring the Fifth Sun to an end.

But there was another orientation, another reaction to the imminent catastrophe. Since Toltec times there had been profound thinkers eager to confront, on the spatial-temporal level, the dreaded destruction which was to come. Working in this milieu, they created a strictly metaphysical concept in regard to the Divine and to a possible life after death. Many speculations and hypotheses on the subject are to be found in the Nahuatl texts.

Salvation was frequently sought in ancient religious doctrines, but these beliefs were often questioned. There was open doubt concerning them, and the problem of the Divine and of the survival and destiny of man was often formulated in a clearly rational manner, independent of myth and tradition. The chapters to follow deal with these speculations—the loftiest aspects of Nahuatl philosophical thought.

III

Metaphysical and Theological Ideas
of the Nahuas

NO testimony speaks so eloquently of the esteem in which the ancient Mexicans held their theological doctrines as the answer made by some surviving Nahuatl wise men in 1524 to an attack by the first twelve missionary friars on the validity of the Indian religion and tradition. This dramatic defense was recorded, along with many of the conversations and discussions on the subject of religion between the native chiefs and wise men and the twelve friars in Mexico-Tenochtitlan, only three years after the collapse of the Aztecs. Based on documents discovered at Tlatelolco and collected and recorded by Sahagún, these discussions constitute a significant part of Sahagún's work, *The Colloquies*.[1]

Contrary to general belief, the *tlamatinime* were neither passive nor submissive. They discussed and questioned the doctrine introduced by the friars. Their public defense of Nahuatl religion and traditions constituted perhaps the last and the most dramatic of their public appearances. The extreme courtesy and prudence of their words show that they were aware of the subordinate position of a conquered people. Although the discussion

[1] Lehmann (ed.), *Colloquies and Christian Doctrine*, 100–106.

certainly could not be undertaken on a basis of equality, none-theless, the *tlamatinime* did not feel that they must refrain from courageously defending their ideas, their religion, and traditions from what they considered to be unjustified attacks.

Their words clearly indicate an organized knowledge of the Divine. Speaking before a large crowd of people and perhaps not wishing to elaborate their explanation beyond the compre-hension of the friars, the *tlamatinime* emphasized only the most relevant points in defense of the Nahuatl concept of the Divine. They were concerned with demonstrating that this concept was worthy of respect because of its richness and high degree of de-velopment, and that it was a solid framework for strict rules of conduct as well as for traditions. The nature and manner of their defense follows:

> Our Lords, our very esteemed Lords:
> great hardships have you endured to reach this land.
> Here before you,
> we ignorant people contemplate you. . . .
>
> And now, what are we to say?
> What should we cause your ears to hear?
> Perchance, is there any meaning to us?
> Only very common people are we. . . .
>
> Through an interpreter we reply,
> we exhale the breath and the words
> of the Lord of the Close Vicinity.
> Because of Him we dare to do this.
> For this reason we place ourselves in danger. . . .
>
> Perhaps we are to be taken to our ruin, to our destruction.
> But where are we to go now?
> We are ordinary people,
> we are subject to death and destruction, we are mortals;
> allow us then to die,
> let us perish now,
> since our gods are already dead.
>
> But calm your hearts . . .

Our Lords!
Because we will break open a little,
we will open a bit now
the secret, the ark of the Lord, our god.

You said
that we know not
the Lord of the Close Vicinity,
to Whom the heavens and the earth belong.
You said
that our gods are not true gods.
New words are these
that you speak;
because of them we are disturbed,
because of them we are troubled.
For our ancestors
before us, who lived upon the earth,
were unaccustomed to speak thus.
From them have we inherited
our pattern of life
which in truth did they hold;
in reverence they held,
they honored, our gods.
They taught us
all their rules of worship,
all their ways of honoring the gods.
Thus before them, do we prostrate ourselves;
in their names we bleed ourselves;
our oaths we keep,
incense we burn,
and sacrifices we offer.

It was the doctrine of the elders
that there is life because of the gods;
with their sacrifice, they gave us life.
In what manner? When? Where?
When there was still darkness.

It was their doctrine
that they [the gods] provide our subsistence,

64

all that we eat and drink,
that which maintains life: corn, beans,
amaranth, sage.
To them do we pray
for water, for rain
which nourish things on earth.

They themselves are rich,
happy are they,
things do they possess;
so forever and ever,
things sprout and grow green in their domain . . .
there "where somehow there is life," in the place of Tlalocan.
There, hunger is never known,
no sickness is there,
poverty there is not.
Courage and the ability to rule
they gave to the people. . . .

And in what manner? When? Where were the gods invoked?
Were they appealed to; were they accepted as such;
were they held in reverence?

For a long time has it been;
it was there at Tula,
it was there at Huapalcalco,
it was there at Xuchatlapan,
it was there at Tlamohuanchan,
it was there at Yohuallichan,
it was there at Teotihuacán.

Above the world
they had founded
their kingdom.
They gave the order, the power,
glory, fame.

And now, are we
to destroy
the ancient order of life?
Of the Chichimecs,

of the Toltecs,
of the Acolhuas,
of the Tecpanecs?

We know
on Whom life is dependent;
on Whom the perpetuation of the race depends;
by Whom begetting is determined;
by Whom growth is made possible;
how it is that one must invoke,
how it is that one must pray.

Hear, oh Lords,
do nothing
to our people
that will bring misfortune upon them,
that will cause them to perish. . . .

Calm and amiable,
consider, oh Lords,
whatever is best.
We cannot be tranquil,
and yet we certainly do not believe;
we do not accept your teachings as truth,
even though this may offend you.

Here are
the Lords, those who rule,
those who sustain, whose duty is to
the entire world.
Is it not enough that we have already lost,
that our way of life has been taken away,
has been annihilated.

Were we to remain in this place,
we could be made prisoners.
Do with us
as you please.

This is all that we answer,

that we reply,
to your breath,
to your words,
Oh, our Lords![2]

The *tlamatinime* skillfully begin their discourse; they humble themselves before the friars, praising them for their voyage "amidst the clouds and the mist" from beyond the sea. But, almost unexpectedly, they declare their determination to contradict and question. In spite of their humble attitude, and acknowledging the possible consequences by their statement, "we place ourselves in danger," the *tlamatinime* openly proclaim that not even the fear of death can keep them from expressing themselves. Rather, it is death that they seek, since, according to the friars, "our gods are already dead."

Following this powerful declaration, the *tlamatinime* refer to the allegations of the friars: "You said that we know not the Lord of the Close Vicinity, to Whom the heavens and the earth belong." Their reaction is first one of wonder, but the reasoning which follows is sound and coherent. The answer is that of any devout follower of a religious faith. "From [our ancestors] have we inherited our pattern of life . . . in truth did they hold . . . our gods, they taught us all their rules of worship, all their ways of honoring the gods."

Having demonstrated the relationship of their beliefs to the ancient knowledge handed down from generation to generation, the *tlamatinime* present a series of varied and profound arguments. The first, perhaps the most meaningful, was easily understood by the majority of the people. It concerned the ancient myth of the creation of the heavenly bodies and of man at Teotihuacán, where the gods assembled to create the Fifth Sun, our present epoch.

"It was the doctrine of the elders," affirmed the Nahuatl wise men, "that there is life because of the gods." Even more significant is the exact specification of the time and manner of the

---

[2] *Ibid.*, 100–106.

creation: "when there was still darkness [*in oc iohuaya*]." These words, as Lehmann notes, mean "in the times preceding all epochs, before anything definite existed."[3] The *tlamatinime* consign the origin of all things to a period of darkness in which no well-defined forms existed. In that vague precosmic interval beyond all determined time and space, the activity of the divine forces began. Such was the antiquity of the existence and the action of the gods.

Other arguments of the *tlamatinime* reinforce the validity of their beliefs and traditions. Not only did the gods create life at a time "when there was still darkness," but throughout all time they maintained life: "They provide our subsistence, all that we eat and drink, that which maintains life: corn, beans . . . ." The gods, the cosmic forces, also determine "the production of things," for they make the rain and water possible. And a clear allusion is made to a marvelous symbol of fecundity, the divine dwelling place "where somehow there is life" in Tlalocan (home of Tláloc, god of rain), and where "things sprout and grow green."

All of these deeply philosophical arguments could be understood by the listening crowd, for repetition of the myths had made them familiar to most of the Nahuas. Historical data, based on what might be called authoritative sources, were also included in the *tlamatinime's* argument. They began by asking: "And in what manner? When? Where were the gods invoked . . . appealed to . . . accepted as such . . . held in reverence?" The answer is clear and direct. "For a very long time this has been so." The most ancient religious and cultural centers, where, according to tradition, "in truth were the gods," are enumerated: Tula, Huapalcalco, Xuchatlapan, Tlamohuanchan, Yohuallichan, and Teotihuacán. Over the entire world (*nohuían cemanáhuac*) the gods ruled.

The conclusion, reinforced by a new argument, is impressive. "Are we to destroy the ancient order of life? Of the Chichimecs, of the Toltecs, of the Acolhuas, of the Tecpanecs?" It is not pos-

[3] *Ibid.*, 103.

sible to obliterate a way of life and of thought whose very roots are tenaciously imbedded in the earliest traditions of the Nahuatl people.

Moving without hesitation from philosophy to history, and manifesting their awareness of the "cultural continuity of the Nahuas," the *tlamatinime* again return to the realm of the metaphysical. In summary manner they set forth certain propositions which appear to be the principal concepts of their theology. "We know," they said, "on Whom life is dependent; on Whom the perpetuation of the race depends; by Whom begetting is determined; by Whom growth is made possible."

Since allusion is made to theological knowledge deliberated beforehand, it is not surprising to discover in the end that the purpose of the *tlamatinime* was to insist that the friars respect the Nahuatl way of thinking and believing. "Do nothing to our people that will bring misfortune upon them . . . ." For what the friars teach "we do not accept as truth," and we say so even though "this may offend you."

It was an unquestionable fact to the *tlamatinime*: their people had been dispossessed of their liberty and their way of life. The conquerors had destroyed their culture; gone were their gods, their art, in fact, their entire civilization. "Do with us as you please. This is all that we answer, that we reply . . . Oh, our lords!" With these final tragic words, the curtain closes on the few *tlamatinime* who had survived the Conquest and about whom we have authentic historical information. The words of the Nahuatl wise men reflect powerfully "the violent clash of the thinking and faith of the Europeans with the spiritual world of the ancient Mexicans." They also prove the existence of an active theological knowledge among the Nahuas.

The available texts will permit, within certain limits, the reconstruction of the elaborate and active theological system of the Nahuas. There is other documentation, however, which is invaluable because it deals with problems of metaphysical knowledge and the Divine in general. An analysis of this information is indispensable to the study of those texts dealing in detail with the rational Nahuatl concepts of the Divine. For, indeed, the Nahuatl philosophers made other affirmations beside those regarding the supreme being. They expressed doubts about and questioned the nature of existence, the Divine, and life after death.

In almost all cultures a common human phenomenon occurs. Profound theological speculation and insight develop alongside the popular religion. The ancient Eleatic philosopher Parmenides distinguished between these two realms of thought by classifying them as two different modes, the one of "opinion," the other of "being" or authentic reality. In the intellectual life of the Nahuas, an analogous development of the two modes took place.

The works of art unearthed by archaeology, the codices, and the chronicles of the early missionaries and historians all speak of countless gods. Outstanding among these were the patron gods such as Huitzilopochtli and Camaxtli. Quite often they are designated by a number of different names. In addition, the myths interweave, overlap, merge, and become tinted with the local color. It follows that whoever attempts to trace and organize the genealogies within the complex Nahuatl pantheon is confronted with no easy task.

The popular religion of the Nahuas was not only polytheistic, it was also an amalgam of diverse regional gods. During the reign of the last king, Motecuhzoma, a great number of the gods of other peoples were freely assimilated by the popular religion. For this diversity of assimilated gods, a special temple called *Coateocalli* (temple of many gods) was erected within the great Tenochtitlan, and, consequently, the number of deities that were worshiped increased day by day. Father Durán's *History* treats this subject in detail:

> The need of a temple to commemorate all of the idols worshiped in the land seems to have been felt by King Motecuhzoma. Motivated by religious enthusiasm, he ordered that it be built within

the temple of Huitzilopochtli, where the houses of Acevedo now stand. They called it *Coateocalli,* which means temple of many gods, because within it, in one room, were located the countless gods of many peoples. . . . Whoever has passed by these houses [of Acevedo] has surely noticed that great was the number of these gods, of many kinds, faces, and workmanship, for they are now strewn all about.[4]

Running parallel to the popular religion were the more profound theological speculations of the Nahuas. Their quest for rational answers ultimately led them to question and to formulate problems in a philosophical manner about the very things the people accepted and believed. They expressed poetically some of the first difficulties they had come upon through rational inquiry. Consciously seeking knowledge "concerning what transcends our powers of understanding, the beyond," the *tlamatinime* compared their metaphysically directed knowledge with the ideal of true knowledge, to the extent that man is able to grasp it. As a result of the comparison, they experienced the intense doubt that has tormented the thinkers of all ages:

Is there perchance any truth to our words here?
All seems so like a dream, only do we rise from sleep,
only on earth do our words remain.[5]

Since what one finds on earth (*in tlaltícpac*) is transitory, "Is one able to find anything on earth which endures?" The question expresses the dubious value of that earthly knowledge which aspires to reach out from the world of illusion in search of a rational explanation for "what transcends our understanding, what might be beyond." From the beginning, the trend of the search is inclined to be negative: "All seems so like a dream [here on earth]." And, further, "only do we awake to dream." This idea appears consistently in the writings of anonymous

[4] Diego de Durán, *Historia de las Indias de Nueva Espana y Islas de Tierra firme,* I, 456.
[5] *MSS Cantares Mexicanos,* fol. 5,v.

Nahuatl thinkers, as well as in poems whose authorship is known:

> So has it been said by Tochihuitzin,
> so has it been said by Coyolchiuhqui:
> It is not true, it is not true
> that we come to this earth to live.
> We come only to sleep, only to dream.
> Our body is a flower.
> As grass becomes green in the springtime,
> so our hearts will open, and give forth buds,
> and then they wither.
> So did Tochihuitzin say.[6]

Several of the poems attributed to the well-known king Nezahualcóyotl show that deliberation on the evanescence of earthly things was a basic theme and point of departure for his speculation. Two of his philosophical poems illustrate this concern:

> Is it true that on earth one lives?
> Not forever on earth, only a little while.
> Though jade it may be, it breaks;
> though gold it may be, it is crushed;
> though it be quetzal plumes, it shall not last.
> Not forever on earth, only a little while.[7]

The other poem, also commenting on the transitory nature of life on earth, is preserved by Ixtlilxóchitl in his *History of the Chichimec Nation*:

> when you depart from this life to the next, oh King Yoyontzin,
> the time will come when your vassals will be broken and destroyed,
> and all your things will be engulfed by oblivion. . . .
> For this is the inevitable outcome of all powers, empires, and
>   domains;
> transitory are they and unstable.
> The time of life is borrowed,
> in an instant it must be left behind.[8]

---

[6] *Ibid.*, fol. 14,v.
[7] *Ibid.*, fol. 17,r.
[8] Ixtlilxóchitl, *Obras Históricas*, II, 235–36.

Cane

Citlaltotonameete

THE SUN OF THE SECOND AGE
"Those who lived under this second Sun were carried away by the
wind." From the *Vatican Codex* A, fol. 6.

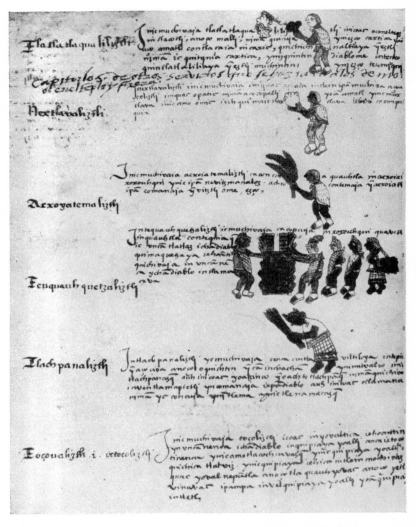

A PAGE OF THE *Códice Matritense del Real Palacio*
the texts of the Indian informants of Bernardino de Sahagún.

Arriving at the unquestionable conclusion that in this earthly life nothing endures, that nothing is "true" in the Nahuatl sense of the word (*nelli,* related to *nel-huá-yotl,* "root, foundation, base"), Nezahualcóyotl and the other *tlamatinime* became even more obsessed with finding an authentic meaning for human activity and thought. If human life is only transitory on *tlaltícpac,* how might one express any truth concerning what is beyond all human experience, concerning the Giver of Life? A paradox exists: If this life is only a dream, our words (because they are earthly) are incapable of coming near to "what transcends us, the beyond." In man's effort to forget that "one day we must go, one night we will descend into the region of mystery,"[9] he can seek consolation in the drunkenness produced by mushroom wine.

The inevitable answer, as the Nahuatl poets and wise men must have conceded, was to live life on earth to the fullest—to derive the maximum pleasure possible:

> One day we must go,
> one night we will descend into the region of mystery.
> Here, we only come to know ourselves;
> only in passing are we here on earth.
> In peace and pleasure let us spend our lives; come, let us enjoy
> ourselves.
> Let not the angry do so; the earth is vast indeed!
> Would that one lived forever; would that one were not to die![10]

This reaction to the possibility of arriving at transcendent truth at least mentally was not the only answer suggested by the Nahuas, nor was it the one the most intensely imbedded in their spirit. Burdened by the paradox, they sought a new form of knowledge—one that would enable man to understand the unchanging principle, founded upon itself, on which thoughts and realities must rest. That foundation of all existing and knowable things might be the supreme deity addressed in the popular

---

[9] *MSS Cantares Mexicanos,* fol. 25,v.
[10] *Ibid.,* fol. 26,r.

religion as "Giver of Life." The *tlamatinime* wondered if dream and illusion could be transcended in the effort to comment truthfully on the supreme being:

> Perchance, oh Giver of Life, do we really speak?
> Even though we may offer the Giver of Life
> emeralds and fine ointments,
> if with the offering of necklaces you are invoked,
> with the strength of the eagle, of the tiger,
> it may be that on earth no one speaks the truth.[11]

This first attempt to escape dream and illusion inquired into the truth of the "Giver of Life" through the medium of religious offerings. "Even though we may offer . . . emeralds and fine ointments . . . it may be that on earth no one speaks the truth." The tone is negative; the offerings to the supreme being do not open the door to truth. And another poem addressed to the Divine repeats the negative tone:

> How many can say that the truth is or is not beyond?
> You, Giver of Life act mysteriously there.[12]

The popular and public cult of the gods as expressed in sacrifice and the mystical militaristic vision of the Aztecs was differentiated from the *tlamatinime*'s search for a new form of knowledge which might embody the truth. In their quest they explored the possibilities of a new way of saying "true words" about what "is above us, what is beyond." The adequate formulation of the theory they developed concerning metaphysical knowledge also found expression in their poetry. One poem in particular describes this attainment. It was recited in the house of Tecayehuatzin, lord of Huexotzinco, on the occasion of a meeting of wise men and poets:

> Thus spoke Ayocuan Cuetzpaltzin
> who without doubt knew the Giver of Life . . .
> "Now do I hear the words of the *coyolli* bird

[11] *Ibid.*, fol. 13,r.
[12] *Ibid.*, fol. 62,r.

as he makes answer to the Giver of Life.
He goes his way singing, offering flowers.
And his words rain down
like jade and quetzal plumes.

Is that what pleases the Giver of Life?
Is that the only truth on earth?"[13]

The meaning of the poem is contained in the last question: "Is that the only truth on earth [*azo tle nelli in tlaltícpac*]?" It is indeed song and flowers that perhaps "please the Giver of Life." This seemingly obscure affirmation may be clarified by an analysis of the idiomatic complex "song and flowers." In *Llave del Náhuatl*, a study of certain stylistic traits of the Nahuatl language, Garibay noted one of the principal and peculiar characteristics of this language. He called it "*difrasismo*":

It is a procedure in which a single idea is expressed by two words, either because they are synonomous or because they are placed next to each other. Several examples in Spanish will more suitably illustrate: *a tontas y a locas,* "recklessly"; *a sangre y fuego,* "by blood and fire"; *contra viento y marea,* "against wind and tide"; *a pan y agua,* "on bread and water," etc. This stylistic form, so rare in our languages, is usual in Nahuatl. . . . Almost all of these expressions are employed metaphorically, and for this reason must be considered within their context. Taken literally, their meaning is distorted or lost completely.[14]

In xóchitl in cuícatl, "flower and song," is one of the many examples of "*difrasismo*" mentioned by Garibay. In addition to the literal meaning, the phrase is a metaphor for poetry or a poem. In the text quoted above, the conclusion of the *tlamatinime* was that "the only truth on earth" was poetry—"song and flowers."

Convinced of the transitory nature of all things existing on earth and of the dreamlike quality of life, the *tlamatinime's*

---

13 *Ibid.*, fol. 9,v.
14 Angel María Garibay K., *Llave del Náhuatl,* 112.

approach to the truth could not have been the Aristotelian "identification of the mind who knows with existing reality." This type of equation was not the path followed by the *tlamatinime*, who had affirmed that "it may be that no one speaks the truth on earth [*ach áyac nelli in tiquitohua nican*]."[15]

Yet this position did not imply universal and absolute skepticism. True poetry derives from a peculiar type of knowledge, the fruit of authentic inner experience, the result of intuition. Poetry is, then, a creative and profound expression which, through symbol and metaphor, allows man to discover himself and then to talk about what he has intuitively and mysteriously perceived. Since he feels that he will never be able to express what he longs to express, the poet suffers. Nevertheless, his words may at times embody authentic revelation. This quality is beautifully illustrated in the following Nahuatl poem, in which the very soul of poetry is discernible:

> Eagerly does my heart yearn for flowers;
> I suffer with songs, yet I create them on earth,
> I, Cuacuauhtzin:
> I crave flowers that will not perish in my hands!
> Where might I find lovely flowers, lovely songs?
> Such as I seek, spring does not produce on earth;
> indeed, I feel tormented, I, Cuacuauhtzin.
> Perchance, will our friends be happy; will they feel pleasure?
> Where might I, Cuacuauhtzin, find lovely flowers, lovely songs?[16]

This yearning for the true expression of poetry—"Eagerly does my heart yearn for flowers . . . . Where might I find lovely flowers, lovely songs?"—tormented the Nahuatl thinker. "I suffer with songs," he says, "yet I create them on earth . . . ." Seldom do his words satisfy his desire to attain "the only truth," for the authentic poetry—"song and flowers"—"spring does not produce on earth." Where, then, does poetry come from? The *tlamatinime*

---

[15] *MSS Cantares Mexicanos*, fol. 13,r.
[16] *Ibid.*, fol. 26,r.

also speculated on this new question. Addressing their priests, they inquired:

> Our priests, I ask of you:
> From whence come the flowers that enrapture man?
> The songs that intoxicate, the lovely songs?[17]

These questions about the origin of poetry attribute to it another unique quality. Poetry "enraptures man," and by intensifying his emotions and his perceptive powers, it enables him to perceive what he ordinarily would not. The answer given by the priests concerning the origin of poetry follows:

> Only from His home do they come, from the innermost part of heaven,
> only from there comes the myriad of flowers. . . .
> Where the nectar of the flowers is found
> the fragrant beauty of the flower is refined. . . .
> They interlace, they interweave;
> among them sings, among them warbles the quetzal bird.[18]

In this way the Nahuas described the divine origin of poetry. It is born of inspiration emanating from beyond—from "what is above us." And it is this inspiration which enables man to speak "the only truth on earth." Another poem also expresses these ideas:

> The flowers sprout, they are fresh, they grow;
> they open their blossoms,
> and from within emerge the flowers of song;
> among men You scatter them, You send them.
> You are the singer![19]

Only he who comes under the divine influence which scatters flowers and songs among men is able to speak of "truth on earth." The wise man is said by Sahagún's informants to possess "a heart

---

[17] *Ibid.*, fol. 34,r.
[18] *Ibid.*, fol. 34,r.
[19] *Ibid.*, fol. 35,v.

made divine [*yoltéotl*]" in their description of the personality of the artist and in their formulation of what might be called an Aztec concept of art.[20]

Inherent in this theory is an affirmation of the lasting quality of poetry. In some mysterious way it is perennial and indestructible. Although flowers, considered the symbol of beauty, perish, when they are related to song, they represent poetry and are everlasting. For, originating in the innermost part of heaven, they constitute "the only truth on earth." Nezahualcóyotl was aware of this belief:

> My flowers shall not cease to live;
> my songs shall never end:
> I, a singer, intone them;
> they become scattered, they are spread about.[21]

And even when Nezahualcóyotl says elsewhere, "It is flowers that wither and perish," he adds that it is "only here on earth." For, he affirms, "beyond, to the gilded house of plumes they find their way," that is, to the dwelling place of the Divine from which they originally came. Referring to the meager immortality to be found on earth, poetry again, "flower and song," is the only thing of value that we may leave behind:

> Destined is my heart to vanish
> like the ever withering flowers?
> What can my heart do?
> At least flowers, at least songs![22]

The passages quoted above affirm that the *tlamatinime* somehow achieved in their poetry an authentic theory of metaphysical knowledge. In spite of the universal evanescence of existence, they concluded, there is a way of knowing the truth, and the way is poetry, for which "flower and song" is both symbol and metaphor. And, as Juan García Bacca noted in his comments on Martin Heidegger's *Essence of Poetry*, "*meta*-phor and *meta*-physics

---

[20] *Códice Matritense de la Real Academia*, VIII, fol. 117,v.
[21] *MSS Cantares Mexicanos*, fol. 16,v.
[22] *Ibid.*, fol. 10,r.

have basically and fundamentally one and the same function: to put things 'beyond.'"[23]

Thus poetry, as a vehicle of metaphysical expression relying on metaphors, is an attempt to vitiate the transitoriness of earthly things, the dream of *tlalticpac*. The wise men did not believe that they could form rational images of what is beyond, but they were convinced that through metaphors, by means of poetry, truth was attainable. This attitude was rooted in their belief in the divine origin of poetry, "it comes from above." In modern terms, poetry is the product of an intuition which moves man's inner being, and in so doing, it enables him to give expression to feelings and experiences which are far beyond the ordinary. Only through poetry is man able to communicate with the Divine:

> Now do I hear the very words of the *coyolli* bird
> as he makes answer to the Giver of Life.
> He goes his way singing, offering flowers.
> Is that what pleases the Giver of Life?
> Is that the only truth on earth?[24]

The richness and precision of the Nahuatl language allowed the *tlamatinime* to embody in their poetry "the only truth on earth." Only through metaphor and poetry could they utter some truth about, and thus communicate with, the Divine.

The *tlamatinime* attributed the beginnings of their loftiest theological ideas to the Toltecs. In the *Annals of Cuauhtitlán* and in the Nahuatl texts collected by Sahagún, this affirmation appears frequently. Was this a symbolic attempt on the part of the Nahuas to identify themselves and their knowledge of the Divine with their rich Toltec background? It is possible, because the Nahuas of the time just prior to the Conquest associated *Toltecáyotl*, "Toltec-ness," with everything superlative in their

---

[23] Juan D. Garcia Bacca, "*Comentarios a La Esencia de la Poesía de Heidegger*," *Revista Nacional de Cultura*, Caracas, Nos. 112–13, p. 226.

[24] *MSS Cantares Mexicanos*, fol. 9,v.

culture. Indeed, the word *toltécatl,* "Toltec," had become a synonym for wise man and artist.

There is in the *Toltec-Chichimec History* an ancient poem which tells something of the original Toltec concept of the Deity. Garibay, who has made a linguistic analysis of this poem, confirms its antiquity.[25] The context demonstrates that the poem was written at a time much earlier than the Aztec period. Certain wandering tribes, probably those uprooted and dispersed by the downfall of the last Toltec empire about the end of the eleventh century A.D., knew and sang the song. The significance of this poem lies in its reference to the same supreme god of duality whose discovery subsequent texts attribute to Toltec sages. This would suggest that "a very ancient philosophical school (one dating from at least Toltec times) held that the origin of all things is one single principle—masculine and feminine—which has begotten the gods, the world and men."[26]

Those ideas of ancient Toltec origin were not simply an inert intellectual heritage in the Nahuatl world. On the contrary, they were the object of intense speculation by the *tlamatinime* during the period immediately before the Conquest. Furthermore, although the *tlamatinime* utilized these ideas as the nucleus of their metaphysico-poetical approach, this does not mean that they simply accepted the ancient theological conception in its entirety. Rather, they formulated a number of problems about it:

Where is the place of light,
for He who gives life hides Himself?[27]

Referring more specifically to the Toltec picture of the supreme being, other questions arose:

Where shall I go?
Oh, where shall I go?
The path of the god of duality.

25 See Angel María Garibay K., *Historia de la Literatura Náhuatl,* I, 128–30.
26 Caso, *La Religión de los Aztecas,* 8.
27 *MSS Cantares Mexicanos,* fol. 62,r.

Is your home in the place of the dead?
In the interior of the heavens?
Or only here on earth
is the abode of the dead?[28]

The *tlamatinime* aspired to discover the path which led to Ometéotl, god of duality. To accomplish their purpose, they suggested three possibilities: Does he live in heaven? Down below in the place of the dead? Or only here on earth?

According to the wise men, Ometéotl dwells in the navel of the earth; he is present in the blue waters, in the clouds, in *Omeyocan*, beyond the heavens, and even in the region of the dead. The *tlamatinime*, with great poetic skill, pointed out once again the multipresence of the Giver of Life:

You live in heaven;
you uphold the mountain,
Anáhuac is in your hands.
Awaited, you are always everywhere;
you are invoked, you are prayed to.
Your glory, your fame is sought.
You live in heaven;
Anáhuac is in your hands.[29]

In this way did the *tlamatinime* picture the Giver of Life, he who is present in every corner of the universe. The poem metaphorically describes the founding action of the Life-Giver—he upholds the mountains and *Anáhuac* is in his hands.

The question concerning the abode and metaphysical "beyond" having been answered, we turn to the Nahuatl philosophical concept of the supreme principle, considered purely as such. Sahagún's natives said:

1. And the Toltecs knew
2. that many are the heavens.
3. They said there are twelve superimposed divisions.
4. There dwells the true god and his consort.

28 *Ibid.*, fol. 35,v.
29 *Ibid.*, fol. 21,v.

5. The celestial god is called the Lord of Duality.
6. And his consort is called the Lady of Duality, the celestial Lady;
7. which means
8. he is king, he is Lord, above the twelve heavens.[30]

COMMENTARY:

LINE 1: *And the Toltecs knew.*
In order to emphasize the antiquity and, perhaps, the profundity of this doctrine the Indian informants began by ascribing a Toltec origin to what they were about to say.

LINES 2–3: *That many are the heavens. They said there are twelve superimposed divisions.*
This is obviously an allusion to the Nahuatl cosmological concept of a vertical universe formed by a series of "celestial floors" through which the stars moved.

LINE 4: *There dwells the true god and his consort.*
This line and the two following explicitly name the supreme principle conceived by Nahuatl thought. He is *in nelli téotl,* "the true god." To understand the significance of this phrase one must remember the connotation of the word *nelli*—true, well-founded, firm. Thus the phrase means that in the twelfth heaven lives the well-founded god, he who is founded in or upon himself—*nelli.* *One* god is being spoken of, for the singular, *téotl,* is used; had the reference been to two or more, the plural, *teteo,* "gods," would have been employed.

Although the "true god" is one, he is immediately described as having a "consort," *i-námic.* This word, derived from the verb *namique* (to find, to help) and the possessive prefix *i* (of him), means literally "his equal," or "a thing which fits or adjusts with some other thing." Adhering to this literal meaning, we translate *i-námic* as "consort," in order to indicate that the *nelli téotl,* the "true god," is related to or complemented by "his equal," or "that which improves him or makes him more complete." The

[30] *Códice Matritense de la Real Academia,* VIII, fol. 175,v.

second entity is not another separate principle, but rather a being which might be described as something united to the supreme deity and sharing the condition of being the *nelli téotl*—the god founded upon himself.

LINES 5–6: *The celestial god is called the Lord of Duality. And his consort is called the Lady of Duality, the celestial Lady.*
Contained in these lines is the key to understanding the idea of "one true god and his consort": "The celestial god [Ilhuicatéotl] is called the Lord of Duality [Ometecuhtli]." Although he is one, at the same time he possesses a dual nature. Therefore, his metaphysical abode is named *Omeyocan*, place of duality, and he is also given the more abstract name Ometéotl (god of duality). Correspondingly, the name of his consort, "his equal," is, as the text says, "Dual Lady (Omecíhuatl)."

The Nahuas, in attempting to explain the origin of all that exists, arrived metaphorically—by the path of "flower and song" —at the discovery of an ambivalent being, an active generating principle which was at the same time a passive receptor capable of conceiving. The powers of generation and of conception— requisites for the appearance of life in our world—were thus combined in a single being. The affirmation is made, first implicitly and later, in other terms, explicitly, that the *nelli téotl* or Ometéotl is the cosmic principle by which all that exists is conceived and begotten. Facing the possible objection that all of this is an anthropomorphic projection of the human reproductive process into the realm of the beyond, the *tlamatinime* themselves acknowledged that "it may be that no one on earth can tell the truth" except through flower and song.[31]

Approaching through figurative language the dynamic essence of the divine being, the Nahuas attributed to him a masculine and feminine ambivalence, origin of life on earth.

LINE 8: *He is king, he is Lord, above the twelve heavens.*
In conclusion comes an affirmation of the transcendent quality of the deity—"he is above the twelve heavens"—and of the power

---

[31] *MSS Cantares Mexicanos*, fol. 13,r.

which he exercises over all things. He is Lord (*tecuhtli*) and he rules (*tlatocati*). These are two fundamental aspects of Ometéotl, the supreme metaphysical principle, who is "above us" and who is master of all that exists because of his perpetual generative faculty and universal sustaining action.

Numerous were the names of the supreme being, and they corresponded to his different roles in the universe. Most abstract of these was Ometéotl, "god of duality." Ometecuhtli-Omecíhuatl, "Lord and Lady of duality," express his masculine-feminine quality. At times he is called Tonacatecuhtli-Tonacacíhuatl, "Lord and Lady of our maintenance." He is also alluded to as *in Tonan, in Tota, Huehuetéotl,* "our Mother, our Father, the old god."

Proof that all these titles refer to the same deity is found in the chronicles of some of the first missionaries. The *"Historia de los Mexicanos"* states that "they had a god whom they called Tonacatecli (Tonacatecuhtli), whose wife was Tonacacíguatl (Tonacacíhuatl) . . . who were self-created, and their dwelling place was always the thirteenth heaven, the beginning of which was never known."[32] Obviously, Tonacatecuhtli and Tonacacíhuatl, Lord and Lady of our maintenance, are none other than Ometecuhtli and Omecíhuatl, Lord and Lady of duality. Torquemada attempts to explain this unified masculine-feminine being: ". . . it might be said, that these Indians wanted the Divine Nature shared by two gods (two persons) who were man and wife."[33]

In their eagerness to describe the double nature of Ometéotl in a manner consistent with their metaphysico-poetical conception, the *tlamatinime* created this diversity of names, which gave new life and strength to their original idea. Two expressive and poetical texts of different origin and date illustrate the eagerness

[32] *"Historia de los Mexicanos . . . Pinturas," loc. cit.,* 228.

[33] Juan de Torquemada, *Los Veintiún Libros Rituales y Monarquia Indiana,* II, 37.

to create a variety of names. Both refer directly to the supreme being.

The first of these texts has been mentioned above. It is a poem included in the *Toltec-Chichimec History*, a work compiled from reports given around 1540 by natives of Tecamachalco (in the present state of Puebla). The Indians of Tecamachalco had in their possession several illustrated manuscripts, from which came much of the data for this *History*, and the works constitute a very reliable source for the study of ancient Nahuatl traditions.

This poem is one of the oldest dealing with the theory of a dual entity and contains several points of major importance to a thorough understanding of Nahuatl theological thought:

1. In the place of sovereignty, in the place of sovereignty, we rule;
2. my supreme Lord so commands.
3. Mirror which illumines things.
4. Now they will join us, now they are prepared.
5. Drink, drink!
6. The god of duality is at work,
7. Creator of men,
8. mirror which illumines things.[34]

COMMENTARY:

LINES 1–2: *In the place of sovereignty, in the place of sovereignty, we rule.*

According to legend, two chieftains of Toltec origin, Icxicóhuatl and Quetzaltehuéyac, went to the mouth of a cave on a rounded hill to invite a group of Chichimecs to join them. "We come," they said, "to take you away from your wandering life." The Chichimecs inside the cave demanded a song which would identify the visitors. After a lively dialogue and an exchange of other comments between the Toltec chieftains and the Chichimecs, the latter recited the poem above. "We rule in the place of sovereignty," they said. "There we have learned that our supreme

---

[34] *Historia Tolteca-Chichimeca* (ed. by Ernst Mengin), 33.

Lord commands it." To assure their being understood by the two who claimed to be of Toltec origin, the Chichimecs made allusion to their supreme being, the dual god.

LINE 3: *Mirror which illumines things: tezcatlanextía.*
That this god is none other than Ometéotl is proved by lines 6–8, for the "mirror which illumines things" is identified with the god of duality, creator of men, whose light illumines all that exists. It should be noted that a clear contrast exists between *tezcatlanextía* and *tezcatlipoca* (smoking mirror); one illumines, the other obscures with his smoke. Tezcatlipoca was also the name given to Ometéotl's four sons, the red, the black, the white, and the blue Tezcatlipocas who inhabit the four corners of the universe. Tezcatlanextía and Tezcatlipoca appear to be two aspects of Ometéotl's role as lord of day and night. The masculine aspect of Ometéotl can also be identified with Citlallatónac, the star "that illumines things"; in his feminine role he was Citlalinicue, whose attire was the starry skirt of the night.

It was precisely at the time of creation, when night and darkness ruled *in oc iohuaya,* that the nocturnal aspect of Ometéotl (Tezcatlipoca) channeled his powers into the four fundamental cosmic energies, his four sons. According to the myths of popular religion in the *"Historia de los Mexicanos"*: "it seems that they had a god whom they called Tonacatecli [Tonacatecuhtli], whose wife was Tonacacíguatl (Tonacacíhuatl). . . . They were self-created and dwelt always in the thirteenth heaven. . . . They gave birth to four sons: The oldest Tlalauque Tezcatlipuca (Tlatlauhqui Tezcatlipoca) . . . was born red. Their second-born was called Yayanque (Yayauhqui) Tezcatlipuca . . . he was born black."[35]

That Ometéotl gave birth to four sons is verified by the informants of Sahagún. They described the supreme being as "Mother and Father of the gods, the old god; he who is in the navel of fire; who is in the circle of turquoise."[36]

---

[35] *"Historia de los Mexicanos . . . Pinturas," loc. cit.,* 228.
[36] *Códice Florentino,* Book VI, fol. 34,r.

The evidence afforded by the texts is clear. Tezcatlipoca and Tezcatlanextía (double mirror which envelops all things with darkness by night and illumines them by day) constituted a double title for Ometéotl in the remotest times of Nahuatl culture. The whole series of prayers contained in Book VI of Sahagún's *History* is further confirmation that Tezcatlipoca, the correlative title for Tezcatlanextía, was originally one of the titles for Ometéotl.

LINES 4–5: *Now they will join us, now they are prepared. Drink, drink!*

The two Toltec chiefs knew and understood the allusion to the "mirror which illumines things." They also felt the words of the Chichimecs to be evidence that the latter would join them. Words of enthusiasm burst forth, "Now they will join us, now they are prepared." Similarity of tradition among the Toltecs and Chichimecs, showing that both participated in the same ancient Toltec culture, gave cause for rejoicing and drinking. "Drink, drink!" they repeated.

LINE 6: *The god of duality is at work.*

The legendary circumstances of the poem enrich the significance of this line. The mutual recognition, which so greatly aroused the enthusiasm of Icxicóhuatl and Quetzaltehuéyac, is considered to have occurred through the intervention of Ometéotl. And because the supreme being was acknowledged by both as the "mirror which illumines things," they joyfully exclaimed, "The god of duality is at work."

LINES 7–8: *Creator of men, mirror which illumines things.*

The two Toltec chieftains ended the poem by chanting two of Ometéotl's attributes. He is *in teyocoyani,* "the creator of men." *In teyocoyani* is a composite term formed by the verb *yocoya,* "to invent" or "to create mentally"; the participial suffix *ni,* "he who"; and the personal prefix *te,* "people," "men." The term *te-yocoyani* as a unit, then, literally means "the one who makes or creates men."

The supreme god is also Tezcatlanextía, the "mirror which

illumines things." This being the term by which Ometéotl was designated, the Chichimecs were able to identify the two chiefs' Toltec origin.

The poem affirms two important facts: the antiquity of the Nahuatl concept of Ometéotl and the variety of titles by which he was designated. He is Tezcatlanextía, he is Tezcatlipoca, and he is also Teyocoyani, the creator of men. In addition, he is the active supreme being—"The god of duality is at work."

The Nahuatl image of the supreme being, considered as an entity in himself, is further explained by a second text. This text, collected by Sahagún, reveals a facet of Ometéotl's being that was perceived by the *tlamatinime* during the time immediately before the Conquest. This theological concept was so important that it became a significant part of Nahuatl birth ceremonies.

The midwife, having finished with her main duty, cut the new-born child's umbilical cord. Next she would wash it and while doing so she would speak to it, and if it were male, she would say:

1. Lord, our master:
2. she of the jade skirt,
3. he who shines like a sun of jade.
4. A male has been born,
5. sent here by our mother, our father,
6. Lord of duality, Lady of duality,
7. he who dwells in the nine heavens,
8. he who dwells in the place of duality.[37]

COMMENTARY:

LINES 1–3: *Lord, our master: she of the jade skirt, he who shines like a sun of jade.*

Two new names for the "Lord, our master" appear here: Chal-chiuhtli-cue, "she of the jade skirt," and Chalchiuh-tlatónac, "he who shines like a sun of jade." These two names, referring to his role as Lord of the waters, closely resemble two other names given the same god of duality: Citlanin-icue, "lady of the skirt of stars," and Lord of the day, Citlallatónac, "whose solar light envelops things."

[37] *Códice Florentino*, Book VI, fol. 148,v.

THE STATUE OF COATLICUE
embodiment in stone of the Aztec cosmology.

*Courtesy Photographic Archives of the National Institute of
Anthropology and History, Mexico City.*

ORNAMENTATION OF THE TEMPLE OF QUETZALCÓATL
creator of man, at Teotihuacán, Mexico.

*Courtesy Photographic Archives of the National Institute of
Anthropology and History, Mexico City.*

Ometéotl has been described as the Lord who "is enclosed in waters the color of the bluebird," *in xiuhtotoatica,* but there has been no specific mention of a dual nature in his role as Lord of the waters. The introduction of the two new names provokes a significant question: Did the *tlamatinime* conceive of Tláloc, the rain god, and his consort Chalchiuhtlicue as two different aspects of the same supreme being? Hermann Beyer has stated that "if we probe deeper into the symbolic language of the myths . . . we shall see that the blatant polytheism which confronts us in ancient Mexico is simply a symbolic reference to natural phenomena. The minds of the priests and wisemen had already conceived religious and philosophic ideas of a much more highly advanced level. The two thousand gods . . . of which Gómara speaks, were, in the minds of the wisemen . . . really many manifestations of only one god."[38]

The identifications of the god in the various texts presented afford partial confirmation of Beyer's opinion. The text above justifies the suggestion that Tláloc and Chalchiuhtlicue represent two other manifestations of Ometéotl. Beyer's statement that the great multitude of Nahuatl gods "were . . . really many manifestations of only one god" offers interesting possibilities for further investigation.[39]

LINES 4–5: *A male has been born, sent here by our mother, our father.*
These lines stress one of the fundamental attributes of Ometéotl. As *teyocoyani,* the "creator of men," he is *in Tonan in Tota,* "our mother and father," and it is he who sends men forth into the world.

LINES 6–8: *Lord of duality, Lady of duality, he who dwells in the nine heavens, he who dwells in the place of duality.*
The allusion here is again to Ometéotl as an entity in himself. He is Ometecuhtli-Omecíhuatl, who dwells above the highest of

[38] Hermann Beyer, *"Das astekische Götterbild Alexander von Humboldt's,"* in *Wissenschaftliche Festschrift,* 116.
[39] *Ibid.,* 116.

the heavens in *Omeyocan,* the place of duality. There are, as this text reveals, differences of opinion concerning the number of heavens. It is probable that different points of view and different schools of thought on the subject existed.

The texts analyzed above agree with Torquemada in "that these Indians wanted the Divine Nature shared by two gods, man and wife."[40] There can be no doubt that the Nahuas assigned a variety of names to Ometéotl, and the diversity of roles which Ometéotl performed corresponds to this variety of names:

1. He is Lord and Lady of duality (Ometecuhtli-Omecíhuatl).
2. He is Lord and Lady of our maintenance (Tonacatecuhtli-Tonacacíhuatl).
3. He is mother and father of the gods, the old god (*in teteuinan, in teteu ita, Huehuetéotl*).
4. He is at the same time the god of fire (Xiuhtecuhtli), who dwells in the navel of fire (*tle-xic-co*).
5. He is the mirror of day and night (Tezcatlanextía-Tezcatlipoca).
6. He is the star which illumines all things, and he is the Lady of the shining skirt of stars (Citlallatónac-Citlalinicue).
7. He is our mother, our father (*in Tonan, in Tota*).
8. Above all, he is Ometéotl who dwells in the place of duality, *Omeyocan.*

Thus the *tlamatinime,* anxious to give greater vitality and richness to their concept of the supreme being, gave him many names, laying the foundation for a comprehensive vision of the dual and ubiquitous divinity. And they did this through "flower and song."

Many of the qualities manifested by Ometéotl have already been noted: his "multipresence"; his function as mother and father of the gods or, in abstract terms, as origin of the cosmic forces; his role as sustainer of the earth (*tlallamánac*); and his identification with the stars, fire, and water. These characteris-

---

[40] Torquemada, *op. cit.,* II, 37.

tics support Beyer's theory of pantheism in Nahuatl thought.[41] Before offering an opinion of Beyer's hypothesis, however, it would be well to examine the several names given by the *tlamatinime* to Ometéotl in describing his relationship to what we call "the essence of things." These titles are an attempt to express the relation between the Lord of duality and everything that exists on earth: *Yohualli-ehécatl*, which Sahagún translates as "invisible and intangible"; *in Tloque in Nahuaque*, "Lord of the Close Vicinity," perhaps "the Lord of the Everywhere"; *Ipalnemohuani*, "He through whom one lives"; *Totecuio in ilhuicahua in tlalticpacque in mictlane*, "Our Lord, master of Heaven, of earth, and of the region of the dead"; and finally, *Moyocoyani*, "He who invents or gives existence to himself."

The expression *Yohualli-ehécatl* (he who is invisible and intangible) appears many times in Sahagún's history. The text gives the impression that *Yohualli-ehécatl* refers to Tezcatlipoca. Sahagún, for example, says that he is going to speak "of the language that they employed in their prayers to their principal deity called Tezcatlipoca or *Yoalli-ehécatl*."[42] However, the "*Historia de los Mexicanos*," speaking of the sons of Ometecuhtli-Omecíhuatl, states that "the third one was called Quizalcóatl or or by another name, Yagualiecatl [that is, *Yohualli-ehécatl*]."[43]

Seemingly disagreeing with both of these references, Sahagún, referring to the origin and traditions of the Nahuas, says: "They had a god whom they worshiped, invoked, and prayed to, asking of him whatever suited them, and they called him *Yoalliehécatl*, which means 'night and air,' or 'invisible,' and they were devoted to him." And elsewhere Sahagún seems to indicate clearly that *Yohualli-ehécatl* was the supreme god of the Nahuas.[44]

The definitive proof is found, perhaps, in the following passage, which gives the supreme deity all three of the titles being analyzed: "*Tlacatle, Tloque Nahuaque, Ipalnemohuani, Yo-*

---

[41] See Beyer, "*Das astekische Götterbild . . . ,*" *loc. cit.*, 116.

[42] Sahagún, *op. cit.*, I, 450.

[43] "*Historia de los Mexicanos . . . Pinturas,*" *loc. cit.*, 228.

[44] Sahagún, *op. cit.*, II, 289.

hualli-ehécatl," "Lord, Master of the Close Vicinity, Giver of Life, Night-and-wind."[45]

It is an established fact that the titles *"Tloque Nahuaque"* and *"Ipalnemohuani"* designate the supreme principle. The equating of *Yohualli-ehécatl* with those names therefore implies that this title also refers to the twofold god. The reason why Tezcatlipoca and Quetzalcóatl were also invoked as *Yohualli-ehécatl* is clear: Tezcatlipoca was originally no more than the nocturnal aspect of Ometéotl, while Quetzalcóatl, one of the four sons of the dual god, also appears in the *"Historia de los Mexicanos"* as the red Tezcatlipoca. Since Quetzalcóatl was identified with Tezcatlipoca, and Tezcatlipoca denoted one aspect of Ometéotl, there remains no doubt that *Yohualli-ehécatl* was a title of the supreme being.

The term *Yohualli-ehécatl* is a *"difrasismo"* like "flower and song." The literal meaning is "night and wind." Symbolically, however, as Sahagún indicates, the phrase means "invisible (like the night) and intangible (like the wind)."[46] This confirms what has already been suggested: the supreme principle is an invisible and impalpable reality. His transcendent nature goes beyond that world of experience so graphically conceived by the Nahuas as the visible and tangible— "what is seen and touched." *Yohualli-ehécatl* is, then, the title that most clearly implies the transcendent character of Ometéotl.

The name *in Tloque in Nahuaque,* like *Ipalnemohuani,* is a common designation for the supreme god. Ixtlilxóchitl notes that Nezahualcóyotl always used these two terms in addressing the deity. *In Tloque in Nahuaque* derives from the two base words, *tloc* and *náhuac. Tloc* means "near," as is proved by several compound words—*no-tloc-pa,* for example, would be "towards my vicinity." *Náhuac* is, literally, "in the circuit of" or "in the ring," as Seler noted in a study of the word.[47] The personal possessive

---

[45] *Códice Florentino*, Book VI, fol. 5,r and *passim.*

[46] Sahagún, *op. cit.*, I, 450–51.

[47] Eduard Seler, *"Ueber die Worte Anauac und Nauatl,"* in *Gesammelte Abhandlungen,* II, 49–77.

suffix *e*, which is appended to both these adverbial forms (*tloqu-e* and *Nahuaqu-e*), connotes that "being near" and the "circuit" or "ring" are "of him." The whole phrase may be interpreted as "the lord of what is near and of what is in the ring or circuit." Fray Alonso de Molina explained the Nahuatl idiom (a pure example of "flower and song") in this way: "It applies to him who is the very being of all things, preserving them and sustaining them."[48] Clavijero, discussing the ancient Mexicans' concept of the supreme being, translated *Tloque Nahuaque* as "he who has everything in himself."[49] And Garibay, bringing Nahuatl thought closer to our own mental atmosphere, rendered it as "the one who is near to everything and to whom everything is near."[50]

From this it may be concluded that the specific attribute applied to Ometéotl under the designation *Tloque Nahuaque* is his multipresence, that quality which has appeared conspicuously in Nahuatl cosmological theory. The deity's ubiquitous presence is not a static quality, but an active principle which gives foundation to the universe—the immense disk surrounded by water (*cem-a-náhuac*)—at the beginning of each new age. *In Tloque in Nahuaque* supports the earth (*tlallamánac*) at its navel or center. Considered in this light, Molina's translation of the double term becomes fully comprehensible: "It applies to the one who is the very being of all things, preserving and sustaining them." Everything belongs to him—from the closest to the most distant part of the ring of water encircling the world. And being of him, everything is produced by his generative action (Lord and Lady of duality), which endlessly gives truth or foundation to all that exists.

Just as *in Tloque in Nahuaque* suggests the sovereignty and sustaining action of Ometéotl, so does *Ipalnemohuani* connote his life-giving function. *Ipalnemohuani* is, in terms of Indo-European grammars, derived from a participial form of the im-

---

[48] Molina, *op. cit.*, fol. 148,r.

[49] Francisco Xavier Clavijero, *Historia Antigua de México*, II, 62.

[50] Garibay, *Historia de la Literatura Náhuatl*, II, 408.

personal verb *nemohua,* "one lives," "everybody lives." To this is added a prefix which connotes causation, *ipal,* "by him," or "by means of him." Finally, to the verb *nemohua* the participial suffix *ni* is appended. The resulting compound *ipal-nemohua-ni* means literally "the one through whom one lives."

Garibay, giving the term a poetic twist, usually translates it "Giver of Life," corresponding to the meaning "the one through whom one lives." Investigating further the meaning of this term, we may infer that the origin of everything associated with movement and life is ascribed to Ometéotl. Thus it complements the title *in Tloque in Nahuaque,* which describes Ometéotl as foundation of the universe and emphasizes that everything is in him. With *Ipalnemohuani* comes the thought that by means of his power (*ipal*) there is movement and life. Once again appears the generative action of Ometéotl, who, after conceiving the universe in his own being, sustains it and creates life.

That is why he was also called—especially in several of the *Huehuetlatolli* (discussions of the elders)—*Totecuiyo in ilhuicahua in tlalticpaque in mictlane,* "Our Master, Lord of the heavens, of the earth and of the region of the dead."[51] This phrase gives a graphic and effective grouping of the three vertical divisions of the universe of which Ometéotl is Lord and Master. Dwelling in the highest of the heavens, in *Omeyocan,* in the navel of the earth, and in the region of the dead, he holds the entire universe, which is, to the eyes of men, "like a marvelous dream." It is actually the fruit of Omecíhuatl's conception, resulting from the generative action of Ometecuhtli. We can now connect these concepts with previously discussed aspects of Ometecuhtli-Omecíhuatl: "Mirrors of night and day," "Star that causes things to appear," "Starry skirt," "Lord of the water and the jade skirt," and "our Father and our Mother." Ometéotl's action, always carried out with his consort, has produced the cosmic stage upon which everything unfolds through the mysterious generation-conception originating beyond the heavens in *Omeyocan,* the place of duality.

[51] Garibay (tr.), *"Huehuetlatolli, Documento A," loc. cit.,* 31–53 and 81–107.

It is this context that *Moyocoyani,* the last of the divine titles to be analyzed, acquires its full meaning. For this word, one of the finest examples of "flower and song" metaphors in the Nahuatl language, contains the supreme explanation of the very essence of Ometéotl.

Among other writers, Mendieta, in his *Historia Eclesiástica Indiana,* has preserved this designation of the god of duality. After discussing the meaning of *Ipalnemohuani,* he writes: "And they also called him *Moyucoyatzin áyac oquiyocux, áyac oquipic,* which means that no one formed or created him, but that he himself and by his own authority and will does everything."[52]

Mo-yucoya-tzin is a word derived from the verb *yucoya* (or *yocoya,* "to invent," "to create mentally"); from the reverential suffix *tzin,* which approximates "our Lord"; and from the reflexive prefix *mo* (self, himself). As a whole the term *mo-yucoya-tzin* means "Lord who mentally conceives or creates himself." The meaning of the other words cited by Mendieta is almost synonymous with, and is explicative of, the concept implied by *moyucoyatzin,* "no one gave him form or existence."

If the *tlamatinime's* search for the Divine culminated in the finding of one ubiquitous dual supreme being, the climax of Nahuatl philosophical thought was the discovery of Ometéotl's self-invention.

The various attributes of Ometéotl and his identification with the celestial bodies, fire, and water led Hermann Beyer to express the opinion that the Nahuatl concept of the Divine and of the world was inclined to be pantheistic.

Xiuhtecuhtli, the god of fire, came to be considered a pantheistic deity who pervades and permeates everything. He was designated by the names Huehuetéotl, "the old god," and *Teteu inan, teteu ita,* "mother and father of the gods." Originally he was the "Blue Lord," god of the sky of day, a solar god. And because the sun was for the Mexicans the source of all terrestrial life, he functioned in

[52] Gerónimo de Mendieta, *Historia Eclesiástica Indiana,* I, 95.

the same role of the old creator god with whom he was identified.[53]

It is true that Xiutecuhtli, "Lord of fire and of time," is identified in several texts with Huehuetéotl, "the old god," and with *in Tonan, in Tota,* "our mother, our father," who are also *in Teteu inan, in Teteu ita,* "mother and father of the gods." The last pair, in other texts, are also synonomous with Ometecuhtli-Omecíhuatl, in other words, with Ometéotl. It is also true that the sun, regarded as the supreme being especially by the Aztecs, was addressed in prayer as "our mother, our father." The following text offers evidence of this. The words were directed to a woman who had died in childbirth:

> Rise, array yourself, stand on your feet,
> partake of the pleasure of the beautiful place,
> the home of your mother, your father, the Sun.
> Good fortune, pleasure and happiness are there.
> Go forth, follow your mother, your father, the Sun.[54]

It is undeniable that Beyer's identification of the various divine titles is well founded. One point, however, is debatable: his statement that Xiuhtecuhtli, who is synonomous with Ometéotl, "came to be considered a pantheistic deity who pervades and permeates everything."[55] In the first place the term pantheism, philosophically speaking, conveys such widely diverse meanings that its use clouds rather than clarifies the nature of Nahuatl theological thought. For this reason, rather than speaking explicitly of pantheism, it is best to outline a specific interpretation of Nahuatl thought.

Certainly, in the *tlamatinime's* eager quest for "the only truth," they arrived at the summit of abstract thought. Ometéotl Moyocoyatzin, the dual god who dwells in *Omeyocan,* the metaphysical place of duality, was self-invented. As Xiuhtecuhtli, Lord of fire and of time, the supreme god reigned beyond the heavens and time.

---

[53] Beyer, *"Das aztekische Götterbild . . . ," loc. cit.,* 116.
[54] *Códice Florentino,* Book VI, fol. 141,v.
[55] Beyer, *"Das aztekische Götterbild . . . ," loc. cit.,* 116.

In *Omeyocan*, "in the thirteenth heaven, of the beginning of which nothing was ever known," dwelled the true god (*in nelli téotl*), founded with and upon himself. Through his generating and conceptive powers, his divine activity came to be. In the first act of his dual being, he begot four sons, and from that moment he was "mother and father of the gods." Because the birth of these four gods took place "when darkness still ruled," they were called Tezcatlipocas, "smoking mirrors." The powers of Ometéotl found further outlet through his four sons; "he spread out" (*ónoc*) over what was to be the navel of the universe (*tlalxicco*) in order to "endow it with truth," to support it, thus allowing his sons to begin the various ages of the world.

In his role as Tezcatlanextía, "mirror which illumines things," he made possible the five creations of the sun. In the four Suns which preceded the fifth, it was Ometéotl who endowed with truth, with a foundation, that which his offspring had accomplished. Perhaps he was also the one who directed the hidden dialectical process inherent in his sons' struggle for supremacy and in the cataclysms that took place in the world.

During the present age, the age of the Sun of Motion, Ometéotl established harmony among the four elements. He endowed with truth a world in which time became oriented and spatialized in terms of the four directions of the universe. Apparently the sons of Ometéotl, in the mind of the common man, had continued to multiply, constantly increasing in number. But the wise men believed that all of the gods who appeared in pairs (man and wife) were manifestations or personifications of the dual god. By day his strength gathers and shines in the life-giving power of the sun.

He was, then, Tona-tíuh, whose path across the sky made the day, and also Ipalnemohuani, the Giver of Life. In addition he was Tezcatlanextía, the mirror that made things appear; Citlallatónac, the celestial body which illumined all things; and Yeztlaquenqui, "he of the red attire," who was ultimately identified by the Aztecs with their war god, Huitzilopochtli. In his nocturnal roles he was invisible and intangible—Yohualli-ehécatl.

In his relation to the moon he was Tezcatlipoca, "the smoking mirror." He was also Citlalinicue, "lady of the luminous starry skirt," and finally Tecolliquenqui, "lady of the black attire"—both referring to the feminine aspect of Ometéotl.

In regard to the earth Ometéotl was Tlallamánac, "she who sustains and upholds the earth." As master of the clouds and heavens over the earth, he was Tlallíchcatl, "he who covers it with cotton." While his presence was in the navel of the earth he was Tlaltecuhtli, "Lord of the earth," and in his maternal role he was Coatlicue, or Cihuacóatl, "Lady of the serpent skirt" or "the Snake Woman." And as Justino Fernández has demonstrated, Coatlicue, expressed in stone, is the marvelous symbol—the embodiment in art—of the creative tension of Ometéotl.

In another aspect of his life-giving role, Ipalnemohuani, he was Chalchiuhtlatónac, who made things "shine like jade." As Tláloc, he was the rain god, the Lord of fertility on earth. His consort in this role was Chalchiuhtlicue, "Lady of the jade skirt," "Lady of the waters that flow," "Lady of sea and lake." In his relationship with man he was Tonacatecuhtli-Tonacacíhuatl, "Lord and Lady of our flesh and of our subsistence." In addition Ometéotl, the Giver of Life, places man on earth, and in the very womb from which each man emerges, the deity preordains his destiny:

It was said, that in the twelfth heaven
our fates were determined.
When the child is conceived,
when he is placed in the womb,
his fate comes to him there;
it is sent to him by the Lord of Duality.[56]

And finally, as a symbol of his intangible quality, as the embodiment of wisdom and of the only truth on earth, Ometéotl was personified in the legendary figure of Quetzalcóatl. As Quetzalcóatl he was sometimes identified with the red Tezcatlipoca and with the inventor and creator of men:

[56] *Códice Matritense de la Real Academia*, VIII, fol. 175,v.

Perchance, is it true? Did he accomplish it, Our Lord, Our Prince,
Quetzalcóatl, inventor of men, creator of men?
Was it perhaps determined by the Lord, the Lady of Duality?
Perchance, was the word conveyed to him?[57]

Concerning the mysterious region of the dead, *Mictlan*, it was
affirmed that Ometéotl "inhabited the shadows" of that region.
And there his masculine and feminine aspects took the roles of
Mictlantecuhtli-Mictecacíhuatl, Lord and Lady of the land of
the dead.

Behind the apparent confusion of the entire Nahuatl pantheon,
was the ever present Ometéotl. Popular religion worshiped, in
ever increasing numbers, a multitude of "gods" of rain, wind,
fire, war, the dead, and others. But the *tlamatinime* went beyond
mere polytheism. In their quest for a symbol, through "flower
and song," which might lead them to comprehend the origin of
all things and the mysterious nature of an invisible and intangible
creator, the *tlamatinime* conceived the most profound of all of
their *"difrasismos,"* Ometecuhtli-Omecíhuatl, Lord and Lady
of duality. Beyond all time, beyond the heavens, in *Omeyocan*,
Ometéotl Moyocoyani existed by self-invention, and continued
to exist by virtue of his perpetual creative activity.

Whatever pantheism there might be in the wise men's concept
of the Divine and of the world could only be described by such
a hybrid term as the dynamic *"Omeyotization"* ("dualization")
of the universe. For to the Nahuatl mind all activity was determined by the intervention of Ometéotl. There was always the
need for an active masculine aspect and a passive or conceiving
feminine counterpart. And that was precisely the origin of the
countless dual deities; in every area they symbolized the activity
of Ometéotl. Generation and conception were moments insep-
arably unified in the dual divinity. They made possible his very
existence and that of all things. From a dynamic point of view,
all existing things received "truth," "foundation," from this time-
less ambivalence of Ometéotl. Duality and truth are inherent
in Ometéotl; all else is "like a dream."

[57] *Códice Florentino*, Book VI, fol. 120,r.

99

The offering to the gods.

The offering of fire.

The offering of copal.

The act of swearing.

The offering of food.

Libation.

AZTEC RITUALS
drawings from the *Madrid Codex*, fol. 254,v.

100

The act of offering food
to the gods.

Payment to the gods
for a favor received.

Offering of branches.

The offering of fire-
wood to the gods.

Sweeping the patio of the Temple.

AZTEC RITUALS
drawings from the *Madrid Codex*, fol. 255,v.

Recognizing that he had his roots in the mysterious duality of the Divine, Nahuatl man acknowledged Ometéotl's transcendency by declaring that he was invisible like the night and intangible like the wind (Yohualli-ehécatl). Feeling all this, the pre-Columbian thinker asked himself if he would someday live in the presence of the Giver of Life, in his dwelling place, from which the "flowers and songs" came. Or was he condemned "to perish in the place of oblivion"? In the face of the acknowledged transcendency of Ometéotl, pantheism would make little sense. The *tlamatinime* accepted the divine omnipresence, but at the same time were able to view it as distinct from the world. Ometéotl was "our mother, our father," "the Giver of Life," "invisible and intangible." Giving truth to all things, he was *Tloque Nahuaque,* "Lord of the Everywhere." But as an entity in himself, he was imperceptible; he was *Yohualli-ehécatl,* night and wind.

It is interesting to observe that this mode of thought concerning the duality of Ometéotl paralleled a dual quality within the Nahuatl language itself. So strongly inclined to conceive in terms of duality were the minds of the *tlamatinime,* that when they wanted to endow an idea with maximum clarity and precision, they always isolated two of its qualities, employing what has been called *"difrasismo."* Thus they evoked in the mind images that were not abstract and cold, but rich in meaning, fresh, vigorous, and dynamic. The following examples of classic *"difrasismos"* are eloquent:

in *cueítl,* in *huipilli*: the skirt, the blouse; the woman from a sexual standpoint.

in *ahuéhuetl,* in *póchotl*: giant cypress, ceiba tree; authority, protective quality.

in *chalchíhuitl,* in *quetzalli*: jade and fine plumes; beauty.

in *atl,* in *tépetl*: water and hill; a town.

topco, petlacalco: in the bag and in the box; a secret.

tlilli, tlapalli: black and red ink; writing or wisdom.

in *topan,* in *mictlan*: what is above us, the region of the dead; the metaphysical beyond.

Yohualli, ehécatl: night and wind; the transcendency of the Divine.
in xóchitl, in cuícatl: flower and song; poetry, the only truth on earth.

In this way was the Nahuatl mind pervaded by dualism. Ometéotl, the dual god, was the cause—or effect—of this view of divinity, man, and the universe.

IV

The Approach to Man in Nahuatl Thought

IT was the *tlamatinime's* duty "to place a mirror before the people, that they might become wise and prudent; to endow with wisdom the countenances of others, so that a face might be assumed and developed . . . to humanize the will of the people."[1]

In their pedagogic mission, the *tlamatinime* encountered several difficulties. More often than not man's reactions and inclinations are unpredictable. That they considered it necessary to teach man to assume a face clearly implies that the Nahuas believed man comes into the world "faceless." He is born without an identity, he is born anonymous.

The *tlamatinime* were also aware that in his eager quest for a "face," for self-identification, man plunged into a questionable existence on *tlaltícpac*. In "surrendering his heart to all things, leading it nowhere [*ahuicpa*], he was in fact losing it,"[2] because on earth it is difficult to aspire to anything of significance. The *tlamatinime* sought a meaning for man and his activities: "Per-

[1] *Códice Matritense de la Real Academia*, VIII, fol. 118,v.
[2] *MSS Cantares Mexicanos*, fol. 2,v.

chance on earth, can anything be found?"[3] And if the quest for truth on earth was difficult, the problem of man in relation to an afterlife presented even more insurmountable obstacles.

Faced with man's precarious situation as a creature born without an identity, full of unsatisfied desires yet lacking a definite goal on *tlaltícpac,* and confronted by the enigma of a beyond, the *tlamatinime* perceived the full import of the riddle of man. The universal question burst forth, "Is there any truth to man?"[4]

With this question, Nahuatl thought moved into what might be called the realm of philosophical anthropology. The wise men began to formulate answers to the questions about the truth of man. To understand the unique complexity of the Nahuatl question, one should remember that *truth* (*neltiliztli*) meant originally support or foundation. The question that they had actually asked was: Is man endowed with any lasting foundation, is he firmly rooted, or is he, too, merely an illusion?

In order to find an answer, the *tlamatinime* followed different paths. Their speculation concerned man as a real being, possessing an origin, a definite nature, and faculties, and aware of the mystery of a life beyond death. They also studied man as the creator of a way of life, author of educational, ethical, legal, and aesthetic principles. The *tlamatinime* finally approached the supreme social and personal ideals—the mainspring of Nahuatl thought and action—the divine spark in man's heart which transforms him into an artist, a poet, or a sage. With this gift man would be capable of making things divine.[5]

Nahuatl speculation on man's origin went through two stages: the mythico-religious and the philosophical. Two myths of the earlier phase which deal with the creation of the first men are particularly interesting.

[3] *Ibid.,* fol. 2,v.
[4] *Ibid.,* fol. 10,v.
[5] See, *Códice Matritense de la Real Academia,* VIII, fol. 117,v.

One of the oldest versions of the story is found in the *"Historia de los Mexicanos."* This account agrees in general with several striking illustrations in the *Codex Vaticanus A* 3738. The *"Historia"* relates that after the first four gods, the sons of Ometecuhtli-Omecíhuatl, had created fire and the sun, they "made a man and a woman. This man and this woman, whom they called Oxomoco and Cipactónal respectively, were sent to till the soil. It was commanded that she spin and weave, that they give birth to *macehuales* [people], and that they always work and not be idle."[6]

In the *Codex Vaticanus A* a drawing depicts this primeval pair. Father Ríos, commenting on this drawing, noted that "According to the opinions of many elders, he [Ometecuhtli] begot Oxomoco with his word and also a woman called Cipactónal. It was they who lived before the flood and who gave birth to others."[7]

Along with the myth of Oxomoco and Cipactónal, which links man's origin with the first gods and, more directly, with Ometecuhtli (the Lord of duality), there is another, completely different account. This version was recorded by Fray Gerónimo de Mendieta:

> They said that when the sun was at nine o'clock, it shot an arrow at the mentioned place [Acolman, which is at a distance of two leagues from Tezcoco and five from Mexico] and a hole was made, from which the first man emerged. He had no body from the armpits down, and afterward an entire woman emerged from the same place. When they [the people of Tezcoco] were questioned as to how that man without a body had been able to beget, they said something foolish and obscene which is not to be written here.[8]

What Mendieta called "foolish and obscene" and refused to record is described in other texts, like the one included by Garibay in his *Epica Náhuatl.*

6 *"Historia de los Mexicanos . . . Pinturas," loc. cit.,* 229–30.
7 *Códice Vaticano A,* fol. 1,v.
8 Mendieta, *Historia Eclesiástica Indiana,* 87–88.

One early morning, the Sun shot an arrow from the sky. It landed on the house of mirrors, and from the opening which it made in the rock emerged a man and a woman. Both were incomplete. They had nothing below the thorax, and through the fields they would skip like sparrows. But merging in a profound kiss, they gave birth to a son who became the origin of men.[9]

These are the two oldest Nahuatl myths concerning man's first appearance, and in them his creation is attributed to the Divine. In other texts rationalization of the myths, leading to the development of philosophical thought, is apparent. The *Manuscript of 1558*, a narration of deep symbolic significance, attributes to Quetzalcóatl the latest creation of man. Commenting on this text, Seler recalls that humanity had been destroyed four consecutive times. If the older myths explained the origin of man in the world's first age, the problem of his origin in the other cosmic periods and especially in the present, remained unsolved. "It was," claims Seler, "a problem of paramount importance to the ancient philosophers to explain the origin of man . . . and the circumstances of his appearance in the present cosmic period."[10]

The answer to this problem is also found in the *Manuscript of 1558* in the narration of Quetzalcóatl's trip to *Mictlan* (the region of the dead). The rationalization of the myth began here and gradually led to philosophical speculation. Other texts present the same idea in its philosophical form.

After the gods had assembled at Teotihuacán and the sun had been created, they asked themselves who would inhabit the earth. It was decided that Quetzalcóatl should make the trip to *Mictlan* to search for the precious bones of man so that he might be recreated to inhabit the earth:

1. And then Quetzalcóatl went to *Mictlan*. He approached Mictlantecuhtli and Mictlancíhuatl [Lord and Lady of the region of the dead]; at once he spoke to them:
2. "I come in search of the precious bones in your possession. I have come for them."

[9] Angel María Garibay K., *Epica Náhuatl*, 7–8.
[10] Seler, *"Entstehung der Welt und Menschen . . . ," loc. cit.*, IV, 53.

3. And Mictlantecuhtli asked of him, "What shall you do with them, Quetzalcóatl?"

4. And once again Quetzalcóatl said, "The gods are anxious that someone should inhabit the earth."

5. And Mictlantecuhtli replied, "Very well, sound my shell horn and go around my circular realm four times."

6. But his shell horn had no holes. Quetzalcóatl therefore called the worms, who made the holes. And then the bees went inside the horn and it sounded.

7. Upon hearing it sound, Mictlantecuhtli said anew, "Very well, take them."

8. But Mictlantecuhtli said to those in his service, "People of *Mictlan!* Gods, tell Quetzalcóatl that he must leave the bones."

9. Quetzalcóatl replied, "Indeed not; I shall take possession of them once and for all."

10. And he said to his *nahualli* [double], "Go and tell them that I shall leave them."

11. And the *nahualli* said in a loud voice, "I shall leave them."

12. But then he went and took the precious bones. Next to the bones of man were the bones of woman; Quetzalcóatl took them.
. . .

13. And again Mictlantecuhtli said to those in his service, "Gods, is Quetzalcóatl really carrying away the precious bones? Gods, go and make a pit."

14. The pit having been made, Quetzalcóatl fell in it; he stumbled and was frightened by the quail. He fell dead and the precious bones were scattered. The quail chewed and gnawed on them.

15. Then Quetzalcóatl came back to life; he was grieved and he asked of his *nahualli,* "What shall I do now . . . ?"

16. And the *nahualli* answered, "Since things have turned out badly, let them turn out as they may."

17. And he gathered them . . . and then he took them to *Tamoanchan.*

18. And as soon as he arrived, the woman called Quilaztli, who is Cihuacóatl, took them to grind and put them in a precious vessel of clay.

19. Upon them Quetzalcóatl bled his member. The other gods and Quetzalcóatl himself did penance.

20. And they said, "People have been born, oh gods, the *macehuales* [those given life or "deserved" into life through penance]."

21. Because, for our sake, the gods did penance![11]

COMMENTARY:

LINE 1: *And then Quetzalcóatl went to Mictlan. He approached Mictlantecuhtli and Mictlancíhuatl; at once he spoke to them.*

Another of the many aspects of the dual god appears here. Quetzalcóatl, symbol of wisdom, begins a dialog with Mictlantecuhtli-Mictlancíhuatl (Lord and Lady of the region of the dead), masks of Ometéotl inhabiting the infernal regions.

LINE 4: *And once again Quetzalcóatl said, "The gods are anxious that someone should inhabit the earth."*

This line gives the reason for Quetzalcóatl's trip to Mictlan. If he went in search of the precious bones, it was because "the gods were anxious," were worried (*nentlamati*) about having humans to inhabit the earth. The existence of man seemed mysteriously necessary to the gods. From this fundamental vision of man as "a being necessary to the gods," two distinct trends of thought derived. One was the mystico-militaristic conception of the Aztecs which affirmed the sun's need for human blood to continue its life. The other was a more abstract philosophical doctrine which called attention to a hidden motive behind the deity's creation of beings different from himself.

LINES 5-6: *And Mictlantecuhtli replied, "Very well, sound my shell horn and go around my circular realm four times." But his shell horn had no holes. Quetzalcóatl therefore called the worms, who made the holes. And then the bees went inside the horn and it sounded.*

The conditions imposed upon Quetzalcóatl by Mictlantecuhtli reflect a mysterious dialectic process within the Divine concerning the creation of man. An internal struggle for and against the

---

[11] Lehmann (ed.), "*Leyenda de los Soles,*" *loc. cit.,* 330–38.

appearance of man takes place within the supreme being. The obstacles that Quetzalcóatl had to overcome were many. He was successful in sounding the shell horn; he mocked the people of *Mictlan*; but finally he fell, temporarily dead.

LINE 15: *Then Quetzalcóatl came back to life; he was grieved and he asked of his nahualli, "What shall I do now ... ?"*

The dualism in Nahuatl thought appears again in the figure of the *nahualli*, a double of Quetzalcóatl. The *nahualli* first helped him to answer Mictlantecuhtli; now his role was that of an adviser.

LINE 17: *And he gathered them ... and then he took them to Tamoanchan.*

The etymology of *Tamoanchan* is obscure, but, as Seler noted, it is probably another name for the place of origin of all that exists:

> ... in this place the beginning of life is concentrated, and because of these gods, it is called *Omeyocan,* the place of duality. From there, the Mexicans believed, the children were sent into the world. For this reason, this supreme heaven was also called *Tamoanchan.*[12]

Inherent in this line is the idea that the bones gathered by Quetzalcóatl could be brought to life only in the place of duality, which was also the place of the origin of man.

LINE 18: *And as soon as he arrived, the woman called Quilaztli, who is Cihuacóatl, took them to grind and put them in a precious vessel of clay.*

Quilaztli, as the text states, was Cihuacóatl. Here she seems to be Quetzalcóatl's consort, another manifestation of what has been called *Omeyotization* or universal dualization. The couple, Quetzalcóatl-Cihuacóatl, creators of man in Tamoanchan, are none other than Ometecuhtli and Omecíhuatl, to whom belonged the title of inventor of men (*Teyocoyani*).

---

12 Seler, *"Das Weltbild der alten Mexicaner,"* loc. cit., IV, 26.

The political organization of the Aztecs offers further proof that Quetzalcóatl and Cihuacóatl acted as the dual principle of life and of the power that governs man. The *Tlacatecuhtli* or "king" was the representative of Quetzalcóatl; his lieutenant or "coadjutor" as the chroniclers called him, was called *Cihuacóatl.* The identification of this pair with the source of supreme power and with the creative wisdom of Ometéotl is not simply hypothetical.

LINE 19: *Upon them Quetzalcóatl bled his member. The other gods and Quetzalcóatl himself did penance.*

The blood of Quetzalcóatl and the penance of the gods brought life to the precious bones from *Mictlan.* Man was therefore the product of the gods' penance. With their sacrifice, the gods "deserved men" back to life. For this reason, the people were called *macehuales,* a word which means "those deserved and brought back to life because of penance."

These are the main ideas contained in the myth of Quetzalcóatl's trip to *Mictlan* in search of the bones for the new creation. This narration poetically relates man's origin in connection with the supreme being Ometéotl in *Tamoanchan,* where Cihuacóatl prepared the material which Quetzalcóatl impregnated by means of his blood.

The same doctrine appears in more abstract form in several texts of the *Florentine Codex.* In these works the identification of the mythical figure of Quetzalcóatl with the wisdom of Ometéotl is unquestionable. A classic speech of congratulations to a pregnant woman points out to whom the creation of man was attributed:

1. Perchance, is it true?
2. Did our Lord, our prince Quetzalcóatl, bring man back to life; he who invents man, he who creates man?
3. Perchance, was it determined by the Lord and Lady of Duality?
4. Was not the word handed down?[13]

[13] *Códice Florentino*, Book VI, fol. 120,r.

COMMENTARY:

LINE 1: *Perchance, is it true?*
From the very beginning there is evidence of the Nahuatl spirit of inquiry. Before they could affirm that something transcended earthly things, they expressed doubt about its truth.

LINE 2: *Did our Lord, our prince Quetzalcóatl, bring man back to life; he who invents man, he who creates man?*
These questions, closely linked to their most elevated meta-physico-theological thought, found answer in "flower and song." The inventor and creator of man was really Ometéotl; here, the same quality is attributed to Quetzalcóatl. Ometéotl, as the universal generating-conceiving principle, is "our mother, our father," and thus our origin. But in order to enhance Ometéotl's role as creator, the Nahuas sought to associate him with Quetzal-cóatl, the ancient Toltec symbol of wisdom.

LINE 3: *Perchance, was it determined by the Lord and Lady of Duality?*
With this question the Nahuatl philosopher asked whether the new creation of man by Quetzalcóatl, the wisdom of Ometéotl, was not also determined by the "Lord and Lady of Duality." In saying that the dual being "determined" or "affirmed" life for man, the *tlamatinime* were in fact repeating the doctrine of the Nahuatl concept of the Divine: Ometéotl was the origin of everything. Generating and conceiving, he determined the existence of all things—in this case, man.

The idea is even more clearly explicated in another text:

Man was born,
sent here [to earth] by our mother, our father,
the Lord and Lady of Duality.[14]

The nature of man and his life on earth was as significant a problem to the Nahuas as the question of his origin. To understand man's life on earth involved careful deliberation. The *tlamatinime* first concerned themselves with the very truth of

[14] *Ibid.*, Book VI, fol. 148,r.

man. The human being as an individual, his free will, his destiny, and a possible afterlife were other problems requiring an answer.

The *tlamatinime,* in their search for the truth about man, discovered his origin in Ometéotl, and thus were able to set forth his first solid roots—his foundation. Turning to the mystery of man's actual and temporal existence, the Nahuatl wise men asked a question of ultimate meaning: What are man's nature and personality? They did not, of course, use the words "nature" and "personality," but chose, in accordance with "flower and song," to embody this idea in a *"difrasismo."*

There are many texts which mention this concept. It appears frequently in the *Huehuetlatolli,* "discourses of the elders," where many ideas about man and his moral life are preserved.

In the *Huehuetlatolli A,* there is a congratulatory speech for a newly married couple containing this *"difrasismo."* Appearing in the Nahuatl marriage ceremony, which consisted of tying the man's cape to the blouse of the woman, the term is used to address the various participants. They all are "owners of a face, owners of a heart." The presiding elder constantly employs phrases like these:

I cause sorrow to your faces, to your hearts.[15]
In reverence do I hold your faces, your hearts.[16]

Addressing himself to those present, to their "faces and hearts," the elder is speaking to their very egos, or intrinsic selves.

Two texts cited above clarify the meaning here. The first one declared that the wise man was "he who teaches people to assume and develop a face (*te-ix-cuitiani, te-ix-tomani*)."[17] The word "face" (*ix-tli*) referred to the ego, the allusion was not anatomical but metaphorical. It described the most individual characteristic of the human being—the very element which removed his anonymity. For the *tlamatinime,* then, "face" was the verbal embodiment of an ego or self assumed and developed through

[15] Garibay (tr.), *"Huehuetlatolli, Documento A," loc. cit.,* 38.
[16] *Ibid.,* 39.
[17] *Códice Matritense de la Real Academia,* VIII, fol. 118,v.

education. In the description of the false *tlamatinime*, additional evidence for this interpretation may be found. He is depicted as "he who destroys the faces of others (*te-ix-poloani*)," and "he who leads them astray (*te-ix-cuipani*)."[18] Beyond doubt, "face" referred to that which most intimately characterized the intrinsic nature of each individual.

The meaning of the other element in the "*difrasismo*," the heart (*yóllotl*), is elucidated by a second text:

> That is why you surrender your heart to each thing;
> aimlessly do you lead it;
> you are destroying your heart.
> On earth, is anything attainable?[19]

To surrender one's heart to something meant to pursue something. The inference is that the word "heart" (*yóllotl*, derived from *ollin*, movement) signified man's dynamism; it was the active searcher of the self. The same idea, related to the deepest longing imbedded in the heart of the *tlamatini*—to discover poetry and wisdom—is beautifully expressed in another poem. The heart is identified with an ego keenly desirous of songs:

> Stealer of songs, my heart!
> Where will you find them?
> You are needy and poor,
> but grasp firmly the black and red ink,
> and perhaps you will no longer be a begger.[20]

The poem's description of the wise man's heart as "destitute" and "stealer of songs" associates the heart with the dynamic quality of the ego, which endeavors to fill its own emptiness by searching for wisdom and art. At times the heart wanders, going nowhere. At other times it arrives at the only truth on earth—poetry, "flower and song."

"Face and heart," the Nahuatl image of the individual, ap-

---

18 *Ibid.*, VIII, fol. 118,v.
19 *MSS Cantares Mexicanos*, fol. 2,v.
20 *Ibid.*, fol. 68,r.

pears to be an equivalent of our own modern idea of personality. Furthermore, this concept was completely in accord with the intuitive nature of the thinking of the wise men. It was not a definition based on cold rationalization, but was fresh and full of vitality. The face reflected the internal physiognomy of man, and the beating of the heart symbolized the source of dynamism in human will.

The Nahuatl idea of man, far from being narrow and limited, was open and broad. It made possible a system of education intended to give shape and meaning to the human face and to humanize the heart and will of man. The Nahuatl educator was rooted so firmly in this tradition that he was called *te-ix-tlamach-tiani,* "teacher of people's faces":

> He makes wise the countenances of others;
> he contributes to their assuming a face;
> he leads them to develop it. . . .
> Before their faces, he places a mirror;
> prudent and wise he makes them;
> he causes a face to appear on them. . . .
> Thanks to him, people humanize their will
> and receive a strict education.[21]

To teach their pupils "to assume a face" and "to humanize their will" was the task undertaken by the wise men in the *Calmécac.* For only with an authentic "face and heart" was each man able to escape the dream world of *tlalticpac.* Only in this manner might he arrive at his own individual truth, and thus be able to follow the path which might lead him to the "only truth on earth." And at the end of this path he might find the answer to that which only "flower and song" could solve: the mystery of human life and suffering on *tlalticpac.*

One of the major problems confronting philosophers of every age is that of man's free will and his destiny, and the *tlamatinime*

[21] *Códice Matritense de la Real Academia,* VIII, fol. 118,v.

were no exception. Nahuatl thought on this subject passed through the magico-religious stage before entering the realm of the philosophical.

The religion of the ancient Nahuas held that human destiny could be predicted with the aid of the *tonalámatl*, "the book of horoscopes." Numerous studies of the *tonalpohualli*, or "day-count," have been made, revealing that the *tonalpohualli* was a special count consisting of twenty groups of thirteen days. There were 20 day-names represented in the codices by hieroglyphs, but only 13 numbers were prefixed to the names of the days. Combining each of the 13 numbers with each of the 20 day-names gives a total of 260 different combinations. The *tonalpohualli*, unlike the solar calendar, had only 260 days, and each day, with its magic combination of a number and a sign, conveyed an omen either bad or good. Man needed to know the meanings of the signs of the most important days of his life: the day of his birth, of his entering the school, of his marriage, and so on. His destiny and his free will were conditioned by this magico-religious pattern. The *tonalámatl*, "book of the days and destinies," told him how he could understand and live in accordance with his fate. Several codices, such as the *Borbonicus*, the *Borgia*, the *Vaticanus B* and the *Telleriano-Remensis*, are in themselves, or at least include, a *tonalámatl*. Equally valuable in this respect is the documentation of the Indian informants of Sahagún, who dealt with the Indians' "judicial astrology or art of prediction" in Book IV of his *History*.

Jacques Soustelle has summarized the essence of the magico-religious configuration of the *tonalámatl*:

> When a man is born or "descends" by virtue of the decision of the supreme dual being, he finds himself automatically situated within a specific order of events, imprisoned by an omnipotent and divine machinery. The sign of the day of the *tonalpohualli* on which he is born will govern him until his death, and even also in his subsequent fate, depending on the nature of his death. Were he to die a sacrificial death, he would then join the Sun's resplendent

retinue; should he drown, he would experience the endless delights of *Tlalocan*; or, finally, he might be destined to nothingness in the dark shadows of the beyond in *Mictlan*. His entire fate was thus subject to the most rigorous predestination.[22]

To determine the fate of an individual, the soothsayers turned to the *tonalámatl*. In this book they read the various favorable and unfavorable possibilities associated with the day on which a child was born or with a day on which some important action was to be carried out. The sources show many of the complicated factors that had to be taken into account in making the calendric diagnosis of a given date.

In the process of making a prediction, consideration of the nature of the year itself was the first step to be taken. This depended fundamentally upon the year's spatial orientation. The Nahuas divided their fifty-two-year cycles into four groups of thirteen years. Each group was associated with one of the four quadrants of the universe. Thus the years controlled by *Acatl* (Reed) enjoyed the fertility and life of the East; the years under *Técpatl* (Flint) were marked by the idea of aridity and death peculiar to the North; and those under *Calli* (House) were identified with the West and with the decline and decadence characteristic of the direction where the sun sets. The years which came under *Tochtli* (Rabbit) were oriented toward the South and were held to be indifferent.

After ascertaining the nature of the year, it was necessary to investigate the peculiar character of each of the various numbers in the group of thirteen, and this system was applied to years as well as to days. The numbers 3, 7, 10, 11, 12, and 13 were thought to bring good fortune; the numbers 4, 5, 6, 8, and 9 were unlucky. The number 1, when introducing a group of thirteen years, was of indifferent value; when the number 2 was related to the sign *Tochtli* (Rabbit), it was considered unfortunate.

It was also necessary to examine the inherent meaning of each one of the twenty signs of the *tonalámatl*. For example, the sign

[22] Soustelle, *La Vie Quotidienne des Aztèques*, 140.

of the Eagle (*Quauhtli*) symbolized warlike inclinations; the sign of the Vulture (*Cozcaquauhtli*), good fortune and the hope of a long life. The sign of the Rabbit (*Tochtli*) was an indication of drunkenness, while the sign of Rain (*Quiáhuitl*) was benevolent. Each of the twenty signs portended a particular type of activity.

To formulate their predictions, then, the soothsayers were required to combine and interpret the many elements which could exert influence on a given day. They had to take into account the spatial orientation, sign, and number of the year; the nature of each group of thirteen days; and finally the character of the particular day itself, determined by its own combination of number and sign as well as by its consecration to a particular deity. On a certain day favorable and unfavorable possibilities might coincide. It was then the soothsayers' duty to weigh and balance the various influential factors in order to formulate and announce the calendric diagnosis.

Of special interest is the fact that when someone "descended to earth" (was born) on an unfortunate day, the fortunetellers, in an attempt to improve or even to change the fate of the child, would set a favorable date for naming him. In this way the ominous signs of the day of birth would be offset. Sahagún has described the process:

After the child was born, they endeavored to know the sign under which it had been born in order to know what his fate was to be. For this reason, they went in search of the fortuneteller, who was called *Tonalpouhqui*, that he might tell them. . . . After being informed of the hour of birth, the priest would then look into his books for the sign under which the child had been born, and for the possibilities under this sign, and . . . perhaps he might tell them: "The child was not born under a good sign, but under a bad one; but there is a reasonable possibility which may offset such a sign, one which should temper and reduce the evil of the main sign." Then he would indicate the day on which it should be given a name. . . . Or he might tell them: "Look, his sign is indifferent, half-good and half-bad." Then he would seek a day that would be favorable. . . . This having been done, the child would receive his name on a day that was favorable.[23]

In this way days of ambivalent nature were balanced, and the negative force was counteracted. The soothsayers felt that in most cases man could be released from a fatal destiny, for although the *tonalpohualli* implied a certain determinism, it was neither so rigid nor so absolute that it would condemn man to a course of action from which he could not deviate. The Nahuatl texts affirm this interpretation; they leave the way open, of course taking into consideration the influence of the day of birth and the day of name giving, for a certain freedom in the exercise of the human will. The following text describes the possibilities for one who had been born on the day 7-Flower:

> If he did worthy things, if he admonished himself,
>   it went well with him. . . .
> If he was negligent, he would accomplish nothing; of
>   nothing would he make himself worthy.
> He would deserve only his humiliation and destruction.[24]

According to this, the reason for "things going well with one" or for deserving only "humiliation and destruction" lay precisely in admonishing oneself (*mo-notza*). In the glossary accompanying the paleographic version from which this text was taken, Schultze Jena translated the word *mo-notza* as "he calls to himself," "he enters within himself," "he disciplines himself," and "he controls himself."[25] Obviously the Nahuas recognized the possibility of modifying their personal destiny by means of their own personal control.

This is not an isolated example. Other texts illustrate the Nahuas' belief in the importance of the individual and in his capacity to alter, by means of his own volition, his fate and

---

[23] Sahagún, *op. cit.*, I, 626–27.

[24] Leonhard Schultze Jena, *Wahrsagerei, Himmelskunde und Kalender der alten Azteken*, 104. This is Schultze Jena's version of the texts of the informants of Sahagún.

[25] *Ibid.*, 302.

destiny. He could even do so negatively; a favorable destiny could be converted into an unfortunate one. The informants of Sahagún described men who did this: "And some conducted their lives wastefully even though they had been born under a favorable sign. They lived a wretched life."[26]

The Nahuas, then, recognized that each man's fate (*tonalli*) could be modified to a significant degree by his own volition. By controlling himself, he could regulate his life so that things might go well for him, but he could also waste his life—even though the signs of his day of birth had been favorable.

This leads us to an evaluation of the popular opinion of Aztec "fatalism." Although the Nahuas certainly believed in the strong influence of the various signs and dates of the *tonalpohualli*, it is also true that they considered self-control an important force in overcoming a destiny. This idea is far from what is normally understood as absolute fatalism or blind belief in predestination.

In conceding man's ability to determine and regulate his life and destiny, the *tlamatinime* passed from the magico-religious to the philosophical realm. As teachers they were directly concerned with the problem of man's free will. Among the many duties of the *tlamatinime* was the explicit task of "humanizing the will of the people," and this implies that they felt it was possible for education to influence man's will. Nahuatl education, leading to the development of a face and a heart, also attempted to impart a humanistic quality to man's will, which, in turn, would free him from a predetermined fate. To this end the *tlamatinime* taught self-discipline:

> Teacher of the truth, the *tlamatini* ceases not to admonish. . . .
> He opens their ears, he enlightens them. . . .
> Thanks to him the people humanize their will
> and receive a strict education.[27]

That a free will capable of being changed by education existed is thus emphatically affirmed. Our knowledge of the reasons for

26 *Ibid.*, 94.
27 *Códice Matritense de la Real Academia*, VIII, fol. 118,v.

the *tlamatinime*'s confidence in the power of education is scant. Perhaps the very results of their educational system, rather than some abstract speculation, were the best proof of their intuitive confidence. For it is undeniably true that men of well-defined moral rectitude—Nezahualcóyotl, the poet-king; Motecuhzoma I, the warrior who gained Aztec independence; and the young Cuauhtémoc, for example—were produced by this system.

Having accepted such a humanistic doctrine of free will, the *tlamatinime* faced that profound problem which confronts all men who acknowledge a supreme being as origin and foundation of man and the universe. It is the old paradox of man who feels himself to be free, yet realizes at the same time his relationship to an all-powerful deity who rules over all things as the "Master of the Close Vicinity."

The problem is no longer the magico-religious one dealing with the possibility of altering a predetermined destiny revealed in the *tonalpohualli* or day count. It is the philosophical question, perhaps unanswerable, of what man's freedom to act might be in the eyes of the Divine. In a Nahuatl text collected by Sahagún, the speculation of the *tlamatinime* concerning this point is lucidly expressed:

1. Our Master, the Lord of the Close Vicinity,
2. thinks and does what He wishes; He determines, He amuses himself.
3. As he wishes, so will it be.
4. In the palm of His hand He has us; at His will He shifts us around.
5. We shift around, like marbles we roll; He rolls us around endlessly.
6. We are but toys to Him; He laughs at us.[28]

COMMENTARY:

LINE 1: *Our Master, the Lord of the Close Vicinity.*
From the very beginning the text positively identifies the one to whom reference is being made. The deity is designated by one

[28] *Códice Florentino*, Book VI, fol. 43,v.

of his most characteristic names, the one which best expresses omnipotence and supremacy over all things—*in Tloque in Nahuaque*, the Lord of the Close Vicinity.

> LINE 2: *Thinks and does what He wishes; He determines, He amuses himself.*

This line mentions what might be considered the fundamental features of divine action. The supreme deity has his own will; his authority and his actions are completely independent; "he determines." The suggestion that the deity amuses himself in this way provides a glimpse of what could be called the ultimate reason for his creative activity. The highest level of Nahuatl thought envisions Ometéotl creating and finding pleasure in the mortal's transitory stay on *tlaltícpac*. The mystico-militaristic approach characteristic of Aztec religion was entirely different, for here it was felt that the purpose of man's creation was to provide blood for the maintenance of the Sun's life.

The *tlamatinime*'s interpretation of the creation perhaps held more meaning than might be supposed. Since it was impossible for man on *tlaltícpac* to know the underlying motive for creation, the wise men attributed it to the Divine's wish for a spectacle, for entertainment—a play which human beings would perform in a world of dreams. In any case this idea should be considered another example of "flower and song," the only way to the many mysteries of what is beyond (*topan, Mictlan*).

> LINE 3: *As He wishes, so will it be.*

This line confirms the absolute independence of the "Lord of the Close Vicinity." Considered in relation to the ideas expressed in line 2, the following description of the supreme being is understandable.

> LINES 4-5: *In the palm of His hand He has us; at His will He shifts us around. We shift around, like marbles we roll; He rolls us around endlessly.*

Granting the universal supremacy of Ometéotl, the *tlamatinime* thus described man's situation on earth. Ometéotl holds man in the palm of his hand (*imácpal iyoloco*) and sustains him within it. He introduces activity into the world, "at His will He shifts us around." We are born never to rest, but to live, to work, to suffer, to fight, and to seek a "face and a heart." Man yearns for what is *true* on earth, for only by finding truth will he put an end to his restlessness and find within himself the foundation he seeks; that is why we shift around, why we roll like marbles. But the most tragic thing about our existence is that, in spite of our feeling of freedom, we do not know our final destiny. No wonder the *tlamatinime* exclaimed, "He rolls us around endlessly."

LINE 6: *We are but toys to Him; He laughs at us.*
Man's condition in the eyes of the Divine is finally established. The line implies an awareness, through "flower and song," that Ometéotl observes man in one way or another. For this reason, perhaps, many of the deities in the Nahuatl pantheon (manifestations of Ometéotl) were represented with a *tlachialoni*, "mirror," through which they could observe the world.

Ometéotl keeps man in view because "we are but toys to Him." The text closes with a highly meaningful sentence describing man's relative importance to the Divine—"He laughs at us." Sahagún called the wise men who conceived all of this "philosophers." They were certainly concerned with questions of ultimate meaning.

If the *tlamatinime* were concerned with the origin, personality, and free will of man, they also faced the urgent question of an afterlife. To appreciate the Nahuatl speculations on this subject one should recall the limited value they placed upon life on earth. A Nahuatl poet reminds us:

It is not true, it is not true
that we came to live here.
We came only to sleep, only to dream.[29]

The reality of this life is like that of a dream, and "this is not the

[29] *MSS Cantares Mexicanos*, fol. 17,r.

place where things are done,"[30] where one finds what is true or firmly rooted.

Here is the invitation of an Aztec poet to those who would try to understand the fugacity of life and the mystery of the beyond:

> Let us consider things as lent to us, oh, friends;
> only in passing are we here on earth;
> tomorrow or the day after,
> as Your heart desires, oh, Giver of Life,
> we shall go, my friends, to His home.[31]

Such was the Nahuatl conviction regarding human life on earth. Death, then, comes as an awakening from a dreamlike existence, after which one enters the world of "the beyond, the region of the dead." But the Nahuas were aware that to give a final answer to the mystery of the beyond was difficult, and a variety of opinions and doctrines can be found in the ancient texts. There are beliefs first of all about the places where the dead might go. Parallel to these beliefs are philosophic doubts, speculation, and the formulation of problems.

The Spanish and Indian chroniclers recorded many ideas concerning the places inhabited or visited by the dead. In the Appendix to Book III, Sahagún includes one example of the purely religious belief. The first dwelling place of the dead was *Mictlan,* according to Sahagún and other sources, and this region was composed of nine levels below the earth. Persons who died a natural death went there, but on the road the dead had to overcome a number of obstacles. The company of a little dog was granted to the dead person; it was cremated along with the corpse. The Nahuas believed that the tests ended after four years, and that this also concluded the wandering existence of the dead. "In this manner," wrote Sahagún, "at this place of the underworld called *Chiconamictlan* (ninth place of the dead), the deceased finally ended."[32]

[30] *Ibid.,* fol. 4,v.
[31] *Ibid.,* fol. 62,r.
[32] Sahagún, *op. cit.,* I, 316.

The idea of man's total disappearance in *Mictlan* after four years was one of the principal factors which led Chavero, the nineteenth-century Mexican positivist historian, to develop his materialistic interpretation of Nahuatl thought. Had Chavero considered the data more carefully, he would have realized that the very fact of a belief in survival after death, even for the short period of four years, implied a faith in the existence of something more than the material body. This faith is also demonstrated by one of the other names used for *Mictlan, Ximoayan,* which means "the place of the fleshless," where men were at last freed from their bodies.

Tlalocan, described by Sahagún as "the earthly paradise," was the second place of the dead. In this place "never is there a lack of green corn, squash, sprigs of amaranth, green chiles, tomatoes, string beans in pods, and flowers; there dwelled some gods called *Tlaloques.*"[33]

The pleasant destiny of going to *Tlalocan* befell those chosen by *Tláloc,* the god of rain. He called them by means of a death which clearly indicated his personal intervention—death by drowning, lightning, dropsy, or gout. The individuals chosen by the god of rain were not cremated but were buried.

Concerning the destiny of those who went to *Tlalocan,* certain verses from the *Tláloc icuic* seem to imply, as Seler noted, "a subsequent development of the souls of those who die through the intervention of *Tláloc.*"[34] It hints at another existence on earth for those who have gone to *Tlalocan:*

In four years, in the beyond, there is a rebirth.
People [here on earth] no longer remember, for long they
    have lost count.
In the place of the fleshless, in the house of quetzal plumes,
there is a transformation of what belongs to the One who
    restores people to life.[35]

This vague allusion to a type of metempsychosis is not com-

[33] *Ibid.*, I, 317-18.
[34] Seler, *Gesammelte Abhandlungen,* II, 993.
[35] Sahagún, *op. cit.*, I, 276.

monly found among the Nahuas as a response to the mystery of the beyond. In opposition to such a doctrine, many texts emphatically maintain that there is but one life, and that on *tlaltícpac*:

> Perchance, are we to live a second time?
> Your heart knows it:
> Only once have we come to live![36]

The third place "to which the souls of the dead went," according to Sahagún, "was a heaven, the dwelling place of the sun [*Tonatiuhilhuícac*]."[37] This was considered a glorious destiny: "Those who went to this heaven were those who died in battle and the captives who had died at the hands of their enemies [sacrificial victims]."[38] Women who died in childbirth met the same favorable fate as the warriors who took captives in battle, for they died with a prisoner in their wombs:

> What the ancients said concerning the women . . . who died from bearing the first child, and who were called *mocihuaquetzque*, and who were also considered along with those who died in battle —all of them go to the house of the Sun and reside in the western part of the sky.[39]

It is for this reason that in addition to being "the home of the Sun," the West was also, for the Nahuas, *Cihuatlampa*, "toward the region of the women." It was the region from which the women who had died in childbirth, the "divine women (*cihuateteo*)," would go out to greet the sun. The warriors, however, triumphantly singing war songs at the side of the Sun, accompanied him from where he rose to the zenith of his voyage. It was only "after four years . . . that they turned into various types of birds of rich plumage and color, and they would sip of all of the flowers of heaven as well as of earth."[40]

---

[36] *MSS Cantares Mexicanos*, fol. 12,r.
[37] Sahagún, *op. cit.*, I, 318.
[38] *Ibid.*, I, 318.
[39] *Ibid.*, I, 596.
[40] *Ibid.*, I, 319.

Such was the nature of the houses of the sun and of *Tlalocan,* and such was the fate of those who went there. In the minds of the Nahuas, these were the two places of delight and triumph beyond earthly life.

One other region of the beyond is illustrated in the *Codex Vaticanus A.* It was called *Chichihuacuauhco.* The name is composed of *chichihua,* "wet-nurse," *cuáuhitl,* "tree," and *co,* "place," so that the word means "in the wet-nurse tree." To this place went the children who died before attaining the age of reason. There they were nourished by the milk which fell in drops from the tree. The destiny assigned to the children must have brought the Christian image of limbo to the mind of the friars.

According to the *Florentine Codex, Chichihuacuauhco* was situated in the house of Tonacatecuhtli (Lord of our Flesh):

> It is said that the little children who died, like jade, turquoise, and jewels, do not go to the frightful and cold region of the dead [*Mictlan*]. They go to the house of Tonacatecuhtli; they live by the "tree of our flesh." They nourish themselves on the tree of our sustenance; they live near the "tree of our flesh"; from it do they feed themselves.[41]

This was the basic structure of the Nahuatl image of the afterlife. They believed that man's final destiny was determined, not on the basis of his moral conduct in life, but by the nature of his death. Those who died by drowning, from lightning, or from dropsy went to *Tlalocan;* those who were sacrificed, those who died in childbirth, and those killed in combat would become the companions of the Sun; and those who died in their infancy would go to *Chichihuacuauhco.* Those who ended their days in any other way went to *Mictlan,* which seemed to be the least desirable of all possible destinies.

To Christians, who believe that moral conduct in life at least partially determines the nature of the afterlife, the Nahuatl view may seem strange, for there was no suggestion of punishment or reward in the hereafter. Nahuatl religion was not simply a

---

[41] *Códice Florentino,* Book VI, fol. 96,r.

doctrine of salvation, for it led the Nahuas to another ethical concept. It urged a way of life in accord with ethical principles which would guarantee the approval of the gods and the immediate social consequence of this approval—the attainable happiness on earth. One's destiny after death was a matter for the gods.

Although they were aware of these popular doctrines, the wise men doubted. If at any point in the development of Nahuatl thought a distinction can be made between the individual who believes and the one who doubts, it is here, concerning the question of the hereafter. Death is inevitable:

> It is true that we leave, truly we part.
> We leave the flowers, the songs, and the earth.
> It is true that we go; it is true that we part![42]

Confronted by the inevitability of death, the doubt which transcends religious faith comes forth:

> Where do we go, oh! where do we go?
> Are we dead beyond, or do we yet live?
> Will there be existence again?
> Will the joy of the Giver of Life be there again?[43]

Death is unavoidable; we shall have to leave "the flowers, the songs, and the earth." The final destiny, though, is uncertain. Even if it is true that we live after death, there is no way of knowing whether there is suffering or joy in the beyond.

The doubts of the *tlamatinime* about human destiny beyond the reality of *tlalticpac* are expressed in many texts. Their insistence on this theme, however, should not be taken as definitive proof of Nahuatl pessimism. The wise men's concept of the individual (face and heart) as a perfectible entity and the possessor of a free will implied a positive attitude in the search for the meaning of death.

Because of the Nahuas' love for "flower and song," symbol of "the only truth," they refused to accept the idea of total destruc-

42 *MSS Cantares Mexicanos*, fol. 61,v.
43 *Ibid.*, fol. 61,v.

tion either by the prophesied end of the Fifth Sun or by the inevitable death, more immediate and personal, of the individual.

The formal religious answer to the problem lay in maintaining the life of the Sun with human blood. But on a personal philosophical level the wise men sought, by means of "flower and song," a different solution.

The poem below is an invitation to inquiry. The *tlamatinime* formulated this invitation at a gathering of poets at Huexotzinco:

Meditate, remember the region of mystery;
beyond is His house; truly we all go
to where the fleshless are, all of us men;
our hearts shall go to know His face.[44]

Suddenly the idea is interrupted, and mistrust appears in the last verses:

What are you meditating?
What are you remembering, oh my friends?
Meditate no longer!
At our side the beautiful flowers bloom;
so does the Giver of Life concede pleasure to man.
All of us, if we meditate, if we remember,
become sad here.[45]

The terrible conviction that the mystery can never be understood is expressed by the Nahuatl philosopher. Looking at the flowers that "open at our side" and feeling his inability to approach the hereafter, the pre-Columbian sage, in an attempt to reconcile man to the limitations of his knowledge, confesses that "if we meditate, if we remember, [we] become sad here."

In spite of this realization, as though he were encouraged by a kind of complacency in the face of mystery, one last evocation of death comes to his mind:

Meditate upon it, oh princes of Huexotzinco;
although it be jade, although it be gold,

[44] *Ibid.*, fol. 14,v.
[45] *Ibid.*, fol. 14,v.

it too must go to the place of the fleshless.
It too must go to the region of mystery;
we all perish, no one will remain![46]

Nahuatl meditation on the theme of death was by no means fruitless. The wise men had learned to face the problem in a positive manner; they could ask themselves about the various possible destinies of man after death:

Where shall I go?
Where shall I go?
Which is the path to the god of duality?

Perchance, is Your home
in the place of the fleshless?
In the innermost of heaven?
Or is the place of the fleshless
only here on earth?[47]

The problem is expressed logically: since "one must go," the path which will lead to life, to Ometéotl, must be sought. There are two possibilities: One, that the path of the "fleshless" (the dead) is only here on earth—that is, the grave marks the end of man's existence; or, two, that the dead follow a path to Ometéotl in a further existence. In the latter case the path must lead either to *Mictlan*, where the dead suffer, or to the "innermost of heaven," the place of happiness and pleasure.

Reduced to a diagram, the Nahuatl statement of the problem is more readily comprehensible:

1. "Only here on earth
   [where the dead are buried
   or cremated] is man's
   last abode."
2. Or the place of the dead
   is beyond earth:
   a. In a place of suffering,
      (*Mictlan . . .*)

46 *Ibid.*, fol. 14,v.
47 *Ibid.*, fol. 35,v.

b. Or, in a place of happiness;
the innermost of heaven:
Omeyocan.

This logical expression of the problem, discovered by means of dilemmas, presents the fundamental possibilities open to one who considers the fact of death. What might, in modern terminology, be called different "schools of thought" were derived from these postulates. Each "school" accepted one of the three possibilities.

The first group believed that "only here on earth [where corpses are buried or cremated] is the place of the dead"; there is no afterlife. And from this arises a logical conclusion:

For only here on earth
shall the fragrant flowers last
and the songs which are our bliss.
Enjoy them now![48]

This "Epicurean" trend in Nahuatl thought appears again and again:

I weep, I feel forlorn;
I remember that we must leave flowers and songs.
Let us enjoy ourselves now, let us sing now!
For we go, we disappear.[49]

Remove trouble from your hearts, oh my friends.
As I know, so do others:
only once do we live.
Let us in peace and pleasure spend our lives;
come, let us enjoy ourselves!
Let not those who live in anger join us,
the earth is so vast.
Oh! that one could live forever!
Oh! that one never had to die![50]

A second school existed alongside the first; it maintained that

[48] *Ibid.*, fol. 61,v.
[49] *Ibid.*, fol. 35,r.
[50] *Ibid.*, fol. 25,v. and 26,r.

man's destination was *Mictlan* or *Ximoayan* (the place of the fleshless), where, perhaps, there is only suffering. Those who held this belief were the poets influenced by traditional religious ideas, but their position was not free from doubt. The lines below, the central theme of a poem, express the fundamental idea of the second school concerning the problem of death:

> I shall have to leave the precious flowers;
> I shall have to descend to the place where those,
>   in one way or another, live.[51]

The very manner of designating the place of the dead—*Quenamican*, "the place where those, in one way or another, live"—testifies to the uncertainty permeating the views of the second school. They wondered:

> Perchance, are we really true beyond?
> Will we live where there is only sadness?
> Is it true, perchance is it not true . . . ?
> How many can truthfully say
> that truth is or is not there?
> Let our hearts not be troubled.[52]

The second group of philosophers, looking fearfully upon human destiny after death, seem to adopt a skeptical attitude. They did not abandon the quest, but never succeeded in answering the question, "How many can truthfully say that truth is or is not there?"

The followers of the third line of thought sought a positive path through "flower and song." They did not boast of definite proof of a happy life in the beyond, but they discovered what might be called, in Pascal's words, "a truth of the heart." The *tlamatinime* expressed it in this way:

> Truly earth is not the place of reality.
> Indeed one must go elsewhere;

[51] *Ibid.*, fol. 5,v.
[52] *Ibid.*, fol. 62,r.

beyond, happiness exists.
Or is it that we come to earth in vain?
Certainly some other place is the abode of life.[53]

Proceeding from the undeniable fact that "earth is not the place of reality," the third school came to the conclusion that to find happiness "one must go elsewhere," unless, as the poem suggests, "we come to earth in vain." Rejecting this last hypothesis, the *tlamatinime* declared, "Certainly, some other place is the abode of life."

One final appeal to Ometéotl, an affirmation of the existence of happiness in the beyond, combines deep philosophical thought, poetry, and mystical inspiration:

Beyond is the place where one lives.
I would be lying to myself were I to say;
"Perhaps everything ends on this earth;
here do our lives end."

No, oh Lord of the Close Vicinity,
it is beyond, with those who dwell in Your house,
that I will sing songs to You, in the innermost of heaven.
My heart rises;
I fix my eyes upon You,
next to You, beside You,
Oh Giver of Life![54]

Thus, in a supreme act of confidence in the Giver of Life, who could not have sent man to earth to live in vain, it is affirmed that "face and heart"—the individual—lifts himself up, escaping the evanescence of a dreamlike world. In so doing, he achieves the desired happiness beyond, "in the place where one truly lives."

Thus did the mind of ancient Mexico conceive of man, his personality, free will, soul, and fate.

[53] *Ibid.*, fol. 1,v.
[54] *Ibid.*, fol. 2,r.

V

Nahuatl Man
Creator of a Way of Life

T
HE Nahuatl wise men were not scientists in the modern sense of the word, but in their effort to develop "faces and hearts" they conceived as systems a social order, an ethical code, and a theory of history, art, and education. In their totality these institutions constituted the basic foundation of all forms of human life. With the passage of time these systems were perfected, and became a chief interest of the Nahuatl thinkers.

A complete study of the systems which consolidated the Nahuas' way of life cannot be undertaken here. We will consider only those aspects which show the Nahuatl philosopher involved in creating and developing the cultural standards to be transmitted from generation to generation through what we call education, a well-defined moral code, history, and art. The principles underlying the Nahuatl institutions reveal that the *tlamatinime* engendered an authentically creative movement of immediate social significance.

The Nahuas had two words for education: *Tlacahuapahua-*

liztli, "the art of strengthening or bringing up men," and *Neixtla-machiliztli,* "the act of giving wisdom to the face." The written sources on the educational practices of the Nahuas are so abundant that a book could be written on that subject alone. Such a book might reconstruct—as did Jaeger's *Paideia* for the ancient Greeks—through the educational system all the richness and profundity of the Nahuatl concept of man.

Among all peoples education is the means of communicating to new generations the experience of the past and the intellectual heritage. Such communication has a twofold purpose: first, to form and develop the individual as a person and, second, to incorporate him into the life of the community.

Greek education, embodied in the *Paideia,* emphasized the personal development of the individual. This was not the case among the Nahuas, who were more interested in the assimilation of individuals into the life and highest ideals of the community. This should not be taken to imply contempt for the individual personality (face and heart), for several texts, speaking of the development of "face and heart," indicate the contrary.

For an understanding of the Nahuatl approach to education one factor is particularly important—the concern of the elders for integrating the individual, from the very beginning, into the life of the group of which he would always be a significant part. Clavijero wrote:

"Nothing," says Father Acosta, "caused me so much admiration and seems to me more worthy of praise and remembering than the care and discipline with which the Mexicans raised their children. In effect, it would be quite difficult to find a nation which in its times of paganism gave more attention to this element of highest importance to the state."[1]

From infancy, parental teaching at home revolved around the idea of strength and self-control. These concepts were instilled in the child by means of long moral talks and rigorous

[1] Clavijero, *op. cit.,* III, 196.

discipline. Thus the *Codex Mendoza* illustrates the child's reduced ration of food, which was intended to teach him to control his appetite.[2] It also depicts his first training in domestic chores, such as carrying wood and water.

The passage below from the Indian informants of Sahagún eloquently describes the primary educational mission of the father:

1. The father, root and origin of the lineage of men.
2. His heart is good, he is careful of things; he is compassionate, he is concerned, he is the foresight, he is support, he protects with his hands.
3. He raises children, he educates, he instructs, he admonishes, he teaches them to live.
4. He places before them a large mirror, a mirror pierced on both sides; he is a large torch that does not smoke.[3]

Many of the functions assigned to the father are analogous to those of the *tlamatini* in his role as educator. He is a man of good heart and foresight, and brings support and protection to his children. Not only does he provide for them, but his principal duty is to teach and admonish them. He is the first to teach his children self-awareness and self-discipline. The same metaphor used to describe the *tlamatinime* appears here: the father "places before them a large mirror," so that they may learn to know themselves, to become masters of themselves.

Thus two fundamental principles guided Nahuatl education in the home: self-control, taught by a series of austerities to which the child must accustom himself, and self-knowledge, as well as knowledge of what he must aspire to be, instilled by repeated paternal advice.

[2] Eusebio Dávalos, discussing Nahuatl educational practices concerning proper eating, notes: "As children they were taught to be moderate in both food and in other things. Self-control seems to have been a characteristic quality of ancient Mexico." Dávalos, *"La alimentación entre los Mexica,"* in *Revista Mexicana de Estudios Antropológicos,* Vol. XIV (1954–55), 107.

[3] *Códice Matritense del Real Palacio,* (ed. of Francisco del Paso y Troncoso), VI, Part 2, fol. 199.

The "Plumed Serpent"
a symbolic representation of one of Quetzalcóatl's many aspects

*Courtesy Photographic Archives of the National Institute of
Anthropology and History, Mexico City.*

AN EXAMPLE OF AZTEC SCULPTURE
the head of a dead man.

Courtesy Photographic Archives of the National Institute of
Anthropology and History, Mexico City.

The next stage in the *Tlacahuapahualiztli* (the art of strengthening or bringing up men) began with the child's entrance into those centers of education which today would be called grammar schools.

According to the *Codex Mendoza*, at the age of fifteen the Nahuatl youth entered either the *Telpochcalli* (house of young men) or the *Calmécac* (a school of higher learning in which nobles and future priests were educated). Soustelle noted that:

> This document [the *Codex Mendoza*] does not agree with the most reliable texts. It seems that the education, strictly parental, ended much earlier [than the age of fifteen]. Some parents took their children to the *Calmécac* from the time they were able to walk, and children entered school between six and nine years of age.[4]

Whatever the case, it is certain that great importance was attached to the child's entering either of the two schools. For at this time the Nahuatl child was actually assimilated into the life and culture of the community. In Book III of his *Historia,* Sahagún recorded the discussions between the father of the student and the director of the school when the child's education was about to become the school's responsibility.

The existence of two types of schools among the Nahuas does not imply a discriminatory criterion like that employed by modern social classes. The son of *macehuales* (common people) was not obligated to attend the *Telpochcalli,* and the son of noble parents did not necessarily attend the *Calmécac.* The *Florentine Codex* speaks clearly on this point, pointing out that the child's entrance into either school depended on the father's choice. He might wish to dedicate the child to the patron divinity of either the *Calmécac* or the *Telpochcalli*:

> When a child was born, his parents would put him in the *Calmécac* or in the *Telpochcalli.* That is, they would promise the child as a gift, and they would take him either to the *Calmécac,* that he might

4 Soustelle, *La Vie Quotidienne des Aztèques,* 199.

become a priest, or to the *Telpochcalli*, in order to become a warrior.[5]

It is clear that the education imparted in the *Calmécac* was superior, for it was there that the intellectual development of the student was emphasized. In this sense the *Calmécac* were the centers of education, where the *tlamatinime* communicated the most elevated aspects of Nahuatl culture. For this reason it is not strange that the sons of kings, nobles, and the rich ordinarily attended the *Calmécac*, but these schools were not exclusively for these classes. The testimony of the informants of Sahagún is clear:

> The chiefs, the nobles, and, in addition, other good fathers and mothers would take their children and promise them to the *Calmécac;* and also all those who so desired.[6]

It is probable that the majority of the people, following perhaps a firmly fixed tradition, did promise their children to the *Telpochcalli*, from which they would emerge as warriors. "The common people [*in macehualtin*]," according to the *Florentine Codex*, "would send their children to the *Telpochcalli*."[7]

The significant point is that all Nahuatl children, without exception, attended one or the other of these schools. Soustelle commented:

> It is admirable that at that time and on that continent, an Indian people of America should have practiced compulsory education for all; that there was not a single Mexican child of the sixteenth century, whatever his social origin, who was deprived of schooling.[8]

An example of the life led in one of these schools, the *Calmécac*

[5] Arthur J. O. Anderson and Charles E. Dibble (trs.), *Florentine Codex*, Book III, 49.

[6] *Ibid.*, Book III, 59.

[7] *Ibid.*, Book III, 49.

[8] Soustelle, *La Vie Quotidienne des Aztèques*, 203. Soustelle refers here to Torquemada's statement that "all the parents in general took care to send their children to these schools, or to others . . . and this was obligatory." (Torquemada, *Monarquía Indiana*, II, 187.)

in this case, is found in Sahagún. He recorded the "customs that were observed in the house called Calmécac."[9] They were directed toward the intellectual growth and development of self-control of the students:

> They would all sweep and clean the house at four in the morning. . . .
> The older boys would go out and look for maguey thorns. . . .
> They would go out to bring wood that was necessary for burning in the house at night. . . .
> They would stop their work a little early, and then they would go straight to their temple school to attend the service of the gods, and the exercises of penitence, and to bathe first. . . .
> The meals they ate, they cooked in the *Calmécac*. . . .
> At the setting of the sun, they would begin to prepare the necessary things. . . .
> Every night at midnight, all would get up to pray, and whoever did not get up would be punished by piercing his ears, his chest, thighs, legs.[10]

After mentioning the punishments imposed upon those who had misbehaved, Sahagún described other aspects of life in the *Calmécac*, finally discussing the most important activity of all—the intellectual education:

> The boys were taught to speak well, and to greet, and to be respectful. . . .
> They were taught all the verses of songs, which were called divine songs, and which were written in their books with characters. . . .
> And in addition, they were taught Indian astrology, and the interpretation of dreams, and the count of the years.[11]

There are three important aspects of the intellectual instruction to consider. It had to do, first of all, with the manner of speaking and of expressing oneself. The *Florentine Codex* men-

---

[9] Sahagún, *op. cit.*, I, 327.
[10] *Ibid.*, I, 327.
[11] *Ibid.*, I, 329.

tions that "they were carefully taught a good language."[12] Education began with what today would be called, in classic terminology, studies in rhetoric. Perhaps the best proof that the young men took advantage of these teachings at the *Calmécac* is afforded by the numerous discourses preserved in the *Huehuetlatolli* and the other texts of the Indian informants. Book VI of Sahagún's *Historia* provides the best example of the *qualli tlatolli* (good language) learned by the students of the *Calmécac*. The difference between this cultured or "noble" manner of speaking and that of the masses is also apparent in the different terms by which they were designated: *macehuallatolli*, "language of the common people," and *tecpillatolli*, "lordly language."

The second point mentioned by Sahagún in describing the intellectual education concerned the teaching of the songs (*cuícatl*), especially the "divine songs" (*teucuícatl*) which "were written in the codices."[13] This teaching trained the students in the Nahuatl religious and philosophical doctrines. For, as has already been demonstrated, the loftiest intellectual concepts were expressed through "flower and song"—poetry. Of the intellectual education among the Nahuas, Durán wrote:

They had masters and teachers who would teach and instruct them in all kinds of arts—military, ecclesiastical, and mechanical—and in astrology based on the knowledge of the stars. About all these things they had large and lovely books of paintings and characters.[14]

Along with the songs in which the most elevated of the *tlamatinime*'s thoughts were embodied, the arts of chronology and astrology formed a significant part of the instruction given to the students:

They were taught the *tonalpohualli*, the book of dreams [*temicámatl*], and the book of the years [*xiuhámatl*].[15]

[12] Anderson and Dibble (trs.), *Florentine Codex*, Book III, 64.
[13] Sahagún, *op. cit.*, I, 329.
[14] Durán, *op. cit.*, II, 229.
[15] Anderson and Dibble (trs.), *Florentine Codex*, Book III, 65.

In order to understand the scope of this third facet of education in the *Calmécac*, is is necessary to recall the complexity of elements involved in interpreting the *tonalámatl*. This training and the mathematical calculations required by their astronomical investigations prepared the Nahuatl students to attain the supreme level of rational abstraction.

To these teachings was added training in history through the *Xiuhámatl* (books of the years), where dates, historical events, and the circumstances under which they took place were recorded in glyphs.

In teaching all these things, the *tlamatinime* were carrying out their mission of "making wise the countenances of others."[16] On the other hand, the rigidity of life in the *Calmécac* was intended to strengthen the dynamic aspect of the personality—the heart. By following the series of prescribed practices and penances, the human will was given shape and directed toward self-control and discipline. The *tlamatinime* sought by means of education to endow the face with wisdom and the heart with strength.

Several ancient texts explain this objective more fully. One, from the informants of Sahagún, describes the ideal man:

The mature man
is a heart solid as a rock,
is a wise face.
Possessor of a face, possessor of a heart,
he is able and understanding.[17]

Such was the goal, profoundly humanistic, to which the *tlamatinime* aspired. That the objective was frequently attained is

[16] *Códice Matritense del la Real Academia*, VIII, fol. 118,v.

[17] *Códice Matritense del Real Palacio*, VI, fol. 215. In an essay entitled "*Apuntes sobre la psicología colectiva y el sistema de valores en México antes de la Conquista*" (in *Estudios Antropológicos publicados en homenaje al doctor Manuel Gamio*), Soustelle reaches a similar conclusion. He emphasizes that self-control was a prime educational objective in the *Calmécac*: "An ideal of moderation, of the middle road, a concept reminiscent of the Greek condemnation of violence (*hubris*)." Soustelle, *La Vie Quotidienne des Aztèques*, 500.

confirmed by the great historical figures, who would make any people proud. Itzcóatl, Tlacaélel, Motecuhzoma I, Cuitláhuac, and Cuauhtémoc certainly possessed stout hearts; while among those who achieved distinction for "wise faces," were Nezahual-cóyotl and his son Nezahualpilli, kings of Tezcoco. A passage from Torquemada illustrates the people's respect for the latter:

> Having reached a discriminating age, he began to show what he would be like, to give an idea of the greatness he would attain in his kingdoms. Exercising great prudence and uniformity of will, he was able to confront all things. In the face of adversity, he demonstrated unflinching courage. Faced with prosperity, he did not exaggerate his pleasure and joy.
>
> It is said that he was a great astrologer; that he was much concerned with understanding the movement of the celestial bodies. Inclined to the study of these things, he would seek in his kingdoms for those who knew of these things, and he would bring them to his court. He would communicate to them all that he knew. And at night he would study the stars, and he would go on the roof of his palace, and from there he would watch the stars, and he would discuss problems with them. I am able to say, at least, that I have seen one place in his house, on the roof of his palace, with four walls no higher than a yard, nor wider than might accommodate one man lying down. And in each corner, he had a hole or opening where poles were placed, on which a canopy was suspended. And asking for what purpose it was used, his grandson (who was showing me the house) answered that it used to belong to the Lord Nezahualpilli, (that it was) where he used to go with his astrologers at night, to study the sky and the stars.[18]

But wisdom as an ideal of Nahuatl education also implied purity of heart. The description of the qualities required of those who would be elected high priest confirms this:

> Even if he were poor and lowly,
> even if his mother and his father were the poorest of the poor . . . .
> His lineage was not considered,

[18] Torquemada, *op. cit.*, I, 188.

only his way of life mattered . . . .
The purity of his heart,
his good and humane heart . . . .
His stout heart . . . .
It was said that he had God in his heart,
that he was wise in the things of God.[19]

This was the highest humanistic ideal to which the *Tlacahua-pahualiztli* (art of strengthening men) aspired. Ignoring all social differences, the *tlamatinime* focused on what is most elevated and significant about man, his person, "his good heart, humane and stout [*in qualli yiollo, in tlapaccaihioviani, in iol-lótetl*]." If it was clear that "he had God in his heart [*téutl yiollo*]" and that he was "wise in the things of God [*in tlateuma-tini*]," the office of high priest could be conferred upon him. He would receive the title *Quetzalcóatl*, personification of wisdom, symbol of the origin of everything precious since the days of the Toltecs.

While the educational system of the Nahuas provided basic standards for their everyday behavior—especially through the post-parental education of the Nahuatl schools—the patterns of behavior were reinforced by a meticulous code of ethics and law.[20] Recognizing the value of the ideals and the way of life taught to the students, Sahagún noted the radical change of customs among Nahuatl youth after the Conquest:

[19] Anderson and Dibble (trs.), *Florentine Codex*, Book III, 67.

[20] For firsthand information about Nahuatl laws and legal precepts, see Chapters XIV and XVII of Book VIII of Sahagún's *Historia*, and the *Códice Mendocino* and *Breve y Sumaria Relación de los Señores de la Nueva España*, both by Alonso de Zurita. For more recent studies, see: Lucio Mendieta y Núñez, "*El Derecho mexicano antes de la Conquista*," *Ethnos*, Vol. I, Nos. 8–12 (1922), 168–86; J. Kohler, *El Derecho de los Aztecas*; Salvador Toscano, *Derecho y Organización social de los Aztecas*; and Carlos H. Alba, *Estudio comparado entre el Derecho azteca y el Derecho Positivo Mexicano*. The last work is particularly interesting in its discussion of the noteworthy similarity between many present-day Mexican laws and those of the Nahuas.

More dutiful in the past were the Indians, regarding matters of the state as well as those dealing with serving the gods; they had organized education in conformity with the needs of the people. For the boys and girls were raised in a strict manner until they were adults. This happened not only in the home of their parents, who, it was felt, were not sufficiently prepared to raise and educate them in the desired manner, but they were also educated collectively. Rigorous and careful teachers taught them, boys and girls separately. And by these teachers they were taught the manner of worshiping the gods and the manner of respecting and obeying the state and its administrators.

There were severe punishments for those who were not respectful and obedient to their teachers. And special care was taken that they . . . not drink *octli* [pulque, native wine]. Day and night they were given many tasks, and they were raised in strict austerity. In this manner the vices and the temptations of the flesh would not overcome either the men or the women. Those who lived in the temples were so busy day and night and were so abstinent that they had no time to think of sensual pleasures. And those who had military obligations frequently found themselves in wars and their demands; they were seldom away from them. This manner of education was very much in conformity with natural and moral philosophy . . . which taught the Indians from experience that, in order to live morally and virtuously, it was necessary to have rigorous discipline, austerity, and continuous work in things beneficial to the state.

All of this ended with the arrival of the Spaniards, because they destroyed and abolished all of the customs and disciplined ways that the Indians had. The Spaniards considered the Indians idolaters and savages and wanted to convert them to the Spanish way of life, both religious and social, and so all of their order and disciplined organization was destroyed.[21]

Later Sahagún said that the new "order [introduced by the Spaniards] was giving rise to people inclined to the vices and other evil doings"[22] which the Indians had been able to avoid.

Sahagún's unusual sense of justice and incisive understanding

---

21 Sahagún, *op. cit.*, II, 242–43.
22 *Ibid.*, II, 243.

led him to say that the Indians' system of education had been, for them, superior to that brought from Europe. He also remarked that it was in the *Calmécac* and *Telpochcalli*, in an active and direct way, that the foundations and standards for the moral and civil life of the Nahuas were laid. There "they were taught . . . the manner of respecting and obeying the state and its administrators." Thus the school instilled in the students at an early age a respect for legal organization and regulations and the knowledge that these were to be obeyed. The *tlamatinime* achieved their objectives through an authentic understanding of human nature; ". . . moral philosophy . . . taught these Indians from experience that in order to live morally and virtuously, it was necessary to have rigorous discipline, austerity, and continuous work in things beneficial to the state."[23] This way of life, in which the Nahuatl youth was trained for several years before marriage, gave men "a stout heart, solid as a rock."

Describing the way "the children were taught morals in the past," an ancient document states that every morning after the children's usual meager breakfast:

1. They would begin to teach them:
2. how they should live,
3. how they should respect others,
4. how they were to dedicate themselves to what was good and righteous;
5. how they were to avoid evil,
6. fleeing unrighteousness with strength,
7. refraining from perversion and greed.[24]

COMMENTARY:

LINES 1–2: *They would begin to teach them: how they should live.*

These lines describe the ethical content of education. The wise men were firmly convinced of the importance of finding "true roots" for man in this life. This was not an easy task, for as one Nahuatl poet remarked:

[23] *Ibid.*, II, 245.
[24] Garibay (tr.), "*Huehuetlatolli, Documento A*," *loc. cit.*, 97.

What does your mind seek?
Where is your heart?
If you give your heart to everything,
you lead it nowhere; you destroy your heart.
Can anything be found on earth?[25]

It was therefore necessary to teach each new generation a rule for living, "how they should live [in iuh nemizque]." The discovery of what was appropriate and right would help men to find themselves and thus escape the worst of all misfortunes—that of losing their own hearts.

LINE 3: *How they should respect others.*
The first ethico-juridical obligation was to respect and obey those invested with authority. Respect and consideration for the "faces and hearts" (personalities) of others came to be so characteristic of the Nahuas that countless examples appear throughout the *Huehuetlatolli,* the "discourses of the elders." The text cited above which records the *tlamatinime's* response to the twelve friars exemplifies this attitude. The politeness and consideration shown by the wise men in this important discussion of controversial points presupposes remarkable self-control as well as a strong conviction of the importance of respect for other people.

LINES 4–5: *How they were to dedicate themselves to what was good and righteous; how they were to avoid evil.*
The ancient rule for living which defined the difference between good and bad was called *tlamanitiliztli.* This word is composed of *tla,* "things," and *mani,* "lasting or remaining permanently." The suffix *liztli* gives the word the character of a substantive, and it becomes, "the totality of things that should last." Or, as Molina translated in his *Dictionary,* "custom or usage of the people, or rules and regulations which they recognize."[26]

[25] MSS *Cantares Mexicanos,* fol. 2,v.

[26] Molina, *op. cit.,* fol. 125,v. The word has the unmistakable meaning of "totality of moral rules and practices" in the text previously cited from Lehmann's edition of the *Colloquies* (*loc. cit.,* 105), where there is mention of the *huehuetlamanitiliztli,* "ancient rule of life."

Tlamanitiliztli offered the absolute criterion for distinguishing between good and evil. In the *Calmécac* a moral doctrine of good and evil was taught both in the abtract and in its practical applications. In the minds of the *tlamatinime*, "good" was *in quállotl in yécyotl*, "what is appropriate and convenient." This phrase is another "*difrasismo*," a "flower and song" metaphor. A brief analysis of this double term establishes its complete meaning. *In quállotl* is a collective and abstract substantive derived from the word *qua*, which means "to eat." The addition of the suffix *llotl* to the verb renders the meaning, "the quality of all that is edible." In a more abstract interpretation, it becomes "the quality of all that is capable of assimilation by the '*ego*' or all that is appropriate for it." To this first term, which metaphorically refers to what "good" should be—"edible, assimilable, appropriate"—a second phrase is added: *in yécyotl*, "righteousness." Derived from the word *yectli*, "straight," in both the physical and moral sense, this word too acquires its abstract meaning from the addition of the suffix *yotl*, which connotes something that cannot be twisted, something that remains straight because of its very nature.

Combining the two terms to form the "*difrasismo*," *in quállotl in yécyotl* (appropriate, righteous), it may be said that the Nahuas defined good in terms of appropriateness to the human being; what is good is edible, assimilable, and it has these qualities because it is "straight" or "as it should be."

Correspondingly, if good is to be equated with appropriateness and righteousness, then moral evil would be, as the line in the text indicates, *in a-quállotl in a-yécyotl* (non-appropriate and non-righteous). That is, to the same "*difrasismo*" the negative *a* (no) is prefixed.

Therefore, in order to find out whether a certain act would or would not conform to the principal moral standard (*tlamanitiliztli*), two questions had to be considered. Would the result of that act be appropriate? That is, would it be "assimilated," and would it enrich or impoverish the life and nature of a man? The second question was: Would the result of that behavior be in itself something straight or something devious? If the act should enrich a man's life, helping him to assume a face and develop a heart, then it could be held that moral good was involved. If, on the contrary, the face and heart were lost in the act, it was not good but evil.

LINES 6–7: *Fleeing unrighteousness with strength, refraining from perversion and greed.*

Perversion (*tlahuelilocáyotl*) and greed (*tlacazólyotl*) are definitely designated as evil here. The first engenders evil because it deprives human behavior of rectitude (*yécyotl*), and the second (abuse of what might be good in itself) corrupts the goodness of things in that it implies lack of self-control. Goodness must be appropriate and righteous, and therefore cannot involve overindulgence or deviousness.

The *tlamatinime* postulated a number of precepts for the purpose of directing men to the path to goodness on *tlaltícpac*. Andrés de Olmos, in the sixteenth century, recorded an ancient *Huehuetlatolli*, or speech of the elders, in which examples of righteous acts are described:

Act! Cut wood, work the land,
plant cactus, sow maguey;
you shall have drink, food, clothing.

With this you will stand straight.
With this you shall live.
For this you shall be spoken of, praised;
in this manner you will show yourself to your parents and relatives.

Someday you shall tie yourself to a skirt and blouse.
What will she drink? What will she eat?
Is she going to live off of the air?
You are the support, the remedy;
you are the eagle, the tiger.[27]

27 Andrés de Olmos, *MSS en Náhuatl*, fol. 116,r. The text cited here was translated and published by Garibay in his *Historia*, I, 434.

Other instructions are also found in the texts. For example, a father counsels his son on greed and vanity:

Receive this word, listen to this word.
I hope that for a little time you will live with Our Lord,
He who is Master of the Close Vicinity.
Live on earth;
I hope you will last for a little time.
Do you know much?
With good judgment, look at things, observe them wisely.
It is said that this is a place of hardship,
of filth, of troubles.
It is a place without pleasure, dreadful, which brings desolation.

There is nothing true here. . . .
Here is how you must work and act;
safely kept, in a locked place,
the elders left us these words
at the time of their departure.
Those of the white hair and the wrinkled faces,
our ancestors. . . .

They did not come here to be arrogant;
they were not seeking;
they were not greedy.
They were such
that they were highly esteemed on earth;
they came to be eagles and tigers.[28]

Just as this text cautions against arrogance and greed, the passage below, addressed again to the son by his father, speaks of the importance of sexual moderation in youth:

Do not throw yourself upon women
like the dog which throws itself upon food.
Be not like the dog
when he is given food or drink,
giving yourself up to women before the time comes.

[28] *Códice Florentino*, Book VI, fol. 85,v.

Even though you may long for women,
hold back, hold back with your heart
until you are a grown man, strong and robust.
Look at the maguey plant.
If it is opened before it has grown
and its liquid is taken out,
it has no substance.
It does not produce liquid; it is useless.
Before it is opened
to withdraw its water,
it should be allowed to grow and attain full size.
Then its sweet water is removed
all in good time.

This is how you must act:
before you know woman
you must grow and be a complete man.
And then you will be ready for marriage;
you will beget children of good stature,
healthy, agile, and comely.[29]

The wise men employed vivid examples and rich metaphors in presenting their idea of "what is appropriate, what is righteous" in life. In this way the *tlamatinime* carried out their mission, as moralists, of developing "a heart solid as a rock," master of itself.

The juridical system of ancient Mexico was inspired by the same view of the human being—"face and heart"—which produced the moral code. Sahagún wrote of this:

The rulers were also concerned with the pacification of the people and the settling of litigations and disputes among them, and for this reason they elected prudent and wise judges, honest people who had been educated in the monasteries of the *Calmécac*.[30]

The integrity of the judges and the principles which guided them in their application of laws were described by the Indian informants of Sahagún and by the celebrated Spanish official Alonso de Zurita. Zurita's discussion of the Indian administration

[29] For the Nahuatl and Spanish versions of this text, see the *Códice Florentino*, Book VI, fol. 97,r., and Sahagún, *Historia*, I, 554.
[30] Sahagún, *op. cit.*, II, 81.

of justice is reminiscent of Sahagún's appraisal of the social and juridical chaos brought about by the Conquest:

> One of the principal Indians of Mexico, when asked the reason for the many fights among them now and for their taking to vice so freely, said: "Because neither do you understand us, nor do we understand you. And we do not know what it is that you want. You have deprived us of our good order and way of government, and the one with which you have replaced it we do not understand. Now all is confusion and without order and harmony. The Indians have given themselves to fighting because you have brought it upon them. . . . Those who are not in contact with you do not fight; they live in peace. And if during the time of our paganism there were fights and disputes, they were very few. And they were dealt with justly and settled quickly because there used to be no difficulties in finding out which of the parties was right, nor were there any delays and cheating as there are now.[31]

Then Zurita described the form of justice practiced before the arrival of the Spaniards:

> At dawn the judges would be seated on their mats, and soon people would begin to arrive with their quarrels. Somewhat early, food would be brought from the palace. After eating the judges would rest a while, and then they would continue to listen until two hours before the sun set. In matters of appeal there were twelve judges who had jurisdiction over all the others, and they used to sentence with the sanction of the ruler.
>
> Every twelve days the ruler would meet with all of the judges to consider all of the difficult cases. . . . Everything that was taken before him was to have been already carefully examined and discussed. The people who testified would tell the truth because of an oath which they took, but also because of the fear of the judges, who were very skilled at arguing and had a great sagacity for examination and cross-examination. And they would punish rigorously those who did not tell the truth.
>
> The judges received no gifts in large or small quantities. They made no distinction between people, important or common, rich

[31] Zurita, *Breve y Sumaria Relacion . . .* , in Icazbalceta (ed.), *Nueva Colección de Documentos para la Historia de México*, III, 110.

or poor, and in their judgments they exercised the utmost honesty with all. And the same was true of the other administrators of the law.

If it were found that one of them had accepted a gift or misbehaved because of drinking, or if it were felt that he was negligent . . . the other judges themselves would reprehend him harshly. And if he did not correct his ways, after the third time they would have his head shorn. And with great publicity and shame for him they would remove him from office. This was to them a great disgrace. . . . And because one judge showed favoritism in a dispute toward an important Indian against a common man and gave a false account to the lord of Tezcoco, it was ordered that he be strangled and that the trial begin anew. And thus it was done, and the verdict was in favor of the common man.[32]

The rigid administration of justice among the the Nahuas shows that the teaching of the principles of justice in the *Calmécac* actually produced "prudent and wise judges."[33] It was not only in the practical application of their precepts that the Nahuas exhibited a "wise face and firm heart," but also in the creation of their laws and juridical organization. The Nahuatl legal system, like that of other ancient cultures, had its origin in custom. Yet there is factual evidence that a number of laws were promulgated by certain kings, including Nezahualcóyotl, whose code has been preserved by the historian Ixtlilxóchitl.[34]

The Aztec system of law embraced the most important aspects of human relations: civil, mercantile, penal, legal procedures, and even such interstate matters as alliances, embassies, and wars. The entire juridical structure reflects a striving toward the fundamental ideal taught at the *Calmécac,* "the manner of respecting others," "giving oneself up to what is appropriate and righteous."

Integrating law and morals on the basis of the single supreme principle expressed in the *Huehuetlamanitiliztli* (the ancient rule for living), the *tlamatinime* perfected a theory of righteous

---

[32] *Ibid.*, 111.
[33] Sahagún, *op. cit.*, II, 81.
[34] Ixtlilxóchitl, *op. cit.*, I, 237–39.

THE AZTEC STATUE OF THE GOD XOCHIPILLI
lord of "flower and song."

Courtesy National Museum of Anthropology.

THE NAHUATL-AZTEC WORLD
of pre-Conquest times.

human behavior, both individual and social. The search for a meaningful moral code, however, was not at all related to a desire for reward in the afterlife, nor did it imply the possibility of determining destiny after death. The Nahuas believed that the destiny of man in the beyond depended only on the inexorable will of Ometéotl. Completely detached from what might be called a "metaphysical utilitarianism," the Nahuatl ethic derived from personal and social needs. It was necessary to discover what was "appropriate and righteous" in order to possess "a true face and heart," for only with these could man be firmly fixed, well founded, and true.

The ideal of personal completeness, however, was not the only incentive for good behavior. The Nahuas also valued social approval:

Not with envy,
not with a twisted heart,
shall you feel superior,
shall you go about boasting.
Rather in goodness shall you make true
your song and your word.
And thus you shall be highly regarded,
and you shall be able to live with the others.[35]

In a slightly different way another text describes the good man's just reward:

If you live uprightly,
you shall be held highly for it,
and people will say of you
what is appropriate, what is just.[36]

A quest for self-completeness and sincere social approbation motivated the conduct of the Nahuas. The two motives were, in essence, one, for true social approval was merited only by the well-developed "face and heart," who practiced on earth what was "appropriate and upright."

[35] Olmos, *MSS en Náhuatl*, fol. 118,r.
[36] *Ibid.*, fol. 112,r.

As we have noted above, the *tlamatinime* were greatly concerned with their task of orienting the people morally and juridically. They were equally interested in preserving the record of the origins, the successes, and the failures of their people. Men with the mission of "placing a mirror before the people that they might know themselves and become wise," the *tlamatinime* realized that men could best know themselves as a group through the mirror of history.

The Nahuas possessed a strong historical consciousness. The texts speak constantly of the role of the *Xiuhámatl*, or "book of the years," in Nahuatl education. Ixtlilxóchitl remarked that in these books, "the historical events of each year were placed in the order of occurrence, by day, month, and hour."[37]

Although most of the books of history were destroyed during and immediately after the Conquest, a few of the originals and several colonial copies are extant. The *Annals of Cuauhtitlán*, the *Codex Aubin* of 1576, the *Tira de la Peregrinación*, and the *Toltec-Chichimec History* have all been preserved.

The reply of the *tlamatinime* to the twelve missionaries reveals another facet of the Nahuas' historical awareness. The Indians speak of the antiquity of their traditions, using history as an argument which they wanted the friars to consider. The roots of their culture were deep in the past, and for this reason they asked:

Shall we now destroy
the ancient way of life?
Of the Toltecs,
of the Acolhuas,
of the Tecpanecs . . . ?[38]

This response to the friars has been discussed above. The *tlamatinime* mentioned the kings and lords who, from the most remote times, had followed the traditional way of life. They then spoke of the ancient sites known to Nahuatl historians—Teotihuacán,

37 Ixtlilxóchitl, *op. cit.*, I, 17.
38 Lehmann (ed.), *"Colloquies and Christian Doctrine," loc. cit.*, 105.

Tula, and other cities. These historical references, presented by the *tlamatinime* under extremely dramatic circumstances, manifest that deep sense of the past which led them to seek arguments through history and tradition.

An incident from the narrative by Sahagún's natives provides further proof of the consciousness of history among the Nahuas. Immediately after the consolidation of the Aztec group through the victories of Itzcóatl (ruler of Mexico-Tenochtitlán 1427–40), it was ordered that the ancient codices containing historical accounts be burned. Itzcóatl wished to establish an official version of the history of the Aztecs, and the destruction of the books shows his sagacity. Realizing the importance of the historical records which assigned the Aztecs a secondary role, he decided that they must be suppressed in order to lay the foundation for a new national pride. He then ordered that the Aztec version of history be taught. And thus the wishes of the Mexican lords who had subdued Azcapotzalco were satisfied:

> They preserved their history.
> But it was burned
> at the time that Itzcóatl reigned in Mexico.
> The Aztec lords decided it,
> saying:
> "It is not wise that all the people
> should know the paintings.
> The common people would be driven to ruin
> and there would be trouble,
> because these paintings contain many lies,
> for many in the pictures have been hailed as gods."[39]

With the intention of suppressing the "lies" of history, Itzcóatl directed himself to the creation of a history which would give an appropriate background to the future glory of the Aztecs. In this way the myths peculiar to the "people of the Sun," particularly those of Huitzilopochtli, their patron deity, originated.

[39] *Códice Matritense de la Real Academia*, VIII, fol. 192,v. We shall refer to this same text in the discussion of the Aztecs' mystico-militaristic world vision.

But Itzcóatl was not successful in suppressing the whole of the ancient historical tradition. Much of it continued to be perpetuated by word of mouth, and it was also preserved by neighboring Nahuatl states, such as Tezcoco, Tlacopan, and Tlaxcala. Yet the very effort to modify the historical records indicates that they were of primary significance in the Nahuatl world. In fact, the Aztec lords felt that "the common people would be driven to ruin" by the old stories.

It now becomes important to examine the *tlamatinime*'s conception of history. In the text quoted above, it is stated that "they preserved their history [*ca mopiaya in iitoloca*]." The term *iitoloca* describes the first aspect of the Nahuatl idea of history. The word is composed of the elements, *i-ito-lo-ca*. The principal root is *ito(a)*, "to say," which, joined with the passive *lo*, means "what is said." The personal prefix *i* (their) causes the term to take on the meaning "what is said of someone." Nahuatl history (*Geschichte*, as Seler translated), then, may be defined as the totality of what is said about those who have lived on the earth.[40]

This definition, "what is said of someone," did not mean that Nahuatl history lacked a written basis. A text in the *Annals of Cuauhtitlán* affirms that "what is to be said is what was put down and painted on paper."[41] This suggests that the wise men narrated what was contained in their codices. Although verbal narration was necessary for the transmission of history, it always presupposed objective documentation based on numerical signs and paintings. It is not strange, therefore, to learn how Ixtlixóchitl wrote the *Historia de la Nación Chichimeca*:

> I had to make use of the paintings and characters with which their histories are written and memorized, because they were painted at the time when the events took place. I also made use of the songs in which they had been preserved.[42]

[40] Eduard Seler, *Einige Kapitel aus dem Geschichteswerke des P. Sahagún*, 435.

[41] Lehmann (ed.), *Annals of Cuauhtitlán, loc. cit.*, 104.

[42] Ixtlilxóchitl, *op. cit.*, II, 17.

There were certain men among the Nahuas who would today be designated "specialists" in the principal branches of history. Ixtlilxóchitl observed that:

> For each type [of history] they used to have writers; some would work with the *Annals* [*Xiuhámatl*], putting in order the things which took place each year, giving the day, the month, and the hour.
>
> Others were charged with the genealogies and ancestries of the kings and lords and persons of lineage. . . .
>
> Others took care of the paintings of the boundaries, the limits, and the landmarks of the cities, provinces, and towns, and [recorded] to whom they belonged.[43]

This enumeration of the various groups of historians charged with recording the events of the past is not the fruit of Ixtlilxóchitl's imagination. In the *Colloquies* and in the "*Historia de los Mexicanos*" there is other evidence of the existence of "schools" or groups of historians.

Proof that historical narratives were known to the common people as well as to the wise men may be found in many texts. The passage below is a popular remembrance of the Aztecs killed in the war with Chalco:

> The death
> which our fathers, brothers, and sons met
> was not because they owed anything;
> nor for stealing or lying.
> It was for the honor
> of our country and nation
> and for the valor of our Mexican Empire;
> and for the honor and glory
> of our god and Lord Huitzilopochtli.[44]

A people who preserved the memory of heroes in this manner and so clearly remembered the events of the past must certainly

---

[43] *Ibid.*, II, 17.

[44] F. Alvarado Tezozómoc, *Crónica Mexicana* (notes by Manuel Orozco y Berra, Chapter XXV), 94.

have had a strong awareness of history. Just as the *tlamatinime* had conceived the idea of personality, "face and heart," on the individual level, so on the social plane they had discovered their people to be a group with special traits and a mission in history. This philosophical discovery was communicated to the people in an effort to lead them to greater achievements.

The Aztecs thus derived from their history the conviction that they were "a people with a mission." This attitude is exemplified by the great Nahuatl historian, Chimalpain, in his predictions of future glory for Mexico-Tenochtitlan:

> As long as the world will endure,
> the fame and glory of Mexico-Tenochtitlan
> will never perish.[45]

This passage typifies the confidence which the awareness of their past had inspired in the Nahuatl people. Their history told of their remotest origins and even attempted to reveal the future, thus enabling the Nahuas to feel themselves an integral part of their world. They were no longer strangers, but creators of and heirs to a culture symbolized by the word *Toltecáyotl*—"the summing up of ancient wisdom and art."

Fully conscious of the importance of history was the fifteenth-century Aztec political figure, Tlacaélel. Without exaggeration he may be called the creator of the mystico-militaristic conception of the Aztecs as "people of the Sun." Since his role has often been minimized or even forgotten by modern historians, it is well to mention here several native documents which speak of this great counselor to Itzcóatl, Motecuhzoma I, and Axayácatl. These include the *Crónica Mexicáyotl*, written in Nahuatl by Tezozómoc, in which the genealogy of Tlacaélel is preserved; the *Séptima Relación* of Chimalpain, which gives the exact date of his birth and other valuable information; the *Anales Tecpanecas de Azcapotzalco*; the *Códice Ramírez*; the *Crónica Mexi-*

---

[45] Domingo Chimalpain Cuauhtlehuanitzin, *Memorial Breve de la fundación de la ciudad de Culhuacán, apud* Lehmann, *Die Geschichte*, 111.

cana; and the *Historia* of Durán. Other sources are the *Códice Cozcatzin*; a Mexican song from the *Manuscript* of the National Library; and two pictographic representations in the *Xólotl* and *Azcatitlan* codices. Chimalpain, in the *Séptima Relación*, tells of the birth of Tlacaélel:

Year 10-Rabbit [1398].
At this time, as the ancient Mexicans knew,
was born
Motecuhzoma the elder, *Ilhuicamina*,
he who shines like resplendent jade,
who came into the world when the sun had risen.
His mother was a princess from Cuauhnáhuac [Cuernavaca].
Her name was Miyahuaxiuhtzin.
And Tlacaélel was
born on the same day, in the morning,
when the sun, as we say, was about to rise.
So it is said that Tlacaélel was older.
His mother was named Cacamacihuatzin;
she was a princess from Teocalhuiyacan.
Each one had a different mother,
But they had the same father, Huitzilíhuitl II,
king of Tenochtitlan.[46]

Tlacaélel's first appearance in the public life of Mexico-Tenochtitlan is described by Durán in his *Historia*. Having elected Itzcóatl king about 1424, the Aztecs found themselves continually vexed by the tyrant Maxtla of Azcapotzalco, and they were forced to decide either to submit or to fight. Facing the danger of annihilation, Itzcóatl and the Aztec lords chose to submit completely to the Tecpanecs of Azcapotzalco. They said it would be best

that they take their god Huitzilopochtli and go to Azcapotzalco and humbly place themselves in the hands of the king, so that he might do with them as he wished. And perhaps he might pardon

[46] Domingo Chimalpain Cuauhtlehuanitzin, *Sixième et Septième Relations* (ed. by Remi Simeon), 85.

them and give them a place in Azcapotzalco where they might live and intermingle with their neighbors if they offered themselves as slaves to those of Azcapotzalco.[47]

It was then that the young Tlacaélel spoke publicly for the first time. He encouraged the Aztecs to fight the tyrant, and this struggle was the beginning of the greatness of Tenochtitlan.

"What is this, Mexicans? What are you doing? You are out of your minds. Wait, be still, let us take further account of this matter. Is there such cowardice that we must mingle with those from Azcapotzalco?" And turning to the King, he said, "Sire, what is this? How can you permit such a thing? Speak to your people. Let some means be sought for our defense and our honor, and let us not offer ourselves so ignominiously to our enemies."[48]

It is unnecessary to speak here of how the Aztecs defeated Azcapotzalco. Our sources attribute the victory to the leadership of Tlacaélel, and the *Códice Ramírez* asserts that Tlacaélel, having become the adviser of King Itzcóatl, influenced him so greatly that "he did only what Tlacaélel advised him to do."

The independence of Mexico-Tenochtitlan assured, Tlacaélel, in three important programs, laid the basis for a restructuring of the Aztec state. He first created a military aristocracy by granting titles of nobility to soldiers who had distinguished themselves in the war against Azcapotzalco. Then he expropriated land from the enemy in order to divide it among the king, the traditional elders of the city, the new military nobility, and the *calpullis*, the corporate groups of kinsmen which were important units in the organization of Mexico-Tenochtitlan. Finally, and perhaps most importantly, Tlacaélel set out to create for his people a new version of their history.

A brief text reports a meeting of Itzcóatl, Tlacaélel, and other Aztec leaders after the victory over Azcapotzalco. They decided immediately to burn their own codices as well as those of Azcapotzalco. Tlacaélel and the other chiefs were determined that

[47] Durán, *op. cit.*, I, 70.
[48] *Ibid.*, I, 70.

in the new history the Aztec people and their state would play heroic parts. They began this project by destroying historical texts which contradicted their ideology. Clearly the later Spanish book-burners had their precursors among the indigenous rulers of Aztec society.

In the rewritten history the Aztecs frequently claimed affinal relationships to Toltec nobility; and their divinities, especially their patron, Huitzilopochtli, god of war, were elevated to the same plane as the creative divinities of the various mythological ages or "Suns." Above all, the new chronicle exalted the military spirit of the "people of the Sun [Huitzilopochtli]," whose mission was to subdue the nations of the earth in order to provide sacrificial blood for the nourishment of Tonatiuh, the heavenly body "which makes the day."

Chimalpain has explained the elevation of the patron deity of the Aztecs, Huitzilopochtli, to the highest rank in the ancient Nahuatl pantheon:

> The first in war, the strong and courageous man Tlacaélel, as it may be seen in the books of the years, went about persuading the people that their supreme god was Huitzilopochtli.[49]

Huitzilopochtli ceased to be the patron deity of a poor and intimidated tribe. Through the activities of Tlacaélel, the prestige and power of this deity increased, so that Huitzilopochtli finally appeared as the most powerful god, the one to whom the ancient prayers of Nahuatl religion were directed. The priests composed hymns in his honor similar to those which had been sung in praise of Quetzalcóatl. Identified with the sun, Huitzilopochtli kept alive, by fomenting war, the age in which we live. One of the ancient hymns alluded to these ideas:

> Huitzilopochtli, the young warrior,
> who acts above! He follows his path!
> "Not in vain did I dress myself in yellow plumes,
> for I am he who has caused the sun to rise."

[49] Chimalpain, *Sixième et Septième Relations* (ed. by Remi Simeon), 106.

161

You, ominous lord of the clouds,
one is your foot!
The inhabitants of the cold region of wings,
Your hand opens.

Near the wall of the region of heat,
feathers were given, they are scattering.
The war cry was heard . . . Ea, ea!
My god is called the Defender of men.

Oh, now he moves on, he who is dressed in paper,
he who inhabits the region of heat; in the region of dust,
he whirls about in the dust.

Those of Amantla are our enemies;
come and join me!
With struggle is war made;
come and join me!

Those of Pipiltlan are our enemies;
come and join me!
With struggle is war made;
come and join me![50]

It was Tlacaélel who insisted on—perhaps originated—the idea
that the life of the Sun, Huitzilopochtli, had to be maintained
by the red and precious liquid. Human sacrifice undoubtedly
existed before the Aztecs, but was probably not practiced as
frequently. Perhaps the explanation lies in Tlacaélel's ability to
convince the various Aztec rulers that their mission was to
extend the dominions of Huitzilopochtli, simultaneously preserving the life of the Sun. Certain words of Itzcóatl, who "did
nothing but what Tlacaélel advised him," clarify this point:

This is the mission of Huitzilopochtli and for this he was born:
to gather and attract to himself and to his service all nations with
the power of his breast and mind.[51]

Construction of a great temple, rich and sumptuous, was

[50] Angel María Garibay K. (ed.), Veinte Himnos Sacros de los Nahuas, 31.
[51] Durán, op. cit., I, 95.

begun in honor of Huitzilopochtli, at the suggestion of Tlacaélel, and many victims were sacrificed in his honor. He had led the Aztecs to important victories and conquests over first the neighboring domains and then over those farther away in Oaxaca, Chiapas, and Guatemala. Tlacaélel, speaking to Motecuhzoma I about the dedication of the great temple, remarked:

> There shall be no lack of men to inaugurate the temple when it is finished. I have considered what later is to be done. And what is to be done later, it is best to do now. Our god need not depend on the occasion of an affront to go to war. Rather, let a convenient market be sought where our god may go with his army to buy victims and people to eat as if he were to go to a nearby place to buy tortillas . . . whenever he wishes or feels like it. And may our people go to this place with their armies to buy with their blood, their heads, and with their hearts and lives, those precious stones, jade, and brilliant and wide plumes . . . for the service of the admirable Huitzilopochtli.[52].

Specifying where such a market might be established, where the Sun might "buy" his nourishment by means of war, Tlacaélel continued:

> This market, say I, Tlacaélel, let it be situated in Tlaxcala, Huexotzinco, Cholula, Atlixco, Tliliuhquitépec, and Tecóac. For if we situate it farther away, in such places as Yopitzinco or Michoacán or in the region of the Huaxtecs, all of which are already under our domination, their remoteness would be more than our armies could endure. They are too far, and, besides, the flesh of those barbaric people is not to the liking of our god. They are like old and stale tortillas, because, as I say, they speak strange languages and they are barbarians. For this reason it is more convenient that our fair and markets be in the six cities that I have mentioned. . . . Our god will feed himself with them as though he were eating warm tortillas, soft and tasty, straight out of the oven. . . . And this war should be of such a nature that we do not endeavor to destroy the others totally. War must always continue, so that each time and whenever we wish and our god wishes to

52 *Ibid.*, 241.

eat and feast, we may go there as one who goes to market to buy
something to eat . . . organized to obtain victims to offer our god
Huitzilopochtli.⁵³

In this manner the *guerra florida*, "flowery war," was viewed
by Tlacaélel. Not only did he introduce reforms in thought and
religion, but he also transformed, as Durán observed, the juridical system, the service of the royal house of Motecuhzoma,
the army, and the organization of the merchants. We know little
of his artistic knowledge, but history assigns to him the creation
of the botanical gardens, including the splendid park of Oaxtepec
in present-day Morelos.

In this way Tlacaélel led the Aztecs to greatness. Although
he was offered the throne after the deaths of Itzcóatl and Motecuhzoma I, he never accepted. Still it was he who always inspired the plans and ideals of the people of the Sun. The words
which he pronounced after the death of Motecuhzoma I were
highly significant. Accompanied by the king of Tezcoco, the
Aztec nobles endeavored to bestow upon him the supreme title
of *tlatoani*. Tlacaélel's reply clearly shows his feelings:

Truthfully, my children, I am grateful to you
and to the king of Tezcoco.
But come here;
I want you to tell me.
For the past eighty or ninety years,
since the war of Azcapotzalco,
what have I been? What position have I held?

Have I been nothing?
Why have I placed a crown upon my head?
Have I not won the royal emblems which the kings use?
Is there no value, then, to all that I have judged and ordered?

Have I not sentenced to death the criminal
and pardoned the innocent?
Have I not been able to set up lords
or remove them, according to my will?

⁵³ *Ibid.*, 242.

Wrongly have I done in attiring myself in the clothing
and in the image of the gods,
and acting as if I were their equal,
and, representing them, taking the knife to kill and sacrifice men?
And if I was able to do it for eighty or ninety years,
it follows that I am king and as such have you held me.
Then what more of a king do you want me to be?[54]

The best commentary on this expressive discourse is found in
the *Códice Ramírez*:

> He [Tlacaélel] was not unjustified, because through his diligence,
> even though he was not king, he could do more than if he were.
> . . . Because in the whole kingdom, nothing was done but what
> he ordered.[55]

The *Crónica Mexicáyotl* applies to Tlacaélel a title not attributed
to any other lord or captain in pre-Hispanic Mexico. The text
refers to the Aztec victory over Tlatelolco:

> It has already been said that the Tlatelolcas were defeated by
> Axayácatl. This occurred when Tlacaélel, the *Cihuacóatl* and con-
> queror of the world [*in cemanáhuac Tepehuan*] was still alive.[56]

The texts quoted above affirm the significance of the plans and
actions of Tlacaélel. A serious study of Tlacaélel, organizer of
what we have called the "mystico-militaristic vision" of the
Aztecs, has yet to be written.

It is interesting that as early as the beginning of the seven-
teenth century, Henrico Martínez, an eminent scientist and a
man not directly dedicated to the study of ancient Mexican history, should describe Tlacaélel as he "who was responsible for
almost all of the glory of the Mexican Empire."[57]

Because of Tlacaélel a world view based on the concept and
reality of struggle came to be an attitude peculiar to the Aztecs.
These ideals were expressed in a number of their poems. Darts

[54] *Ibid.*, 326.
[55] *Códice Ramírez*, 85.
[56] F. Alvarado Tezozómoc, *Crónica Mexicáyotl*, 121.
[57] Henrico Martínez, *Reportorio de los Tiempos e Historia Natural de Nueva España*, 129.

and shields, symbols of struggle and of the roots of Mexico-
Tenochtitlán, embody the substance of Tlacaélel's mystico-militaristic thought:

> With our darts,
> with our shields,
> the city lives.[58]

> There, where the darts are dyed,
> where the shields are painted,
> are the perfumed white flowers,
> flowers of the heart.
> The flowers of the Giver of Life
> open their blossoms.
> Their perfume is sought by the lords:
> this is Tenochtitlan.[59]

It has been difficult for modern man to understand and enjoy
"the message" of Nahuatl art. A number of scholars have attempted to formulate an "indigenous aesthetic," but many of
their works are disappointing. The degree of success achieved
has depended on the extent of their ability to divest themselves
of modern Western intellectual and emotional attitudes in an
attempt to visualize the cultural artifacts in their original context. Of definite value to this approach would be a study of the
rich documentation in the Nahuatl language gathered from
native informants in the sixteenth century.

These texts speak of a certain predestination or fate (*tonalli*)
with which the artist is endowed, and of what he seeks and experiences when he produces a work of art. They define the several
classes of artist in the pre-Hispanic Nahuatl world: painter,
sculptor, goldsmith, potter, singer, gem carver, and others. A
careful study of a number of these texts reveals that they contain something approaching a Nahuatl concept of art. The material is abundant and extremely interesting; it deserves a much
fuller treatment than can be attempted here.

[58] *MSS Cantares Mexicanos*, fol. 20,v.
[59] *Ibid.*, fol. 18,r.

Sahagún's informants traced the origins of their culture back to the "golden age" of the Toltecs, a time when everything was good and beautiful. The word *Toltecáyotl* had come to signify for them the sum total of all the arts and ideals inherited from the Toltecs. After tracing the history of the wanderings of the Toltecs, they spoke of the remains of the ancient capital at Tula:

> Truly they were all there together,
> lived there together.
> The remains of what they made and left behind
> are still there and can be seen, among them
> the works not finished, among them
> the serpent columns, the round columns of serpents
> with their heads resting on the ground,
> their tails and rattles in the air.
> The mountain of the Toltecs can be seen there
> and the Toltec pyramids, the structures
> of stone and earth, with stucco walls.
> The remains of Toltec pottery also are there;
> cups and pots of the Toltecs can be dug from the ruins;
> Toltec necklaces are often dug from the earth,
> and marvelous bracelets, precious green stones,
> emeralds, turquoise. . . .[60]

The Nahuas claimed to be the heirs of the Toltecs, and they described them in this way:

> The Toltecs were a skillful people;
> all of their works were good, all were exact,
> all well made and admirable.
>
> Their houses were beautiful, with turquoise mosaics,
> the walls finished with plaster,
> clean and marvelous houses, which is to say,
> Toltec houses, beautifully made,
> beautiful in everything. . . .
>
> Painters, sculptors, carvers of precious stones,
> feather artists, potters, spinners, weavers,

[60] *Códice Matritense de la Real Academia*, VIII, fol. 172 r.–v.

167

skillful in all they made, they discovered
the precious green stones, the turquoise;
they knew the turquoise and its mines, they found
its mines and they found the mountains hiding
silver and gold, copper and tin,
and the metal of the moon.

The Toltecs were truly wise;
they conversed with their own hearts. . . .
They played their drums and rattles;
they were singers, they composed songs
and sang them among the people;
they guarded the songs in their memories,
they defied them in their hearts.[61]

These texts show how highly the Nahuas of the early Conquest period regarded their Toltec ancestors. They held that all their art originated in the Toltec period, as well as their highest religious, ethical, and philosophical concepts.

For them the word *toltécatl* had come to mean "artist." In the descriptions of characteristic features of singers, painters, sculptors, potters, and other artists, it is always stated that they were "Toltecs," that they worked like "Toltecs," that their creations were the fruit of *Toltecáyotl*. There is even a text in which the artist is described and referred to precisely as a *toltécatl*:

The artist: disciple, abundant, multiple, restless.
The true artist, capable, practicing, skillful,
maintains dialogue with his heart, meets things with his mind.

The true artist draws out all from his heart;
works with delight; makes things with calm, with sagacity;
works like a true Toltec; composes his objects; works dexterously;
    invents;
arranges materials; adorns them; makes them adjust.

The carrion artist works at random; sneers at the people;

[61] *Ibid.*, VIII, fols. 172,v. and 176,r.

makes things opaque; brushes across the surface of the face of
  things;
works without care; defrauds people; is a thief.[62]

The Nahuas believed that artists were born and not made.
One could become like the Toltecs only if it had been so ordained.
The artist's destiny was marked by two characteristics: first, the
possession of a series of particular qualities—most importantly,
a face and a heart, a well-defined personality; and, second, a
propitious date of birth—one of the several days which, according
to those who knew the prophetic calendar, were favorable to
artists and the production of their works. This second element
was necessarily conditioned by the fact that the artist had to
keep his destiny always in mind, to make himself worthy of it,
and to learn to converse with his own heart. Otherwise he would
destroy his own happiness, lose his place as an artist, and turn
into a foolish and dissolute fraud:

He who was born on those dates
  (*Ce Xóchitl*: the day named One Flower),
whether a noble or not, became a lover of songs,
an entertainer, an actor, an artist.
He bore this in mind, he deserved his well-being,
he lived joyfully; he was contented
as long as he bore his destiny in mind,
as long as he guided himself and made himself worthy of it.
But he who did not heed this,
if he considered it of no account,
if he scorned his destiny,
even though he was a singer, an artist, a craftsman,
he thereby ruined his happiness, he lost it.
(He did not deserve it.) He held himself above others;
he squandered all of his destiny,
which means he grew conceited and insolent.
He looked down on others; he became a fool,
dissolute in appearance, in his heart,

---

[62] *Ibid.*, VIII, fols. 115,v. and 116,r.

in his songs and thoughts;
he became a poet of foolish and dissolute songs.[63]

Another text supports this view and defines what might be
called the moral milieu of the artist. It describes the rewards
that awaited the artist if he worked wisely and observed the
religious traditions of his people. It shows the solemnity of the
celebration of the calendar day "Seven Flower":

And the symbol Seven Flower
was said to be both good and bad.
When good, they celebrated it
with great devotion;
the painters honored it,
they painted its image,
they made offerings to it.
The embroiderers were also joyful
under this symbol.
First they fasted in its honor,
some for eighty days, or forty,
or they fasted for twenty days.

And this is why they made these supplications
and performed these rites:
to be able to work well,
to be skillful,
to be artists like the Toltecs,
to order their works well,
whether embroidery or painting.

For this reason they all burned incense
and made offerings of quail.
And they all bathed and sprinkled themselves
when the fiesta began,
when the symbol Seven Flower was honored.

And when this symbol was bad,
when an embroiderer broke her fast,
they said that she deserved to become a woman of the streets,

63 *Ibid.*, VII, fol. 300.

this was her reputation and her way of life,
to work as a prostitute.

But for the one whose actions were good,
who worked well, who guided herself,
all was good; she was esteemed,
she made herself worthy of esteem
wherever she might be.

It was also said
that whoever was born on that day
would thereby be greatly skilled
in the several arts of the Toltecs.
He would work like a Toltec,
he would bring things to life,
he would be wise of heart,
all this, if he guided himself well.[64]

The *Cantares Mexicanos* in the Mexican National Library
contain several documents describing gatherings of poets,
singers, and dancers. In the *Historia Chichimeca*, Ixtlilxóchitl
also speaks of something very much like what we might today
call academies of music and of literature. Almost all of the ancient
chroniclers and historians affirm that there were many different
types of artists in the pre-Hispanic Nahuatl world. A whole section of the Sahagún documents is devoted to the categories of
artists: the feather artist, the painter, the potter, the goldsmith,
the silversmith, and others.

One narrative describes the *amantécatl*, "the feather artist,"
who devised the magnificent headdresses, fans, robes, and
draperies used by the nobles. As the poem indicates, the Nahuatl
artist was expected to have a well-defined personality, a "face
and heart," and the ability to achieve the supreme end of art—
to "humanize the will of the people."

Amantécatl: the feather artist.
He is whole; he has a face and a heart.

The good feather artist is skillful,

---

[64] *Ibid.*, VII, fols. 285–86.

is master of himself; it is his duty
to humanize the desires of the people.
He works with feathers,
chooses them and arranges them,
paints them with different colors,
joins them together.

The bad feather artist is careless;
he ignores the look of things,
he is greedy, he scorns other people.
He is like a turkey with a shrouded heart,
sluggish, coarse, weak.
The things that he makes are not good.
He ruins everything that he touches.[65]

The *tlacuilo,* "the painter," was of utmost importance in
Nahuatl culture, for it was he who painted the codices. He knew
the different kinds of Nahuatl writing as well as all the symbols
of mythology and tradition. He was a master of the symbolism
that could be expressed in red and black ink. Before he began to
paint, it was necessary for him to learn how to converse with
his heart. He had to become a *yoltéotl,* one with "a heart rooted
in God," into which had entered all the symbolism and creative
force of Nahuatl religion. With God in his heart, he would then
attempt to transfer the symbols of divinity to his paintings,
codices and murals. And in order to be successful in this, he had
to know better than anyone else the colors of all the flowers, as
though he were a Toltec.

The good painter is a Toltec, an artist;
he creates with red and black ink,
with black water. . . .

The good painter is wise,
God is in his heart.
He puts divinity into things;
he converses with his own heart.

He knows the colors, he applies them and shades them;

[65] *Ibid.,* VIII, fol. 116,r.

he draws feet and faces,
he puts in the shadows, he achieves perfection.
He paints the colors of all the flowers,
as if he were a Toltec.[66]

These descriptions of the feather artist and the painter list a number of the traits of the Nahuatl artist. The *zuquichiuhqui*, or potter, is "he who gives shape to clay," "he who teaches it to lie," so that it will learn to take countless shapes. The clay figure is not a puppy, but it looks like one; it is not a squash, but it seems to be one. The potter also converses with his heart; "he brings things to life." His skill gives life to things that seem dead. "He teaches the earth to lie," so that all kinds of figures seem to take shape and live in it.

He who gives life to clay:
his eye is keen, he molds
and kneads the clay.

The good potter:
he takes great pains with his work;
he teaches the clay to lie;
he converses with his heart;
he makes things live, he creates them;
he knows all, as though he were a Toltec;
he trains his hands to be skillful.

The bad potter:
careless and weak,
crippled in his art.[67]

Similarly the goldsmiths and silversmiths worked to create an image of life in motion:

Here it is told
how a work was cast
by the smiths of precious metals.
They designed, created, sketched it

[66] *Ibid.*, VIII, fol. 117,v.
[67] *Ibid.*, VIII, fol. 124,r.

with charcoal and wax, in order
to cast the precious metal,
the yellow or the white;
thus they began their works.

If they began the figure of a living thing,
if they began the figure of an animal,
they searched only for the similarity;
they imitated life
so that the image they sought
would appear in the metal.

Perhaps a Huaxtec,
perhaps a neighbor
with a pendant hanging from his nose,
his nostrils pierced, a dart in his cheek,
his body tattooed with little obsidian knives;
thus the charcoal was fashioned,
was carved and polished. . . .

Whatever the artist makes
is an image of reality;
he seeks its true appearance.

If he makes a turtle,
the carbon is fashioned thus:
its shell as if it were moving,
its head thrust out, seeming to move,
its neck and feet
as if it were stretching them out.

If it is a bird
that is to be made of the precious metal,
then the charcoal is carved
to show the feathers and the wings,
the tail-feathers and the feet.

If it is a fish,
then the charcoal is carved
to show the scales and fins,
the double fin of the tail.
Perhaps it is a locust or a small lizard;

the artist's hands devise it,
thus the charcoal is carved.

Or whatever is to be made,
perhaps a small animal, or a golden neckpiece
with beads as small as seeds
around its border,
a marvelous work of art,
painted and adorned with flowers.[68]

A rich study of Nahuatl art could be based on texts such as those cited above. One could also examine the codices, which represent pictorially much of what is to be found in the histories themselves, and in this respect the *Mendocino* and *Florentine* codices would be especially valuable. This material could then be related to works of art which archaeological investigation has discovered. Only by reconstructing the Nahuatl world through an assimilation of the codices, texts, chronicles, and archaeological findings will it be possible to understand the forms and symbols peculiar to the art of the Nahuas.

Such a study would present a detailed analysis of the Nahuatl artist, heir to the great Toltec tradition—a man of foreordained destiny, according to the *Tonalámatl.* The artist would emerge as a man able "to communicate with his own heart [*moyolnonotzani*]," who ponders over the ancient myths, the traditions, and the great doctrines of his religion and philosophy. By communicating with his own heart, he discovers and activates his potential destiny; he is divinely inspired, he is transformed into a *yoltéotl,* a "deified heart"; he has become a visionary, eager to transmit to objects his divine inspiration. He may choose the *amate* paper of the codices, the surface of a wall, precious metals, plumes, or clay as the material for his art and symbol. With these soulless substances he devises a metaphor of "flower and song." Thus the artist permits the people to see and "to read" in the stone, on the walls, and in all works of art a meaning for their lives on earth.

[68] *Ibid.,* VIII, fol. 44,v.

The approach to the soul of the Nahuatl artist and his art should not be an inert experience. It could constitute a lesson of surprising originality to contemporary aesthetic thought, for in the Nahuatl concept of art there are images and ideas of unsuspected depth. That the Nahuatl sages considered the only way of embodying truth on earth to be through "flower and song," that is, by means of symbolism expressed in art, is sufficient proof that the Nahuas possessed a unique and effective aesthetic.

VI

Conclusion

AZTEC religion, on the mystico-militaristic level, sought to preserve the life of the Sun, threatened by a fifth and final cataclysm, through ceremonial warfare and human sacrifice. The supreme ideal of the Aztec warriors was to fulfill their mission as the chosen people of Tonatiuh, the Sun, who needed the precious liquid if he were to continue to shine over *Cemanáhuac,* the world. At the same time, however, many of the wise men, living in the shadow of the great symbol of Nahuatl wisdom, Quetzalcóatl, attempted to discover the meaning of life on an intellectual plane. These almost diametrically opposed attitudes toward life and the universe existed side by side—a situation similar to that of Nazi Germany in our time, where a mystico-militaristic world view and a genuinely humanistic philosophy and literature coexisted. Indeed, such a mixture of humanism and barbarism seems to be an inherent quality of the so-called rational animal.

In the face of this duality of attitudes, it is necessary to isolate that fundamental element which colored and gave direction to Nahuatl thought.

The *tlamatinime*'s point of departure was the ephemeral and fragile quality of all that exists. "Although it be jade, it is broken; although it be gold, it is crushed; although it be quetzal plumes, it is torn asunder." Obviously, "this is not the place where things are made; here nothing grows green," and "we only dream, all is like a dream."

Convinced of the evanescence of earthly life, the Nahuatl wise men posed two questions, one of a practical nature, the other more speculative: "On earth, is the striving for anything really worth while?"; "Do we perhaps speak any truth here?" Since truth is that which gives support or foundation to all things, the second question led to two even more urgent problems: "What is it perchance that stands?" "Are men really true?" In other words, do things and men have a real truth or foundation, or are they merely dreamlike, as are those things which come into one's semiconscious mind at the moment of awakening?

The problems were formulated cosmologically in the language of the ancient myths, and they were given impetus by the need of finding an answer before the imminent end of the Fifth Sun. For man, here on earth without "a well-formed face and heart," the question of his own truth is the most pressing, since this reality embraces his origin, his personality, and his final destiny.

Lengthy and profound were the meditations of the Nahuatl wise men. Instead of creating numerous hypotheses, they first asked themselves—in spite of their religious beliefs— whether it were at all possible "to speak the truth on earth." Giving their thought a metaphysical turn, they concluded that if everything on earth is temporary and dreamlike, then "it is not here where truth is to be found." Truth must be sought "farther on," "beyond the visible and tangible," "in that place that lies beyond us, in the region of the dead and of the gods."

But how to find this road to the beyond, to reach "that which is true?" The religious approach, through sacrifice and offerings, was rejected by some because the Giver of Life seemed to them to be always inexorable and inscrutable. Nor could the problem be solved satisfactorily by the attempt of human reason to reach the essence of things. For if everything on earth "changes, perishes, and is like a dream," the Nahuas' ultimate question—"How many say that the truth is or is not here?"—must remain unanswerable.

Thus the *tlamatinime* crossed the borders of doubt. Some of them, despairing of ever finding an answer, formulated a Nahuatl version of Epicureanism—to live pleasurably this short while on earth.

In opposition to this attitude of intellectual despair, there finally appeared a philosophical answer to the question of metaphysical knowledge. The answer came through intuition; there is only one way by which we may babble the "truth" occasionally, and that is through poetic inspiration—"flower and song." By means of metaphors conceived within the very depths of one's being or perhaps emanating from the "interior of heaven," one may attain certain glimpses of the truth.[1]

"Flower and song," then, could reveal the universe to man and allow him to explain it in poetry. There was first the supreme metaphor of Ometéotl, God of Duality, the self-created, the generating-conceiving cosmic principle, Lord of the Close Vicinity, invisible as the night and the wind—origin, foundation, and goal of all things and of man.

Many aspects had Ometéotl: "mother and father of the gods"; "in his circle of turquoise, in the waters colored as the bluebird; it is he who dwells in the clouds, on earth and in the realm of the

---

[1] It seems extraordinary that we find this same affirmation in one of the recent works of the German philosopher Martin Heidegger. In his *Aus der Erfahrung des Denkens* (1945), he states: "Three possibilities hover over the process of thinking: one—a good and beneficial one—the possibility of becoming a singer or poet. A second possibility—bad and therefore subtle—thought itself being used to think against itself; this is rarely hazarded. But the most dangerous possibility is philosophizing [that is, cold and abstract thinking]" (*op. cit.*, 15). And, in fact, as he asserts later on, "until now the poetic character of thinking has remained hidden" (*ibid.*, 23).

But we should like to add, keeping in mind the evidence of the Nahuatl texts, that this quality was not hidden from the *tlamatinime*, because for them the only real kind of knowledge was that of poetry—"flower and song."

dead, the Lord of fire and of the year"; "in whose hands rests Anáhuac." He is the mirror of night and day, able both to conceal and to illuminate; he gives all things their truth and then makes them vanish "into the region of oblivion." He is "the inventor of man, the one who drops him into the maternal womb; he holds men and the world in the palm of his hand and, rocking them to and fro, amuses himself and laughs." This then is Ometéotl, the metaphysical configuration of God, seen through "flower and song."

The wise men then conceived a theory about man himself; he is "face and heart." Concerning man's free will, his destiny, and his moral goodness, the sages felt that his supreme ideal should be the development of "a wise countenance and a heart firm as a rock." Man, in reality a beggar, needed a light, a truth. These he could find, perhaps, through the symbols of and along the path of "flower and song."

> Oh stealer of songs, my heart!
> Where will you find them?
> You are needy and poor,
> but grasp firmly the black and red ink [wisdom],
> And perhaps you will no longer be a beggar.[2]

In order to escape this poverty, this lack of metaphysical knowledge, the Nahuatl sages meditated. Their final answer was that "flower and song" placed God in man's heart, making it true and causing it to create what today we call art. So, for instance, in the description of the painter, the artist appears as a man with God in his heart, a man in possession of the truth and of the very roots of his being. Having a deified heart, he converses with it so that he can "give a divine quality to things"; he creates art:

> The good painter is wise;
> God is in his heart.

2 MSS *Cantares Mexicanos*, fol. 68,r.

He puts divinity into things;
he converses with his own heart.
He paints the colors of all the flowers
as if he were a Toltec.[3]

The painter, the singer, the sculptor, the poet, and all those worthy of the title Toltec, artist, were "deified hearts," visionaries who, having truth themselves, were empowered to create divine things. Such men, having realized the supreme Nahuatl ideal, were called upon to fill high posts, such as that of director of the *Calmécac*, the greatest centers of learning.

Memorizing the divine hymns, contemplating the heavens and "the orderly motions of the stars," admiring painting and sculpture, the students of the *Calmécac* were taught to awaken in their hearts a thirst for the light and the creative power of Ometéotl. They began to see the world and man actively through "flower and song." They became aware that only this "calms and delights men."

Opening his own window to the universe, a youthful student described the essence of his being as a spring from which inspiration flowed:

Who am I?
As a bird I fly about,
I sing of flowers;
I compose songs,
butterflies of song.
Let them burst forth from my soul!
Let my heart be delighted with them![4]

By allowing the "butterflies of song" to be born in himself, the Nahuatl wise man began to express "that which is true on earth." And the painter, "the artist of the black and the red"; the sculptor, carver of the signs that measured time and of the images of gods and myths; all of the philosophers, musicians, architects, and

[3] *Códice Matritense de la Real Academia*, VIII, fol. 117,v.
[4] *MSS Cantares Mexicanos*, fol. 11,v.

astronomers sought the same thing—their own truth and that of the universe.

Nahuatl philosophic thought thus revolved about an aesthetic conception of the universe and life, for art "made things divine," and only the divine was true. To know the truth was to understand the hidden meanings of things through "flower and song," a power emanating from the deified heart.

The philosophy of metaphors did not pretend to explain the mystery completely, but it did lead man to feel that beauty was perhaps the only reality. It sought to give wise faces to human beings, to awaken in them the desire to "steal flowers and songs."

This was the core of Nahuatl philosophical thought. Perhaps in its essence there is meaning for our tormented modern world. "Flower and song" is a pattern for men conscious of their own limitations, yet unwilling to conceal or hoard that which may give meaning to life.

Upon this world view the Nahuatl sages based their way of life. Their spirit rose to the heights of true mathematical knowledge, through which they contemplated "the motions of the stars along the paths of the heavens." The same spirit lifted them to the heights of philosophy and self-understanding. But their very status as captives of beauty, enamored of the stars and of poetry, was perhaps the main reason for their destruction in the Spanish Conquest. It was almost as though the transient world of *tlaltícpac* had taken its revenge. Their culture of metaphors and numbers was overthrown by weapons of steel and fire. It vanished like a dream—"the quetzal plumes were torn asunder, the jade was broken"—and only memory remained. The beautiful world, the vision divine and true, was forced to flee back to the place of its origin, to "that place which is beyond us," when the wise men were cast out, when the books were burned, when the temples and statues were smashed to pieces.

Even in the midst of misfortune the Nahuatl image of man, "wise countenance, stout heart," retained its greatness. In their final appearance before Cortés and the twelve friars, the *tlama-*

tinime, bringing the drama of their dying culture to its climax, exclaimed, "If, as you say, our gods are dead, it is better that you allow us to die too."[5]

These were the last words spoken by a people who had discovered a beautiful way to think, to live, and to die—the way of "flower and song."

[5] Lehmann (ed.), *Colloquies and Christian Doctrine,* 102.

Appendix I

The Sources

REPEATED references to the existence of Nahuatl wise men appear in several of the first chronicles and histories. For example, in the ancient text *Origen de los mexicanos,* it is affirmed that "writers and wise men who understand these matters are many . . . most of whom do not venture to show themselves."[1] There are also allusions to Nahuatl sages in the histories and accounts of Sahagún, Durán, Ixtlilxóchitl, Mendieta, Torquemada, and others.[2]

Nonetheless, although their testimony has great historical importance, these writers cannot be considered in themselves as sources for the study of what, in the strictest sense, we call Nahuatl philosophy. Other, more direct sources present the opinions of the native thinkers expressed in their own language. These sources will now be briefly listed and evaluated.

[1] *"Origen de los mexicanos,"* in Icazbalceta (ed.), *Nueva Colección de Documentos para la Historia de México,* III, 283.

[2] See: Sahagún, *Historia General de las cosas de Nueva España,* Introduction to Book I; Book VI; Book X, 144, 242–46, 276–80; Durán, *Historia de las Indias de Nueva España,* I, 6; Ixtlilxóchitl, *Obras Históricas,* II, 18, 178, *etc.*; Mendieta, *Historia Eclesiástica Indiana,* I, 89; Torquemada, *Monarquía Indiana,* II, 146–47, 174, *etc.*

Appendix I

1. *Texts in Nahuatl given by the informants of Sahagún.*
These are documents compiled by Fray Bernardino de Sahagún, beginning in 1547, in Tepepulco (Tezcoco), Tlaltelolco, and Mexico, from the narratives of Indian elders who repeated what they had learned by memory in their schools, the *Calmécac* and the *Telpochcalli.* In this immense compilation of data there are entire sections which speak of the Nahuatl mythico-religious world view and of the wise men, their opinions, and their theories.

The first question about these documents is inevitable: Was the Indians' knowledge of their own beliefs and traditions reliable? One might also question their own personal veracity, for they may have distorted the truth because of ill-will toward the Conquerors.

Regarding the first question, it is well to remember that Sahagún began his research at Tepepulco in 1547, only twenty-six years after the fall of Mexico-Tenochtitlan. He could easily have found not a few adults between fifty and seventy years of age—in Tezcoco and Tlatelolco as well as in the Aztec capital—who had lived in the Nahuatl world for several decades before the arrival of the Spaniards.

Although many of these elders probably had not been priests but simply the sons of high-ranking nobles, most were undoubtedly former students of the *Calmécac.* In the absence of a system of writing such as ours, doctrines, traditions, and the technique of understanding the illustrated manuscripts were taught by rote. The course of study for these Nahuatl youths included the highest expression of their thought, often molded into songs and speeches to be learned by heart.

Since they had been in contact with the living traditions of the *Calmécac* and had learned its doctrines from memory, it is logical to suppose that many of the elders who gave information to Sahagún had an adequate knowledge of their traditions.

But were they truthful in their reports? Or did they distort the truth? It is necessary to remember that Sahagún never accepted the testimony of only one informant, but established the authen-

ticity of his knowledge by questioning "from ten to twelve leading elders" in Tepepulco. And the investigation did not end
there. He also compared these data with those obtained later
from inquiries made at the College of Tlatelolco, where "they
chose for him eight or ten elders from among those most informed about their antiquities, and with four or five trilingual
students . . . ."[3] Finally, as though the verification made in
Tlatelolco were not enough, Sahagún made another anaylsis,
in the monastery of San Francisco in the City of Mexico, of what
he had gathered at Tepepulco and Tlatelolco. Of this triple critical process to which he submitted all of his data, Sahagún said:
"And so it was that the first screening of my material took place
in Tepepulco, the second in Tlatelolco, the third in Mexico.[4]

Having found that the various reports did, indeed, form a
coherent whole, Sahagún became convinced of the authenticity of what the Indians had told him. To several skeptics who
had attacked him, he answered:

> In this book it will be seen very clearly that the claims of some
> rivals, who have said that everything written in this *History* is
> lies and inventions, are themselves intolerant lies. It would not be
> within the power of the human mind to invent what is written here,
> nor could any living man counterfeit the language set forth herein.
> If we were to question all the well-versed Indians, they would con-
> firm that this language is indeed that of their ancestors and that
> it describes their way of life.[5]

Further evidence of the authenticity of these texts is the fact
that they reflected the intellectual culture of the Nahuas so vividly that some friars began to view them as a dangerous instru-
ment, fearing that they might revive ancient beliefs and practices. Their protests to Madrid resulted in the enactment of a
Royal Cedula of Philip II in 1577, which stated:

> From letters written in those provinces we have learned that Fray

---

[3] Sahagún, *op. cit.*, I, 2.

[4] *Ibid.*, I, 3.

[5] *Ibid.*, I, 445–46.

Bernardino de Sahagún of the Order of Saint Francis has composed a Universal History of the most noteworthy things in New Spain. It is an abundant collection of all the rites, ceremonies, and idolatries practiced by the Indians when they were unbelievers, divided into twelve volumes and written in the native language. Although it is understood that the zeal of said Fray Bernardino has been commendable, and that his intention was for the book to bear wholesome fruit, it seems that it is not proper that this book be published or disseminated in those places, for several reasons. We thus command that, upon receiving this Cedula, you obtain these books with great care and diligence; that you make sure that no original or copy of them is left there; and that you have them sent in good hands at the first opportunity to our Council of Indies in order that they may be examined there. And you are warned absolutely not to allow any person to write concerning the superstitions and ways of life of these Indians in any language, for this is not proper to God's service and to Ours.[6]

Fortunately Sahagún kept a copy of his texts and thus saved them from possible destruction. Of the documents which he gathered, what has been preserved may be found today in Madrid and Florence. The oldest texts, the fruit of his investigations in Tepepulco and Tlatelolco, are preserved in the two *Códices Matritenses,* one of which is in the Library of the Royal Palace in Madrid, the other in the Royal Academy of History. In the Laurentian Library of Florence there is another bilingual copy in four volumes with numerous illustrations. This copy, although more complete, is of a later date.

From 1905 to 1907, the Mexican scholar Francisco del Paso y Troncoso prepared a magnificent facsimile edition of all the material contained in the *Códices Matritenses.* Of the manuscripts in Florence he succeeded in publishing only the illustrations. The reproduction of the *Códices Matritenses* done by Hauser and Menet in Madrid appeared through 1905–1907 in an edition of 420 copies. The earliest information gathered by Sahagún was thus made available to investigators for the first time.

[6] "*Códice Franciscano, siglo XVI,*" in Icazbalceta (ed.), *Nueva Colección,* II, 249–50.

There are also editions of certain sections of some of the texts accompanied by paleographic versions and translations. The first to interest himself in this type of study was Eduard Seler, who translated into German, with extensive and erudite commentary, the twenty hymns transcribed in Nahuatl by Sahagún in Book II of his *History*.[7] Seler's wife published a posthumous bilingual edition—in Nahuatl and German—of the original information contained in Book XII of the *History*, as well as other chapters Seler had translated.[8]

Many years later John Hubert Cornyn translated into English the legend of Quetzalcóatl, taken from the Nahuatl material used by Sahagún for his third book. A work of considerable merit, this was to be the forerunner of new investigations.[9]

In 1940, Angel María Garibay K. published his grammar, *Llave del Náhuatl* (*A Key to Náhuatl*), in which some of the Sahagún material was carefully paleographed for the purpose of making classic passages available to students of this tongue.[10] Continuing this type of investigation, Garibay published a poetic translation of thirteen of the twenty hymns collected by Sahagún.[11] Later he published other texts based on the Tepepulco compilations, translating them into Spanish for the first time.[12] Finally, in his monumental work, *Historia de la Literatura Náhuatl*, Garibay offers a direct translation of numerous texts gathered by Sahagún, presenting them as literary examples.[13]

A new edition of Sahagún's *Historia General de las Cosas de*

[7] Seler, *Gesammelte Abhandlungen zur amerikanischen Sprach und Altertumskunde*, II, 420ff. and 959ff.

[8] Seler, *Einige Kapitel aus dem Geschichtswerk des P. Sahagún, aus dem Aztekischen ubersetzt von Eduard Seler* (see Bibliography).

[9] John H. Cornyn, *The Song of Quetzalcóatl* (Yellow Springs, Ohio, 1930).

[10] Garibay, *Llave del Náhuatl* (see Bibliography).

[11] Garibay, *Poesía Indígena de la Altiplanicie*, Bibl. del Estudiante Universitario (Mexico City, Universidad Nacional Autónoma de México, 1940), and *Epica Náhuatl* (see Bibliography).

[12] Garibay, "*Paralipómenos de Sahagún*," *Tlalocan*, Vol. I (1943–44), 307–13, and Vol. II (1946), 167–74 and 249–54; also "*Relación Breve de las Fiestas de los Dioses*," *Tlalocan*, Vol. II (1948), 289–320.

[13] Garibay, *Historia de la Literatura Náhuatl*, see especially: Vol. I, Chapters II, V, VI, VII, IX, and X; Vol. II, Chapters II and III.

Nueva España, which is an adapted presentation in Spanish of the original native texts, was edited by Garibay in 1956.

Another work of special merit is the paleographic version of numerous Nahuatl texts from the *Códices Matritenses*, with a German translation, prepared by Leonhard Schultze Jena. It corresponds in part to the material which served Sahagún as a basis for Books II, III, IV, V, and VII of his *History*. These texts were published under the title *Auguries, Astrology and Calendar of the Ancient Aztecs*.[14] Later he published texts corresponding to Books VIII and X of the *History* under the title *Family, Social and Professional Organization of the Ancient Aztec People*.[15]

Finally we should call the reader's attention to the Nahuatl-English edition of the *Florentine Codex* produced by Charles E. Dibble and Arthur J. O. Anderson, of the School of American Research at Santa Fe, New Mexico. Nine volumes had been published by 1962, containing the Nahuatl text corresponding to Books I, II, III, IV-V, VII, VIII, IX, X, and XII of Sahagún's *History*.[16]

2. *El Libro de los Colloquios.*

A work of highest importance, the complete title is *Colloquies and Christian Doctrine with which the Twelve Friars of Saint Francis Sent by Pope Adrian VI and Emperor Charles V Converted the Indians of New Spain, in the Mexican and Spanish Languages.*

[14] Leonhard Schultze Jena, *Wahrsagerei, Himmelskunde und Kalender der Alten Azteken* (see Bibliography).

[15] Schultze Jena, *Gliederung des Alt-Aztekischen Volks in Familie, Stand und Beruf* (see Bibliography).

[16] Arthur J. O. Anderson and Charles E. Dibble (trs.), *Florentine Codex*, Books I, II, III, IV, V, VII, VIII, IX, X, and XII of Sahagún's *Historia* (see Bibliography). The Seminar of Nahuatl Culture at the Institute of History (National University of Mexico) began in 1958 the publication of the *Codices Matritenses* in a Nahuatl-Spanish edition. Three volumes have appeared to the present time: Miguel León-Portilla (ed.), *Ritos, Sacerdotes y Atavíos de los dioses*, (see Bibliography); Angel María Garibay K. (ed.), *Veinte Himnos Sacros de los Nahuas* (see Bibliography); and Garibay (ed.), *La Vida Económica de Tenochtitlan* (Mexico City, Universidad Nacional Autónoma de México, 1961).

This work is significant because it presents the last public appearance of the learned men of the Nahuas. In the year 1524, they defended their opinions and beliefs from the attacks of the first twelve Franciscan friars in New Spain.

The original manuscript is mutilated, and only fourteen chapters of the original thirty are extant. The text was discovered in the secret archives of the Vatican in 1924 by Father Pascual Saura, and was published for the first time by Father Pou y Martí in Volume III of *Miscelánea Fr. Ehrle* (pages 281–333) under the auspices of the celebrated Duke of Loubat. In 1927, Zelia Nutall published a xylographic edition of the *Colloquies* in the *Revista Mexicana de Estudios Históricos*, appendix to Volume I (pages 101 and following).

In 1949 the *Iberoamerikanische Bibliothek* of Berlin included in its series on historical sources dealing with the ancient history of America a careful edition of the original text paleographed by Walter Lehmann, and accompanied by a literal German version of the Nahuatl. This brought to light the wealth of data contained in the Indian text but not in the Spanish résumé. Lehmann gave this edition the significant title, *Gods that Die and the Christian Message, Discussions between Indians and Spanish Missionaries in Mexico, 1524.*[17]

In regard to the origin and historical value of the *Colloquies*, and to Sahagún's own participation in the editing of the work, the missionary himself supplies the following information in a foreword addressed to the reader:

For the purpose of understanding this present work, prudent reader, I will have it known that this doctrine with which those twelve apostolic preachers—of whom we have spoken in the prologue—began to convert the inhabitants of New Spain has been preserved in the form of papers and memoranda until this year of 1564. Before this time there was no opportunity to put it in order or to transcribe it into suitably polished Nahuatl. This translation has now been made in the College of Santa Cruz of Tlatelolco this

17 Walter Lehmann, *Sterbende Götter und Christliche Heilsbotschaft* [*Colloquies and Christian Doctrine*] (see Bibliography).

same year by the most capable students, well versed in Latin, who have to this time been educated in this school. They are: Antonio Valeriano, resident of Azcaputzalco; Alfonso Vegerano, of Cuauhtitlan; Martín Iacobita and Andrés Leonardo of Tlatelolco. It was also polished by four elders well versed in their language and their antiquities.

The treatise is divided into two separate books: the first, of thirty chapters, contains all the discussions, sermons, and talks between the twelve priests and the native princes, lords and wise men.[18]

3. *The Colección de Cantares Mexicanos.*

This manuscript is preserved in the National Library of Mexico and appears to be a copy of an older transcription. It was recorded in the 1560's. Not a few of the Nahuatl songs and poems included express profound ideas of a philosophical character.

The Americanist Daniel G. Brinton first noted the importance of these *Cantares*. Having obtained a Spanish translation of twenty-eight of them prepared by the Indian scholar of the nineteenth century, Chimalpopoca, he published them in English in his *Ancient Nahuatl Poetry*.[19] In spite of the defects due to errors of paleographic transcription and to an inaccurate first translation into Spanish, Brinton's work has the unquestionable virtue of having opened a new field.

In 1904 these poems were published in their entirety in a photoengraved edition by Antonio Peñafiel.[20] This work, which made available the Nahuatl text of the *Cantares*, is the one which has been used in this study.

Concerning the origin and authenticity of the *Cantares*, we refer to the authoritative opinion of Garibay, who was the first to translate and make a critical study of them:

The exact origin of this valuable book has not been determined. From internal evidence, one may deduce that it is a copy of an older collection or, perhaps, of several native manuscripts which

18 *Ibid.*, 52.
19 Daniel G. Brinton, *Ancient Nahuatl Poetry* (see Bibliography).
20 Brinton, *Rig Veda Americanus* (Philadelphia, 1890).

contained ancient poems. The frequent inclusion of the same song two or even three times indicates that the transcriber, with clear and elegant handwriting, had no other specific goal in mind than to compile those documents. It is almost positive that the copy belongs to the third part of the sixteenth century.

That the collector was an Indian is clearly seen from certain grammatical errors in Spanish in the new phrases which appear in that language. That it was destined for a missionary is also obvious from one of the notations, but who this cleric was cannot be stated with certainty. Although some are inclined to believe that the collection was gathered for Sahagún, it could well have been for Father Durán, who was also engaged in collecting similar material. . . .

There have been some who, with little understanding, have believed that this is a post-Conquest collection. . . . They base this belief on finding in the repertoire a few poems of post-Cortesian times of a Christian character and also on certain corrections and additions in which Christian saints and other personalities are mentioned. However, the flavor and nature of these poems, as the reader may judge, are in perfect harmony with the ideas of the Nahuatl peoples, and the corrections themselves are so awry that they proclaim the authenticity of these texts.[21]

In the *Cantares* there is a repetition of that phenomenon found in the philosophico-religious thinking of India and even among some Greeks, such as Parmenides. The wise man expresses himself in verse; he uses metaphor and poetry to give voice to what he has discovered in solitary meditation. For this reason the poems are a fertile source for the reconstruction of the philosophical vision of the Nahuas.

4. *Huehuetlatolli, or the Talks of the Elders.*

Under this title are included several documents of different derivation, whose contents are of pre-Hispanic origin. They are didactic talks or exhortations addressed to the boys of the *Calmécac* or the *Telpochcalli*, and also to adults upon such occasions as marriage and funeral rites, for the purpose of incul-

21 Garibay, *Poesía Indígena de la Altiplanicie*, X–XI.

cating moral ideas and principles. Under the title *Huehuetla-tolli, Document A,* Garibay has published a collection of formulas and short discourses in which may be found many moral ideas of extreme importance to the comprehension of the Nahuatl ethic. In his introduction to the *Huehuetlatolli,* Garibay discusses at length its authenticity and historical value.[22]

Other collections of talks—or *Huehuetlatolli*—of even greater importance are the result of the investigations of Fray Andrés de Olmos. A small number of them were included in his *Arte,* which appeared in Paris in 1875.[23] Others were published by Father Juan Baptista in 1600, with a condensed Spanish version.[24]

These collections and others preserved at the National Library of Mexico contain, along with the Christian ideas interpolated into the primitive text, the authentic moral philosophy of the Indians. There is also abundant material with which to form an idea of the Nahuatl concepts of death, free will, the human person, good and evil, and social obligations and duties.

5. *The Codex Chimalpopoca (Annals of Cuauhtitlán and the Legend of the Suns).*

These texts, named *Codex Chimalpopoca* by Abbé Brasseur de Bourbourg and called *Historia de los Reinos de Colhuacán y México* by Boturini, actually contain three documents from very distinct sources. The first is the anonymous *Annals of Cuauhtitlán* in the Nahuatl language. The second, *Breve Relación de los Dioses y Ritos de la Gentilidad,* was written in Spanish by Pedro Ponce. The third is the anonymous Nahuatl *Manuscript of 1558,* to which Paso y Troncoso gave the title *Leyenda de los Soles (Legend of the Suns).* The first and third of these documents are of special interest.

The *Annals of Cuauhtitlán,* collected before 1570, are mentioned in the catalogue added by Boturini as an appendix to his

[22] Garibay, *"Huehuetlatolli, Documento A," Tlalocan,* Vol. I, No. 1 (1943–44), 31–53 and 81–107.

[23] Andrés de Olmos, *Arte para aprender la lengua mexicana* (see Bibliography).

[24] Juan Baptista, *Huehuetlatolli o Platícas de los viejos* (Mexico City, 1600).

Idea de una Nueva Historia de la América Septentrional (Madrid, 1756). The original manuscript belonged to Fernando de Alva Ixtlilxóchitl. Although compiled in Cuauhtitlán and known as the *Annals* of that town, they contain information about Tezcoco, Tenochtitlan, Chalco, Tlaxcala, Cuauhtitlán, and others. Robert H. Barlow has made a study of this subject. (See: *Hispanic American Historical Review,* Vol. XXVII, pp. 520–26).

The first Spanish version of a part of the *Annals* was made by Faustino Galicia Chimalpopoca, who was commissioned by José Fernando Ramírez. This translation, together with one by Mendoza and Sánchez Solís, was published in an appendix to the third volume of the *Anales del Museo Nacional* in Mexico in 1885.

Walter Lehmann, in 1906, published in the *Journal de la Societé des Americanistes de Paris* (Volume III, pages 239–97) a version of the manuscript of 1558 together with other texts. He gave this the title *Traditions des Anciens Mexicains.*

In 1938, Lehmann also offered investigators a new edition, in which he included a careful transcription of the original Nahuatl text, accompanied by a German version of the complete *Annals,* as well as the *Manuscript of 1558.*[25]

Finally, under the title *Codex Chimalpopoca (Anales de Cuauhtitlán y Leyenda de los Soles),* there is a photoengraved edition and translation by Primo Feliciano Velázquez, published by the National University of Mexico Press in 1945.

The so-called *Leyenda de los Soles* (or *Manuscript of 1558*) is probably the explanation of an Indian codex, no longer extant, which seems to have expressed pictorially the various suns or ages.

The *Leyenda de los Soles* was first transcribed, translated, and published by Francisco del Paso y Troncoso in Florence in 1903. It was also included in the Lehmann and Velázquez editions. Unless otherwise specified, the references made in this study are to Lehmann's paleographic version of the text of both the *Annals* and the *Manuscript of 1558.*

25 Walter Lehmann, *Die Geschichte der Königreiche von Colhuacan und Mexico* (see Bibliography).

Appendix I

6. The Historia Tolteca-Chichimeca.

Of this anonymous work, compiled around 1545, Heinrich Berlin says:

It contributes valuable data toward the clarification of many problems in ancient Mexican history, such as the abandonment and destruction of Tula, the waves of migrations in the valleys of Mexico and Puebla, the origin and nature of the Chichimecas, the location of the famous Chicomóztoc, the history of the Olmec-Xicalancas and their relationship to Cholula, the expansion of the Aztec empire . . . .[26]

This work also includes several brief poems—strongly archaic —containing a complete philosophical conception of divinity and the world's relation to it. We owe our first knowledge of this work to Lorenzo Boturini. The well-known French collector Aubin later owned this manuscript. It was finally acquired by the National Library of Paris, where it is now preserved (*Manuscrit Mexicain, 46–58 bis*).

Konrad Th. Preuss and the noted Americanist Ernst Mengin published this manuscript in the *Baessler Archiv, Band* XXI, *Beiheft* IX, *Die Mexikanische Bilderhandschrift, Historia Tolteca-Chichimeca* (Part I, Introduction, paleography and German translation; Part II, Commentary; Berlin, 1937–38).

In 1942 Mengin also edited a facsimile reproduction of the *Historia Tolteca-Chichimeca*, which was the first volume of his valuable *Corpus Codicum Americanorum Medii Aevi* (Sumptibus Einar Munksgaard, Havniae, Copenhagen, 1942).

7. Other ancient Nahuatl sources.

The following documents, important in themselves, contain minor references to ancient Mexican thought:

Unos Anales Históricos de la Nación Mexicana (*The Annals of Tlatelolco*). Facsimile edition in Volume II of *Corpus Codicum Americanorum Medii Aevi* (Copenhagen, 1945).

Diferentes Historias Originales de los Reynos de Culhuacán y

[26] *Anales de Quauhtinchan, Historia Tolteca-Chichimeca* (see Bibliography).

México y de otras Provincias. The author is Domingo Chimalpain (MS Mexicain 78 of the Bibl. Nat. de Paris). Translation and commentary by Ernst Mengin, in *Mitteilungen aus dem Museum für Völkerkunde in Hamburg* (Volume XII, Hamburg, 1950).

The Sixth and Seventh Accounts of Chimalpain. See: Chimalpain, Cuauhtlehuanitzin, Domingo Francisco de S. Antón Muñón, *Sixième et Septième Relations (1358-1612)*, translated and published by Remi Simeón (Paris, Maisonneuve et Ch. Leclerc, 1889).

The *Crónica Mexicáyotl*, by Fernando Alvarado Tezozómoc; paleography and Spanish version by Adrián León (Mexico City, University Press, 1949).

8. *Documents in languages other than Nahuatl.*

Other ancient writings in Spanish and French provide important data for the comprehension of the world view of the ancient Nahuas:

Fray Andrés de Olmos (?), "*Historia de los Mexicanos por sus Pinturas,*" in the *Nueva Colección de Documentos para la Historia de México*, III, Pomar, Zurita, *Relaciones Antiguas*, published by Joaquín García Icazbalceta (Mexico City, 1891, pages 228-63); and a second edition by Editorial Salvador Chavez Hayhoe (Mexico City, 1942).

The anonymous manuscript entitled *Origen de los Mexicanos*, also in *Nueva Colección . . .* , pages 281-308.

The anonymous manuscript, *Estas Son las Leyes que Tenían los Indios de la Nueva España*, in *Nueva Colección . . .* , pages 308-15.

An anonymous document, *Histoyre du Mechique*, in a sixteenth-century translation made by A. Thévet, published by De Jonghe in *Journal de la Societé des Americanistes de Paris* (Volume II, pages 1-41).

Other authors who wrote in Spanish and who have been cited previously are: Motolinía, Durán, Pomar, Muñoz Camargo, Tovar, Ixtlilxóchitl, Mendieta, Zurita, Hernández, Acosta, and

Torquemada. Bibliographical references appear at the end of this book.

9. *The Codices.*

The codices are perhaps best defined as illustrated Indian manuscripts. Only those of definite Nahuatl origin and which contribute pertinent data to the study of Nahuatl philosophical thought will be mentioned here.

The *Codex Vaticanus A*, known also as *Codex Ríos*, consists of three principal parts: the first describes cosmic origins, the thirteen heavens, the gods, the cosmogonic suns, *etc.*; the second contains a ritual calendar; the third includes historical data from the Conquest to 1563.[27]

The first section, painted after the Conquest, is undoubtedly a copy of a pre-Hispanic codex. The commentaries of Father Ríos which accompany it, written in an Italian saturated with Hispanicisms, although often the product of his imagination, are not without interest.

The *Codex Vaticanus A* was first reproduced in Volume II of Lord Kingsborough's monumental work, *Antiquities of Mexico* (London, 1831). In 1900 the *Codex* was republished in color (photoengravings), under the auspices of the Duke of Loubat.

An important complement to the *Vaticanus A* is the *Codex Telleriano-Remensis*, which derives its name from the Archbishop of Reims, Le Tellier, to whom it belonged. The *Codex Telleriano-Remensis* also contains references to the calendar and to mythology. The first part seems to be a copy of the same pre-Hispanic book which inspired the paintings of the *Vaticanus A*. Although the *Telleriano-Remensis* is not as complete, it offers some data not found in the Vatican manuscript. The publication of the *Telleriano-Remensis* also resulted from the patronage of the Duke of Loubat.[28]

The *Codex Borgia* in the Vatican Library also contains pictorial material of great interest. Much has been written about

[27] *Codex Vaticanus A* (Ríos) (see Bibliography).
[28] *Codex Telleriano-Remensis* (see Bibliography).

the origin of this manuscript. Eduard Seler stated that it was Zapotec, while on other occasions he suggested that it was possibly Nahuatl. Today the authoritative opinion of Alfonso Caso, formulated after a close study of the paintings of Tizatlán, is accepted:

> The analogy is so extraordinary that we may believe that the same culture produced the Tezcatlipocas of the Borgia and the paintings of Tizatlán.[29]

Since Tizatlán was a Nahuatl center in Tlaxcala, it follows that the origin of the *Codex* is also Nahuatl.

The *Borgia* is one of the most remarkable codices, both in its rich color and in the artistic conception of its paintings. Along with its calendaric contents, it contains marvelous stylizations of the Nahuatl concept of the universe, with its center and four cardinal directions. The Duke of Loubat financed a reproduction of the *Codex* in colored photoengravings.[30]

The *Florentine Codex* also contains pictorial material useful to the student of the thought and life of the ancient Mexicans. It was published by Paso y Troncoso in the fifth volume of the facsimile edition of the Nahuatl texts collected by Sahagún. Although there is a marked European influence in the illustrations which depict the various crafts, plants, animals, calendar tables, *etc.*, there are still strong elements of the ancient pictorial art.

Of equal importance to the study of Nahuatl thought are the *Codex Borbonicus* and the *Codex Mendoza*. The *Borbonicus*, with its clear style, is in part a *tonalámatl*—a sacred book of divination. It is therefore an excellent source for the study of astrological and religious beliefs. The extant edition was published by E. T. Hamy.[31]

The *Codex Mendoza*, compiled about 1541 by order of Viceroy Antonio de Mendoza, preserves historical information about the

---

[29] Alfonso Caso, "*Las ruinas de Tizatlán*," *Revista Mexicana de Estudios Históricos*, Vol. I, No. 4 (1927), 139.

[30] *Codex Borgia* (see Bibliography).

[31] *Codex Borbonicus* (see Bibliography).

foundation of Tenochtitlan, the Aztec Confederation, the tributes which the Aztecs imposed, and their systems of education, law, *etc.* Important to our theme is the last part of the codex, which describes, among other things, the juridical organization of the ancient Mexicans. Preserved in the Bodleian Library of Oxford, the *Codex Mendoza* was first edited in Mexico by the National Museum of Archaeology, History, and Ethnography in 1925, and was edited later in London by James C. Clark.[32]

10. *Archaeological testimony.*

A valuable complement to the written sources are the archaeological discoveries, particularly the stone sculptures. Two extraordinary examples—the celebrated Aztec calendar stone and the monumental sculpture of the mother goddess Coatlicue—are in the National Museum in Mexico City.

The importance of such works of art to the study of the mind of ancient Mexico becomes apparent if we realize that in their symbolism they often express fundamental aspects of the pre-Columbian world view. An example of this may be found in the penetrating study of Justino Fernández, who, in analyzing the statue of Coatlicue, has discovered the basic elements of the mystico-militaristic concept of the "people of the Sun."[33]

[32] *Codex Mendoza* (see Bibliography).

[33] Justino Fernández, *Coatlicue, estetica del arte indigena antiguo* (see Bibliography); see also Salvador Toscano, *Arte Pre-colombino de Mexico y de la America Central* (see Bibliography).

Appendix II

Investigators of Nahuatl Thought

APPENDIX I describes the most important native sources for this study as well as the early Colonial chroniclers who dealt with the mind of ancient Mexico. We now turn to the opinions of later authors—chiefly those writing after 1700—who, using the Indian sources and the post-Conquest chronicles, were to some degree concerned with the philosophical ideas of the Nahuas.

1. *Eguiara y Eguren.*

Juan José de Eguiara y Eguren (1696–1763), a Mexican bibliographer and professor at the Royal and Pontifical University of Mexico, has been justly described as "the father of the history of ideas in Mexico."[1]

Prior to Eguiara y Eguren, Carlos de Sigüenza y Góngora (1645–1700) and the Italian traveler Giovanni F. Gemelli Carreri (1651–1725) wrote about the ancient indigenous cultures. Sigüenza y Góngora's work on this subject, including his *Historia del Imperio de los Chichimecas*, has unfortunately been lost.

---

[1] See Juan Hernández Luna's article, "*El Iniciador de la Historia de las Ideas en México*," *Filosofía y Letras*, Nos. 51–52 (July–December, 1953, pp. 55–80.

We know only of his reputation as a great investigator and collector of Mexican antiquities, and we have some data which Carreri included in his *Giro del Mondo*, published in 1700. This work, although it contains valuable information, cannot be compared in excellence with the achievements of Eguiara y Eguren.

In the prologue to his most important work, *Bibliotheca Mexicana* (1755),[2] Eguiara y Eguren refutes vigorously the opinions of a certain Manuel Martí, dean of Alicante, who had denied the most elementary level of intellectual culture to the people (ancient and modern) of the New World in general and of New Spain in particular. After explaining his motives in replying to Martí, the author devotes a good part of his prologue to what he considers to be the real culture of the ancient Mexicans. He calls upon the testimony of the chroniclers and historians of the Indies. He admits that "to be sure, the Indians did not possess the use of an alphabet. But this is no reason to say that they were crude or uncultured, or completely lacking in science, codices, or illustrated manuscripts."[3] And he goes on to say with equal truth that "the Mexicans cultivated history and poetry, rhetorics, arithmetic, astronomy, and all those sciences of which they have left evident proof."[4]

As further corroboration, he cites the indigenous books collected by Sigüenza y Góngora, in which are found the annals of the Indians, data concerning their laws, chronology, rites and ceremonies, ordinances dealing with the collecting of tribute, and so on. He also quotes writers who had delved into these codices—Torquemada, Betancourt, Gómara, Solís, Acosta, Henrico Martínez, Gemelli, *etc.*

Eguiara y Eguren studied the native educational system. He speaks of the poet-king Nezahualcóyotl, whose wisdom he praises, and he even quotes the first Nahuatl words of one of the

---

[2] Juan José Eguiara y Eguren, *Prólogos a la Biblioteca Mexicana*, with an introductory note by Federico Gómez de Orozco (Spanish version annotated with a biographical study and bibliography of the author by Agustín Millares Carlo; Mexico City, Fondo de Cultura Económica, 1944).

[3] *Ibid.*, 61–62.

[4] *Ibid.*, 61–62.

songs attributed to the great poet. He deals also with the physical, medicinal, and theological knowledge of the Nahuas:

> We do not believe that the ancient Indians were unacquainted with the study of physics. . . . And if we examine their codices written in hieroglyphics, we shall find that not a few of them deserve being called theological treatises. All this being so, we may indeed picture the Mexican Indian—no less than we do the Egyptian—as being well-versed in a superior type of knowledge and wisdom.[5]

This study, little known in modern times, can be considered the first attempt to synthesize the most valuable elements of Nahuatl culture and thought.

2. *Boturini.*

A contemporary of Eguiara y Eguren was the learned Italian voyager Lorenzo Boturini. He arrived in New Spain in 1736 and gathered an impressive collection of manuscripts and codices, which he listed in catalogue form in his *Idea de una Nueva Historia General de la América Septenrional.*[6]

Although Boturini does not specifically deal with Nahuatl philosophy, there are in his writings several allusions to the characteristics of Nahuatl thought and culture, and he also suggests a new and objective method for their study. "Upon writing this historical *Idea*," he states, "it has been necessary for me to meditate about the scientific accounts of the Indians, and to use—especially in discussing the First and Second cosmogonic Ages—their own concepts to explain them."[7] Following this criterion, he studies, among other things, the Nahuatl symbols of the four seasons, the calendar, the astronomy, the metaphors which enrich the Nahuatl language—"which in my opinion is superior in elegance to Latin." He also discusses the songs and poems and declares that "whoever reflects about them attentively will find

[5] *Ibid.*, 95–96.
[6] Lorenzo Boturini Benaducci, *Idea de una Nueva Historia General de la América Septentrional* (see Bibliography).
[7] *Ibid.*, 162.

some extraordinarily subtle myths woven in lofty metaphors and allegories."[8]

It is a great misfortune that Boturini was unable to utilize the great collection of documents which he had gathered, since they were confiscated by royal orders. Nevertheless his name remains an important one for those desirous of understanding the mind of ancient Mexico.

3. *Clavijero.*

More important than Boturini in the study of the culture and traditions of the Nahuas is the Jesuit Francisco Xavier Clavijero (1731–87). His foremost work, *Historia Antigua de Mexico*, conceived and begun in New Spain, was published in Italy during his exile, a result of the expulsion of the Mexican Jesuits in 1767.[9]

Clavijero's great achievement lay in summarizing and putting in order—both in his *Historia* and *Disertaciones*—the material handed down by the first chronicles regarding the religious ideas of the Indians, their concept of a supreme being, their chronology, their cosmogonic myths, and their tales and discourses. Clavijero also analyzed their educational system, laws, social organization, language, poetry, music, medicine, painting, and so on.

His comments about the Mexican language are of particular interest: "I venture to state that it would not be easy to find a language more apt for dealing with metaphysical matters than Nahuatl. For where can one be found that is richer in terms conveying abstract ideas? To give an idea of what this tongue is like, and to satisfy the curiosity of my readers, I give below a number of words that express metaphysical and moral concepts, and yet are understood by the most unlearned Indians."[10]

In spite of the acuteness of such observations, Clavijero did

---

[8] *Ibid.*, 57–58.

[9] The title of the Italian version is *Storia Antica del Messico Cavata Da'Manoscritti E Dalle Pitture Antiche degl'Indiani*. Only in recent times did an edition based on the original Spanish text appear (4 vols. Colección de Escritores Mexicanos; Mexico City, Editorial Porrúa, 1945).

[10] Francisco Xavier Clavijero, *Historia Antigua de México*, IV, 328–29.

not actually study Nahuatl philosophy as such. Nevertheless, out of the mass of details which he presents about their myths, religion, and art, there emerges a vivid picture of life of the times and the universe as it was probably visualized by the Nahuas. The objectivity and the manifest "Mexicanism" of Clavijero make his *Historia* and *Disertaciones* the first serious attempt to show Europe an unbiased picture of the cultural values of ancient Mexico.

Clavijero's search for knowledge was soon to be reflected in his successors—some of them foreign—such as the great Humboldt. The latter's *Vista de las Cordilleras y de los Monumentos de los Pueblos Indígenas de América* demonstrates repeatedly his romantic desire to understand the Aztec way of life and world view.[11]

Another European influenced by Clavijero was the ill-starred Lord Kingsborough, who, in his *Antiquities of Mexico* (London, 1830–48), made available to students throughout the world many of the indigenous codices adequately reproduced.

In spite of such works as the above, the first real attempts to study Nahuatl philosophy as such do not come until almost the closing years of the nineteenth century.

4. *Orozco y Berra.*

It was Manuel Orozco y Berra who, in his *Historia Antigua y de la Conquista de México*, first gave careful attention to Nahuatl myths and philosophical ideas.[12]

Beginning with the cosmogonic ideas expressed in *Codex Vaticanus A*, he analyzes the myth of the Suns, the origin of the stars and gods, the belief in *Tloque Nahuaque*, and the concept of the *Ométotl* or divine ambivalence. He is then concerned with the Nahuatl ideas about the earth, the heavens, the moon, and the sun, and states that "the Mexicans worshipped the four

---

11 Alexander von Humboldt, *Vues des Cordillères et Monuments des Peuples de l'Amérique* (Paris, 1813).

12 Manuel Orozco y Berra, *Historia Antigua y de la Conquista de México* (see Bibliography).

elements as well as the heavenly bodies." Orozco y Berra describes the Nahuatl theory of the origin of the various tribes composing the Aztec empire, noting that the Aztecs affirmed the existence of a single ancestor common to them all. This monogenistic theory, according to Orozco y Berra, was expressed platonically through myths. As an example he cites the legend of Iztacmixcóatl (Serpent of White Clouds) and his six sons, and declares: "The Mexican philosophers held that all the various tribes of the empire, disregarding their ethnographic differences, were of a single stock or origin."[13]

Comparing the Aztec and Pythagorean attitudes, he asserts that for both of them "the sublunar earth was the theater of endless combat between life and death. . . . It was the region of the four elements—earth, air, water, fire—which through their incessant uniting, separating, and transformations produced all the transitory phenomena which are visible to us."[14]

Orozco y Berra's comparison of Aztec thought and Pythagorean philosophy and his comparison of Aztec thought and that of India, are stimulating, but most interesting is his attempt to reveal the universal values and meanings in Nahuatl philosophy. Unfortunately this scholar was not acquainted with the texts and Nahuatl poems collected by Sahagún, not one of which had been published at that time. This is especially regrettable, for, considering Orozco y Berra's competence as a historian, he could have bequeathed to us the first book on Nahuatl philosophy studied from the original sources.

5. *Chavero.*

A few years after the publication of Orozco y Berra's *Historia*, there appeared a work in which an attempt was made to study Nahuatl philosophy. This was Alfredo Chavero's *Historia Antigua y de la Conquista,* Volume I of *México a Través de los Siglos* (1887).[15]

[13] *Ibid.,* I, 31.
[14] *Ibid.,* I, 41.
[15] Alfredo Chavero, *México a través de los siglos* (see Bibliography).

After dedicating the second and third chapters of Book I to Nahuatl myths and religious ideas, in Chapter IV, Chavero considers "Nahuatl philosophy." The following excerpt gives an idea of Chavero's interpretation of Nahuatl thought:

> Many noted writers have gone astray in their attempts to attribute every possible perfection to the Nahuatl people. They do not hesitate, for example, to declare that the first tribes, the Toltecs themselves, were deists. But their cosmogony indicates the contrary. They conceived a being, Ometecuhtli, but that creator was the material element, fire, and creation was produced by the material force, the *Omeycualiztli*. The creative being was the Eternal, the *Ayamictlan*, but that which was imperishable continued to be the element fire. The gods are the four material beings, the four stars. . . . In order to explain the appearance of man, they referred to the physical action of fire upon earth, the symbolic marriage of Tonacatecuhtli and Tonacacíhuatl. The idea of a spiritual being is never even remotely conceived. The Nahuas were not deists, nor may it be said that their philosophy resembled Asiatic pantheism; it was simply materialism based on the eternal nature of matter. Their religion was the Sabaist worship of four stars and, like their philosophy, was materialistic.[16]

Referring to the Nahuatl concept of the hereafter, he adds:

> Much as we would like to idealize the Nahuatl people, we must conclude that the road of the dead and their perishing in the Mictlan reveal an indubitable materialism.[17]

The following paragraph, embodying a viewpoint of negation and pessimism, presents something of a résumé of Chavero's appraisal:

> No matter how much we should prefer to maintain that the Nahuas had achieved a great philosophy, that they were deists and believed in the immortality of the soul—all of which we too had thought before—we must nevertheless confess that their civilization, as a consequence of the social medium in which it developed,

16 *Ibid.*, I, 105.
17 *Ibid.*, I, 106.

did not reach such heights. Their gods were material; eternal fire was eternal matter; men were sons of, and had been created by, their father the sun and their mother the earth; fatalism was their philosophy of life.[18]

Such was Chavero's interpretation of Nahuatl philosophy. He does, to be sure, explicitly vouch for its existence. However, perhaps imputing some of his own positivist convictions to the Nahuas, he declares them to be materialists. He does not seem to realize that he thus contradicts the positivist thesis of the three stages and history itself, which tells us that the world concept of the peoples of antiquity always tended toward animism, or toward different metaphysical conceptions. Therefore, recognizing some merit in Chavero's work, we cannot refrain from judging his interpretation of Nahuatl thought as superficial and ill-founded. The fact is that his source material was incomplete, and, as was the case with Orozco y Berra, he was unable to consult the texts dictated by Sahagún's Aztec informants. It is these documents which reveal a deep philosophical thought that cannot by any stretch of the imagination be termed materialistic. More than in anything else, Chavero's merit lies in having pointed out a theme which needed more profound research.

6. *Valverde Téllez.*

Limiting himself to the small amount of really dependable information he had available, Emeterio Valverde Téllez, the first historian of colonial and modern philosophical thought in Mexico, dedicated three short pages of his *Apuntaciones Históricas* to what he calls "pre-Conquest philosophy."[19] A much more cautious observer than Chavero, he testifies to the existence of philosophers among the ancient Mexicans:

> We do not doubt that the pre-Conquest Mexicans, as rational men, had their philosophers. It was unlikely that their philosophy dif-

[18] *Ibid.*, I, 94.
[19] Valverde Téllez, *Apuntaciones Históricas sobre la Filosofía en México* (Mexico City, Herrero Hnos., 1896), 36.

ferentiated sharply from their religious ideas on one hand and their astronomical and physical ideas on the other.

Valverde then offers as proof of this a quotation from Clavijero in which the latter, basing his interpretations on Ixtlilxóchitl, speaks of Nezahualcóyotl's knowledge of astronomy, natural science, and philosophy. Nezahualcóyotl, the wise king of Tezcoco, is credited not only with having discovered the idea of a single creator of all that exists, but with being at the same time a student of the stars, an investigator of nature, and a profound thinker. Valverde Téllez uses Nezahualcóyotl to emphasize the well-known fact that it is most difficult "to draw a dividing line between the subject matter and the aims of the various sciences" of the ancient peoples. This is true not only of the former inhabitants of Mexico, but also of the first Greek philosophers, such as Thales, Anaximander, Anaximenes, and Heraclitus, who are considered to have been simultaneously philosophers, physicists, astronomers, *etc.* Not until recent times has a more or less definite line been drawn between the subject matters of the different sciences. Precisely because Copernicus fixed clear-cut limitations to his own field of investigation is he called the father of astronomy. The same is true of Newton for physics and Lavoisier for chemistry. All these sciences were at one time related as parts of philosophy.

It is lamentable that the original sources of Nahuatl philosophical thought were unknown to Valverde Téllez. This source material was not made available until several years after the appearance of his *Apuntaciones.*

7. *Parra.*

A well-known Mexican thinker and logician, Porfirio Parra, a pupil of Gabino Barreda, was steeped even more than Chavero in the positivism then in fashion. Parra wrote, at the beginning of this century, the history of what he called "the luminous reign of Science" in Mexico.[20] In this work Parra first devotes a

---

[20] Porfirio Parra, *"La Ciencia en México,"* in *México, su Evolución Social* (Mexico City, 1902), Book I, Vol. II, pp. 417–66.

few pages to a rapid and—we venture to say—aprioristic examination of ancient Nahuatl culture. Arguing that "the scientific movement in our country is exclusively of Spanish origin,"[21] he avows that, considering the imperfect nature of Nahuatl writing, the Indians could not "express the abstract ideas of space, time, divisibility—all indispensable elements in mathematics, which in turn is the basis for all science."[22] As though to confirm this, Parra describes what he supposes to be the defective Nahuatl system of counting:

> The Nahuatl tribes found an equal, if not greater, obstacle to the cultivation of pure science in their imperfect system of numbering, if indeed we can even call it such. . . . Direct examination of the method the aborigines used for counting, and the testimony of reputable authorities . . . reveal to us that the Indians could not count beyond twenty without error.[23]

He goes on to deny any scientific value to their chronology and astronomy without even naming those "reputable authorities" who had informed him that "the Indians could not count beyond twenty without error" and that the Nahuas "did not express the abstract ideas of space, time, divisibility . . . ."

Such fantastic affirmations are comparable only to those of the Prussian philosopher Paw—of whom Clavijero speaks—who maintained that the Nahuatl numbering system only reached the number three! To this absurdity, Clavijero scornfully replied:

> I learned the Mexican language and heard the Mexicans speak it for many years. However, I did not know that it was so deficient in number words and in meaningful terms for universal ideas until Herr Paw came along to enlighten me. I had thought that the Mexicans gave the name *centzontli*, four hundred, or rather *centzontlatole* (the one who has four hundred voices) to that bird so esteemed for the incomparable sweetness and variety of its songs.

---

21 *Ibid.*, Book I, Vol. II, p. 424.

22 *Ibid.*, Book I, Vol. II, p. 424.

23 *Ibid.*, Book I, Vol. II, pp. 424–25.

... I thought I knew, in short, that the Mexicans had number words to express as many thousands and millions as they wished.[24]

This answer, which Parra should have been familiar with, makes it almost impossible to believe that he—a professor of logic and a positivist to boot—should pass such judgments on the Nahuas, who, according to him, "could not count beyond twenty without error."

In contrast to such frivolous pronouncements, there are the contemporaneous publications, the fruit of direct investigation, of Francisco del Paso y Troncoso, Antonio Peñafiel, and Joaquín García Icazbalceta, all outstanding scholars in research and in the printing of unedited texts, many of them in the original Nahuatl. Since these texts have been discussed in Appendix I, we will not list them again.

8. Seler.

Founder of a group of investigators known as the "German School" was Eduard Seler (1849–1922). His work as translator and editor of the Nahuatl texts gathered by Sahagún and others has already been noted. This activity was continued by such scholars as Lehmann, Schultze Jena, and Mengin.

Seler's opinions of Nahuatl philosophical thought are found in a number of articles originally scattered through various journals and other publications. These were finally brought together in that encyclopedia of Middle American cultures, his *Gesammelte Abhandlungen*.[25] Pertaining to the subject of this work, there is a study entitled *Einiges über die natürlichen Grundlagen mexikanischer Mythen*, an essay attempting to determine the Toltec elements in sixteenth-century Nahuatl mythology.

His studies on several of the ancient codices also contain ideas important to the understanding of the Nahuatl vision of the universe. Four of his papers are of special interest: "The Mexican Concept of the World"; "The Appearing of the World and of Men, Birth of the Sun and Moon"; "The First Men and the

---

24 Clavijero, *op. cit.*, *Disertación* VI, Vol. IV, 324.
25 Seler, *Gesammelte Abhandlungen* (see Bibliography).

Celestial World"; "The Principal Myth of the Mexican Tribes."
In all these works Seler draws directly from the chroniclers and
illustrated manuscripts. As an example of Seler's manner of deal-
ing with his subject, we quote from his *Mexican Concept of the
World*. After citing his source—the *Codex Vaticanus A* (folio 8)
—Seler writes of:

> . . . the two gods whose name is Tonacatecuhtli, Tonacacíhuatl,
> "Lord and Lady of our Subsistence," or Ometecuhtli, Omecíhuatl,
> "Lord and Lady of Duality." The goddess is also called Xochi-
> quétzal, "flowers and adornment of plumes." These gods, who were
> for the Mexicans the gods of love, procreation, birth, and—in a
> corresponding way—of all that exists in life, of sustenance, of corn,
> *etc.*, dwelt in the thirteenth heaven. This material from the *Codex
> Vaticanus* is in complete agreement with Sahagún (Book X,
> Chapter 29), where he states that the source or principle of life is
> concentrated in this place which, because of these gods, is called
> *Omeyocan*, or place of duality. And it was from there, the Mex-
> icans believed, that children were sent into this world (Sahagún,
> Book VI, Chapter 32). For this reason this supreme heaven was
> also called *Tamoanchan*, "Place of origin," that is, of birth. So this
> name, as I have shown, indicated the mythical place of origin for
> the Nahuas as a people, because, indicating the source of indi-
> vidual life, it was natural that it should also refer to the region
> from which the peoples came.[26]

In this careful way Seler proceeds, always building upon the
codices, texts, and archaeological discoveries. He prepared the
way for a continuation of his work, which would be the study
of how myth is rationalized and turned into philosophy.

9. *Lehmann and Beyer.*

A student of Seler and, like him, an investigator of ancient
Nahuatl texts, Walter Lehmann, who died in 1939, produced,
among other works, the first translation from the original Nahuatl of the book of the Colloquies, as well as a careful paleographic version of the *Anales de Cuauhtitlán*. His interest in the

[26] *Ibid.*, IV, 25–26.

philosophies of the Mayan and Nahuatl cultures was outlined in an interesting study published posthumously.[27] In this work he insists on the need for a more comprehensive use of archaeological data in the reconstruction of the ancient cultures, one that will lead to their very soul—their philosophy.

Another exponent of the humanistic tendencies of this German school was Hermann Beyer. Of extreme interest is his study entitled *The Aztec Image of Alexander von Humboldt*. In it Beyer declares that if:

> . . . we penetrate further into the symbolic language of the myths and the images portrayed in the illustrated manuscripts, we shall note that the blatant polytheism which appears to be characteristic of ancient Mexico is simply a symbolic reference to natural phenomena. The thought of the priests had conceived philosophico-religious ideas of much greater scope. The two thousand gods of that great multitude of which Gómara speaks were for the learned priests and the priestly initiates only so many manifestations of the *One*. In the figure of the god Tonacatecuhtli we find a substitute for monotheism. He is the old creator god who reigns in the thirteenth heaven and from there sends forth his influence and heat, thanks to which children are conceived in the maternal wombs. In order to express the idea that the cosmic forces were emanations of the divine principle [*Urgottheit*], the gods of nature were called children of Tonacatecuhtli. . . . And the fact that the ancient god should appear (at times) in feminine form is as much and as little a contradiction to the monotheistic principle as the Christian Trinity. We find in the Mexican pantheon a divine pair conceived as the single and identical fundamental principle of the universe. The fact that the sun was for the Mexicans the source of all terrestrial life means that it performs the same function as the old creator god and that therefore the two are identical. Fire, or heat, is for the primitive philosophers the vitalizing power which pervades all that exists.[28]

27 See Walter Lehmann, "*Die Bedeutung der Altamerikanischen Hochkulturen für die allgemeine Geschichte der Menschheit*," *Ibero-Amerikanisches Archiv*, April-July, 1943, pp. 65–71.

28 Hermann Beyer, "*Das aztekische Götterbild Alexander von Humboldt's*," in *Wissenschaftliche Festschrift*, 116.

This analysis, revealing Beyer's opinion that the Aztec vision of the cosmos was monistic-pantheistic, contrasts with Chavero's contention that Nahuatl thought was materialistic in essence. Beyer's study concludes as follows:

> And we may say that the day is not distant when there may be attained—at least, fundamentally—an understanding of the mythological system of the thinkers of Anáhuac.[29]

Finally there are a number of contemporary scholars whose contributions to the study of Nahuatl philosophy are of considerable value. We regret that the scope of this study does not allow us to speak of such writers as Herbert J. Spinden, Miguel Othón de Mendizábal, Theodor W. Danzel, George C. Vaillant, Salvador Toscano, Paul Westheim, and others—all authorities in fields less restricted than that of the present work.

10. *Gamio.*

Manuel Gamio (1883–1960), in *Forjando Patria*, clearly points out the importance of the studies on indigenous thought.[30] Commenting on Indian art, Gamio admits that a great abyss lies between the aesthetic standards of modern Western man and those of the Indians. He later shows why indigenous art often does not awaken aesthetic emotion in Occidentals. This happens "because one cannot, in any real sense appreciate things one does not understand. What is observed for the first time cannot be appreciated or evaluated sufficiently to allow a valid judgment."[31] In order, therefore, to understand indigenous art, it is necessary to become saturated with the aboriginal mentality, to learn about its antecedents, its myths, its cosmogony, its philosophy—in other words, to acquire knowledge of the typical patterns or molds manifest in indigenous thought. Although this idea of Gamio's refers to art, it implies a more universal mean-

---

[29] *Ibid.*, 119.

[30] Manuel Gamio, *Forjando Patria* (see Bibliography), note especially "*El Concepto del Arte Prehispánico*," 69–79.

[31] *Ibid.*, 74.

ing; in order to comprehend thoroughly any aspect or manifestation of culture, it is necessary to reconstruct on a humanistic
basis all the facets of its concept of the cosmos and, as far as possible, of the highest elaboration of that concept—its philosophy.

11. *Caso*.

Alfonso Caso has produced a number of studies about the ideas
and world concept of the Aztecs. His interpretations are presented in *La Religión de los Aztecas* (1936 and 1945), "*El Aguila
y el Nopal*" (1946), and finally in *The People of the Sun* (1953
and 1958).[32]

Caso begins his appraisal of Aztec religion by noting the
fact that:

> in the uneducated or uncultured classes there was a tendency to
> exaggerate polytheism, picturing as a number of deities what in
> the minds of the priests were manifestations and names all belong-
> ing to one and the same god.[33]

There is, then, a contrast between what may be called the religious attitude of the people and that of the priests and wise
men:

> The efforts of the Aztec priests to reduce the numerous divinities
> to aspects of one god are unmistakable; upon adopting the gods of
> conquered races, or of more advanced cultures, they consistently
> strove to incorporate them—as did the Romans—into their own
> national pantheon. Often the Aztecs considered them different
> manifestations of the gods they had inherited from the great civil-
> izations from which they had derived their own culture.[34]

Caso also refers to:

> . . . a very ancient school of philosophy which maintained that the
> origin of all things lies in one single dual principle, masculine and
> feminine, which had begotten the gods, the world, and men.
> Certain exceptional men, such as Nezahualcóytol, king of Tezcoco,

---

32 Alfonso Caso, see Bibliography.
33 Caso, *La Religión de los Aztecas*, 7; see also Caso, *El Pueblo del Sol*, 16–17.
34 Caso, *La Religión*, 8, and *El Pueblo*, 17.

went even further and worshiped an invisible god who could not be represented physically; he was called *Tloque Nahuaque* or *Ipalnemohuani,* "the Lord of the Everywhere," "the Giver of Life."[35]

But since "the gods conceived by philosophers have never achieved great popularity," the religious world vision of the Aztec people continued to develop in its own way.

An analysis of the data provided by Caso reveals in the pre-Columbian world vision three different layers or substrata: (1) the popular, which was polytheistic; (2) the priestly substratum, which attempted to establish the multiple gods as aspects of a single deity; and (3) *the philosophical,* a very ancient school, which affirmed the existence of the dual cosmic principle and even produced isolated thinkers who approached monotheism.

Having thus emphasized the complexity of certain elements in Aztec thought, Caso is concerned with the first two substrata—the popular and the priestly. He refers only peripherally to the strictly philosophical level, since, after all, his purpose is the study of Aztec religion. He then narrates the myths pertaining to the creation of the gods, the spatial distribution of the cosmos in relation to the four quarters of the world, the creation of man, the four Suns, the mission of Quetzalcóatl and his battles with Tezcatlipoca, and the attributes of the gods of fire, water, vegetation, the soil, and death.

Probing more deeply into the religious vision of the cosmos, Caso discovers the key or *leit-motiv* of Aztec thought—man viewed as the collaborator of the gods, particularly of the sun, Huitzilopochtli:

... the youthful warrior who is born every morning from the womb of the old earth goddess and dies every night in order to illumine the world of the dead with his faded light. But upon being born the god has to fight with his brothers, the stars, and with his sister, the moon; and, armed with the fire serpent—the solar rays—every day he puts them to flight, and his victory signifies a new day of life

[35] Caso, *La Religión,* 8, and *El Pueblo,* 18.

for men. Upon the consummation of his victory, he is carried in triumph to the middle part of the sky by the souls of the warriors who have died in battle or on the sacrificial block, and when the afternoon begins, he is met by the souls of the women who died in childbirth. Such women are comparable to the men because they died upon taking a man—the newly born—as prisoner. . . . Every day this divine battle takes place; but in order for the sun to triumph it is imperative that he be strong and vigorous, for he must fight against the countless stars. . . . Therefore man must give food to the sun, which, being a god, disdains the coarse food of man, and can be sustained only by life itself, by the magic substance which is found in man's blood, the *chalchíuatl*, the "precious liquid," the terrible nectar which nourishes the gods.

The Aztecs, people of Huitzilopochtli, are the chosen people of the sun, entrusted with nourishing him. War for the Aztecs became thus a form of religious ritual and a necessary activity.[36]

This concept, establishing the Aztecs as "the people of the Sun," is further confirmed by the author's analysis of the old Aztec symbol of the eagle and the cactus. Combining in his study the archaeological contributions with the data furnished by the chroniclers, Caso concludes that:

The eagle on the cactus signifies that the Sun has rested on the spot where he is to receive his food. The prickly-pear cactus, the spiny tree which produces the fruit, is the tree of sacrifice. According to their mythology only human sacrifice can nourish the Sun, only by offering him the red fruit will the solar bird be able to continue his flight.[37]

Caso shows that the very meaning of the life and behavior of the Aztecs was derived from this fundamental idea—that of being "a people with a mission." They believed that the survival of the universe depended upon them, since if the sun was not fed, he would be unable to continue his endless battle. And the Aztecs' feeling that they were collaborating with the sun made them allies of the good in the moral combat against the evil. This, then,

---

[36] Caso, *La Religión*, 10–11.
[37] Caso, *"El Aguila y el Nopal,"* loc. cit., 102.

is the essence of the Aztec mythico-religious concept of the cosmos and the motivating force which led them to create the Mexican Empire and the great lake city of the Tenochca world. Caso's investigations on the mythico-militaristic world view of the Aztecs prepared the way for subsequent research on the philosophical ideas of the great Nahuatl thinkers.

12. *Soustelle.*

A study complementary to that of Caso is *La Pensée Cosmologique des Anciens Mexicains,* by Jacques Soustelle.[38] This work may be described as a summary of the fundamental conceptions of the Nahuas regarding the origin of the world, the four Suns, the stars and heavens, the earth, the dwelling place of the dead, the four quadrants of the universe, and space and time. In relation to these themes, Soustelle's reflections on Nahuatl language and culture are very interesting. Concerning the nature of the Nahuatl language, he states:

> It may be characterized as an instrument for the transmission of traditionally associated ideas, of combinations, of swarms—if you choose—of images. . . .
> What really gives Mexican cosmological thought its own peculiar quality is this binding together of traditionally associated images. The world is a system of symbols—colors, time, the orientation of space, stars, gods, historical events—all having a certain interacting relationship. We are not faced with a long series of ratiocinations, but rather with a continuous and reciprocal complex of the various aspects of a whole.[39]

After commenting upon the principal Nahuatl cosmological ideas, Soustelle gives a succinct interpretation of their space-time world:

> And so, Mexican cosmological thought does not make a sharp distinction between space and time. It refuses, above all, to think of space as a neutral and homogeneous medium independent of

[38] Jacques Soustelle, *La Pensée Cosmologique des anciens mexicains* (see Bibliography).
[39] *Ibid.,* 9.

the unfolding of time. Time unfolds in the form of heterogeneous events whose peculiar characteristics follow one another with a predetermined rhythm and in a cyclical manner. In Mexican thought space is not one thing and time another, but rather there is the concept of space-time, in which natural phenomena and human acts are immersed and saturated continuously with their own qualities. Each "place-moment," a complex of location and action, determines in an irresistible way everything found within it. The world can be compared to a great stage upon which different multi-colored lights, controlled by a tireless mechanism, project reflections that follow one after the other and overlap, maintaining for a limitless period an unalterable sequence. In such a world, change is not conceived as the result of a gradual evolving or "becoming" in time, but rather as a brusque and complete mutation: today it is the East that rules, tomorrow it will be the North; today we still live under a favorable sign and we shall, without any gradual transition, pass into the fatal days of the *nemontemi*. The law of the universe is the succession of different and radically separated qualities which alternately prevail, disappear, and reappear without end.[40]

In addition to *La Pensée Cosmologique*, we should mention another work by Soustelle, *La Vie Quotidienne des Aztèques*.[41] Written for the reading public, it is a popular presentation of, among other things, the Aztec *Weltanschauung* and religion, educational system, ethics and social organization, arts, commerce, literature—in fact, a summing up of Aztec life in the past.

13. *Ramos.*

On the subject of Aztec cosmological thought and to "that very ancient philosophical school" mentioned by Caso, reference should be made to the first chapter of the *Historia de la Filosofía en México*, by Samuel Ramos.[42] In this chapter—entitled "Did

[40] *Ibid.*, 85.
[41] Soustelle, *La Vie quotidienne des Aztèques à la Veille de la Conquête Espagnole* (see Bibliography).
[42] Samuel Ramos, *Historia de la Filosofía en México* (see Bibliography). The same work, "*¿Hubo Filosofía entre los antiguos Mexicanos?*" is in *Cuadernos Americanos*, Año I, Vol. II, 132–45.

Philosophy Exist among the Ancient Mexicans?"—Ramos asks a basic question: Are there authentic sources for a possible study of pre-Columbian thought?

> The astronomy of the Aztecs and Mayas, although closely tied to religious ideas, represents beyond any doubt a rational effort to understand the universe. . . .
> The astronomical concepts reveal a rational aspect in the points which served as frames of reference for chronology. Pre-Columbian astronomy is, then, necessarily bound to arithmetic in forming the Calendar, and the latter demonstrates how these peoples conceived time in the universe.[43]

Aware of the necessity for a thorough knowledge of the source material, Ramos refers to a short study by Salvador Domínguez Assiayn, the "Filosofía de los Antiguos Mexicanos."[44] Domínguez Assiayn's laudable intentions led him to the extreme of giving the Nahuas credit for knowledge about the "immortality of energy and matter." Unfortunately he does not name any sources in which this type of thought of the ancient Mexican wise men would be found.

Only the Nahuatl philosophical texts, including those collected by Sahagún, could answer Ramos' question. This scholar's merit lies in his having asked the question and in his insistence that the answer must depend upon authentic source material.

14. *Garibay.*

It was Angel María Garibay K., the great Nahuatl scholar, paleographer and translator of many texts, who first indicated the existence of genuine sources for the study of Nahuatl philosophy. All those who have read his anthology of lyric and epic Nahuatl poetry or his more inclusive work on Nahuatl literature in general have surely come upon verse or prose lines in which doubts and problems of deep philosophic import are obvious.

---

[43] *Ibid.*, 11, 13.

[44] Salvador Domínguez Assiayn, *"Filosofía de los antiguos Mexicanos,"* *Revista Contemporáneos*, Nos. 42–43 (1931), pp. 209–25 (quoted by Ramos in *op. cit.*, 14).

To cite an example, in his *Historia de la Literatura Náhuatl* there is an ancient poem in which a pre-Hispanic wise man responds to the metaphysical urge to answer the eternal and often agonizing question about the reality and value of the present life on earth:

Do we speak the truth here, Giver of Life?
We merely dream, we are only awakened from dreams.
All is like a dream. . . .
No one speaks here of truth. . . .[45]

A series of questions about the hereafter, in which there is the implied confession that nothing is known for sure, appears later in the poem:

Are flowers carried to the kingdom of death?
It is true that we go, it is true that we go!
Where do we go? Where do we go?
Are we dead there or do we still live?
Do we exist there again?[46]

Elsewhere in Garibay's works are speeches and poems that are as genuinely philosophical as the pronouncements of Heraclitus, or Parmenides' poem, or the Vedaic hymns.

When the author decided to investigate the sources of Nahuatl thought, he discovered that Garibay himself had already been selecting—with a keenly critical eye—many texts of purely philosophical content from the vast amount of material which he had paleographed and translated. These texts (generously made available by Garibay) together with others discovered and translated by the author, constitute the source material for the present study.

15. *Fernández.*

In addition to the study of written sources, much can be learned about Nahuatl thought through its plastic arts. No one has accomplished more in this field than Justino Fernández who,

---

[45] Garibay, *Historia de la Literatura Náhuatl*, I, 147.
[46] *Ibid.*, I, 186.

in his stimulating study, *Coatlicue, estética del arte indígena antiguo,* demonstrated and explained the symbolism implicit in the celebrated statue of Coatlicue, goddess of the earth. Fernández describes the purpose of his investigation in the following way:

> The important thing here is to ascertain the historic *being* of the Aztec *world vision;* that is to say, the *being* of the gods and the being of human life, as fundamentally interrelated, in order to attain an understanding of the historic *being* of Coatlicue's beauty, which is our objective.
>
> The Aztecs lived out the principle of movement, which they saw in their gods, in life, in man, and in all created beings and things. That is why their culture and art have a deep dynamism hidden beneath an apparently static quality. The essence, the *being* of their concept of the world is dynamic. But it is essential to discover the deep significance of that dynamism, to understand exactly how they felt it, imagined it, and thought about it. And to do that, one must return to Coatlicue in order never to stray from our points of departure and destination.[47]

Fernández achieved his objective of discovering, through sculpture, the Aztec concept of the world. Evidence of this is found in his phenomenological approach to and analysis of Coatlicue, and in the conclusions he draws at the end of his study.

In the Bibliography the reader will find a number of other works by investigators who, in a less direct way, have been concerned with the mind of ancient Mexico.

[47] Fernández, *Coatlicue,* 249–50.

Bibliography

I. PRIMARY SOURCES

Anales de Cuauhtitlán, in *Códice Chimalpopoca*. Photographic edition and translation by Primo F. Velázquez. Mexico City, Imprenta Universitaria, 1945. See also Walter Lehmann, *Die Geschichte der Königreiche von Colhuacan und Mexico.*

Anales de Quauhtinchan, or *Historia Tolteca-Chichimeca*. Ed. and annotated by H. Berlin in collaboration with Silvia Rendon, and with a Prologue by P. Kirchhoff; *Colección Fuentes para la Historia de México*. Mexico City, Robredo, 1947.

Anderson, Arthur J. O., and Charles E. Dibble, trs. *Florentine Codex* (Sahagún's *History*). Books I, II, III, IV, V, VII, VIII, IX, X, XII. Santa Fe, the School of American Research and the University of Utah, 1950–61.

Chimalpain Cuauhtlihuanitzin, Domingo. *Diferentes Historias originales de los reynos de Culhuacan y México, y de otras provincias*. Tr. and ed. by Ernst Mengin. Hamburg, 1950.

———. *Sixième et Septième Relations* (1358–1612). Tr. and published by Remi Siméon, Paris, 1889.

Clavijero, Francisco Xavier. *Historia Antigua de México*. 4 vols. in *Colección de Escritores Mexicanos*. Mexico City, Editorial Porrúa, 1945.

Codex Borbonicus. Mexican manuscript in the Library of the Palais Bourbon. Facsimile ed. with commentary by E. T. Hamy. Paris, 1899.

Codex Borgia. Mexican manuscript *Borgia* of the Ethnographic Museum of the S. *Congr. di Prop. Fide.* Reproduced in facsimile by the Duke of Loubat with the permission of the Vatican Library. Rome, 1898.

Codex Fejérváry-Mayer. Pre-Columbian Mexican manuscript in the Free Public Museum of Liverpool (M 12014). Chromophotographic ed. published by the Duke of Loubat, Paris, 1901.

Codex Mendoza. Ed. and tr. by James Cooper Clark. London, 1938. The Mexican manuscripts known as the Collection Mendoza are in the Bodleian Library, Oxford.

Codex Telleriano-Remensis. Mexican manuscript of the office of Ar. M. le Tellier, archbishop of Rheims, now in the Bibliothèque Nationale (MS Mex. 385). Paris, E. T. Hamy, 1899.

Codex Vaticanus A (Ríos). Vatican Mexican manuscript 3738, called the Ríos codex. Reproduced in facsimile by the Duke of Loubat with the permission of the Vatican Library. Rome, 1900.

Codex Vaticanus B. Vatican Mexican manuscript 3773. Reproduced in facsimile by the Duke of Loubat with the permission of the Vatican Library. Rome, 1896.

Códice Florentino (illustrations). Facsimile ed. of Vol. V by Francisco del Paso y Troncoso. Madrid, 1905.

Códice Florentino (Bernardino de Sahagún, *General History of the Things of New Spain*). Book VI and Book XI are unpublished; see Arthur J. O. Anderson and Charles E. Dibble, *Florentine Codex*, for published translation.

Códice Franciscano, Siglo XVI, in Icazbalceta (ed.), *Nueva Colección de Documentos para la Historia de México.* Mexico City, Chávez Hayhoe, 1941.

Códice Matritense del Real Palacio (Nahuatl texts of the Indian informants of Sahagún). Facsimile ed. of Vol. VI (Part 2) and Vol. VII by Francisco del Paso Y Troncoso. Madrid, Hauser y Menet, 1906.

Códice Matritense de la Real Academia de la Historia (Nahuatl texts of the Indian informants of Sahagún). Facsimile ed. of Vol. VIII by Francisco del Paso y Troncoso. Madrid, Hauser y Menet, 1907.

Códice Ramírez. The origin of the Indians of New Spain, according to their histories. Mexico City, Editorial Leyenda, 1944.

Díaz del Castillo, Bernal. *Historia verdadera de la Conquista de la Nueva España.* 3 vols. Mexico City, Robredo, 1939.

Durán, Diego de. *Historia de las Indias de Nueva España y Islas de Tierra firme.* 2 vols. and atlas. Mexico City, Jose F. Ramírez, 1867–80.

García Icazbalceta, Joaquín, ed. *Nueva Colección de Documentos para la Historia de México.* 5 vols. Mexico City, 1886–92.

Garibay K., Angel María. *Epica Náhuatl. Bibl. del Estudiante Universitario,* No. 51. Mexico City, 1945.

———. *Historia de la Literatura Náhuatl.* Mexico City, Editorial Porrúa, 1953–54.

———, tr. "Huehuetlatolli, Documento A," *Tlalocan,* Vol. I (1943), 31–53, 81–107.

———. *Llave del Náhuatl, Colección de Trozos Clásicos con Gramática y Vocabulario, para utilidad de los Principiantes.* Mexico City, Otumba, 1940 (2nd. ed., 1961).

———. "Paralipómenos de Sahagún," *Tlalocan,* Vol. I (1943–44), 307–313, Vol. II (1946), 167–74, 249–54.

———. Prologue and introductions to each book of Sahagún, *Historia General de las cosas de Nueva España.* 4 vols. Mexico City, Editorial Porrúa, 1956.

———. "Relación Breve de las Fiestas de los Dioses" (compiled by Bernardino de Sahagún), *Tlalocan,* Vol. II (1948), 289–320.

———. *Veinte Himnos Sacros de los Nahuas* (Informants of Sahagún 2). *Seminario de Cultura Náhuatl, Instituto de Historia.* Mexico City, National University of Mexico, 1958.

"Historia de los Mexicanos por sus pinturas," (Olmos?) in Icazbalceta, ed., *Nueva Colección de Documentos para la Historia de México,* III.

Ixtlilxóchitl, Fernando de Alva. *Obras Históricas.* 2 vols. Mexico City, 1891–92.

Jonghe, Edouard de. "Histoire du Mechique" (MS de Thevet), *Journal de la Societé des Americanistes de Paris,* Vol. II (1905), 1–41.

Bibliography

Kingsborough, Lord Edward King. *Antiquities of Mexico.* 9 vols. London, 1831–48.

Lehmann, Walter. *Die Geschichte der Königreiche von Colhuacan und Mexico.* Vol. I in *Quellenwerke zur alten Geschichte Amerikas.* Contains texts of *Annals of Cuauhtitlán* and *Leyenda de los Soles* with German translation by Lehmann. Stuttgart, 1938.

———. *Sterbende Götter und Christliche Heilsbotschaft, Wechselreden Indianischer Vornehmer und Spanischer Glaubenapostel in Mexiko, 1524* [*Colloquies and Christian Doctrine*]. Spanish and Mexican text with German translation. Stuttgart, 1949.

León-Portilla, Miguel. *Ritos, Sacerdotes y Atavíos de los Dioses* (Informants of Sahagún 1). *Seminario de Cultura Náhuatl, Instituto de Historia.* Mexico City, National University of Mexico, 1958.

Mendieta, Geronimo de. *Historia Eclesiástica Indiana.* Mexico, 1870; 2nd. ed., Mexico City, Chávez Hayhoe, 1945.

Mengin, Ernst, ed. *Historia Tolteca-Chichimeca.* Vol. I of the *Corpus Codicum Americanorum Medii Aevi.* Cophenhagen, Sumptibus Einar Munksgaard, 1942.

———, and Konrad Preuss. *Die Mexikanische Bilderhandschrift Historia Tolteca-Chichimeca, übersetz und erläutert von* . . . . Parts 1 and 2. Berlin, Baesler Archives, 1937–38.

Molina, Alonso de. *Vocabulario en lengua castellana y mexicana.* Facsimile ed. is Vol. IV of the *Colección de Incunables Americanos.* Madrid, 1944.

Motolinía, Toribio. *Memoriales.* Paris, 1903.

———. *Historia de los Indios de la Nueva España.* Mexico City, Chávez Hayhoe, 1941.

Muñoz Camargo, Diego. *Historia de Tlaxcala.* Mexico City, Chavero, 1892.

Olmos, Andrés de. *MSS en Náhuatl (Huehuetlatolli).* The original is preserved in the Library of Congress, Washington, D.C.

———. *Arte para aprender la lengua mexicana* (includes first part of *MSS en Náhuatl*). Paris, 1875.

Paso y Troncoso, Francisco del, ed. *Leyenda de los Soles.* Florence, 1903.

Peñafiel, Antonio. *Colección de Cantares Mexicanos.* MSS in the

National Library of Mexico. Photographic ed., Mexico City, 1904.

Pomar, Juan Bautista. *Relación de Texcoco*, in Icazbalceta, ed., *Nueva Colección de Documentos para la Historia de México*, III. Mexico City, 1891.

Sahagún, Bernardino de. *Historia General de las Cosas de Nueva España.*
Ed. by Carlos María de Bustamante. 3 vol. Mexico City, 1829.
Ed. by Robredo, 5 vols., Mexico City, 1938.
Ed. by Miguel Acosta Saignes. 3 vols. Mexico City, 1946.
Ed. by A. M. Garibay. 4 vols. Mexico City, Porrúa, 1956.
All quotations in this book are from the Acosta Saignes edition.

Schultze Jena, Leonhard. *Alt-aztekische Gesänge, nach einer in der Bibl. Nacional von Mexiko aufbewahrten Handscrift, übersetz und erläutert von* . . . . Vol. VI in *Quellenwerke zur alten Geschichte Amerikas.* Stuttgart, 1957.

———. *Gliederung des alt-aztekischen Volks in Familie Stand und Beruf, aus dem aztekischen Urtext Bernardino de Sahagún's.* Vol. V in *Quellenwerke zur alten Geschichte Amerikas.* Stuttgart, 1952.

———. *Wahrsagerei, Himmelskunde und Kalender der alten Azteken, aus dem aztekischen Urtext Bernardino de Sahagún's.* Vol. IV in *Quellenwerke zur alten Geschichte Amerikas.* Stuttgart, 1950.

Seler, Eduard. *Einige Kapitel aus dem Geschichtswerk des P. Sahagún, aus dem Aztekischen übersetzt von Eduard Seler.* Ed. by C. Seler-Sachs in collaboration with Walter Lehmann. Stuttgart, 1927.

———. *Gesammelte Abhandlungen zur Amerikanischen Sprach und Altertumskunde.* 5 vols. Berlin, Ascher und Co. and Behrend und Co., 1902–23.

Tezozomoc, F. Alvarado. *Crónica Mexicana.* Mexico City, Vigil, reprinted by Editorial Leyenda, Mexico City, 1944.

———. *Crónica Mexicáyotl.* Paleography and Spanish version by Adrián León. Mexico City, Imprenta Universitaria, 1949.

Thevet, A. See Edouard de Jonghe.

Torquemada, Juan de. *Los Veintiún Libros Rituales y Monarquía*

Indiana. 3 vols. 2nd ed., Madrid, 1723, published in facsimile, Mexico City, 1943.

Tovar, Juan de, S. J. *Historia de los indios mexicanos* (*Códice Ramirez*). Mexico City, 1944.

Zurita, Alonso de. *Breve y Sumaria Relación de los Señores de la Nueva España* in Icazbalceta, ed., *Nueva Colección de Documentos para la Historia de México.* Mexico, 1891.

II. SECONDARY SOURCES

Acosta, Joseph de, S. J. *Historia Natural y Moral de las Indias.* Mexico City, Fondo de Cultura Económica, 1940, 1962.

Alba, Carlos H. *Estudio comparado entre el Derecho azteca y el Derecho Positivo Mexicano.* Mexico City, Instituto Indigenista Interamericano, 1949.

Barlow, Robert H. *The Extent of the Empire of the Culhua Mexica.* Iberoamericana 28. Berkeley and Los Angeles, University of California Press, 1949.

Beyer, Hermann. "*Uber Namenshieroglyphe des Kodex Humboldt,*" and "*Das aztekishe Götterbild Alexander von Humboldt.*" In *Wissenschaftliche Festschrift zu Enthüllung des von Seiten S. M. Kaiser Wilhelm II, dem Mexicanischen Volke zum Jubiläum, seiner Unabhängigkeit Gestifteten Humboldt-Denkmals, von . . . .* Mexico City, Müller hnos., 1910.

Boturini Benaducci, Lorenzo de. *Idea de una Nueva Historia General de la América Septentrional.* Madrid, 1748.

Brinton, Daniel G. *Ancient Nahuatl Poetry.* Philadelphia, 1887.

Campos, Rubén M. *La Producción Literaria de los Aztecas.* Mexico City, 1936.

Carochi, Horacio, S. J. *Arte de la Lengua Mexicana.* Mexico City, 1892.

Casas, Bartolomé de las. *Historia de las Indias.* 2 vols. Mexico City, 1877.

Caso, Alfonso. "*El Aguila y el Nopal,*" *Memorias* of the Mexican Academy of History, Vol. V (1946), 93–104.

———. "*El Paraíso Terrenal en Teotihuacán,*" *Cuadernos Americanos,* Vol. VI (1942), 127–36.

———. *El Pueblo del Sol.* Mexico City, Fondo de Cultura Económica, 1954; English ed., Norman, University of Oklahoma Press, 1958.

————. *La Religión de los Aztecas*. Mexico City, Enciclopedia Ilustrada Mexicana, 1936.

————. *"Las Ruinas de Tizatlán," Revista Mexicana de Estudios Históricos*, Vol. I (1927), 139–72.

————. *Trece obras Maestras de la arqueología Mexicana*. Mexico City, 1938.

Chavero, Alfredo. *México a través de los siglos. Historia Antigua y de la Conquista* is Vol. I. Mexico City and Barcelona, Ballesca, Espasa y Cía., n.d.

Comas, Juan. *"Influencia indígena en la medicina hipocrática," América Indígena*, Vol. XIV (1954), 327–61.

Cornyn, John H. *The Song of Quetzalcóatl*. Yellow Springs, Ohio, 1930.

Dávalos H., Eusebio. *"La alimentación entre los Mexica," Revista Mexicana de Estudios Antropológicos*, Vol. XIV (1954–55), Pt. 1, p. 107.

Domínguez Assiayn, Salvador. *"Filosofía de los antiguos Mexicanos," Revista Contemporáneos*, Nos. 42–43 (1931), 209–25.

Edman, Irwin. *Arts and the Man*. New York, New American Library, 1949.

Fernández, Justino. *Coatlicue, estética del arte indígena antiguo*. Prologue by Samuel Ramos. Mexico City, Centro de Estudios Filosóficos, 1954; 2nd ed., 1959.

Gamio, Manuel. *Forjando Patria*. Mexico City, Librería de Porrúa, 1916, 1960.

————, and others. *La Población del Valle de Teotihuacán*. 3 vols. Mexico City, Dir. de Talleres Gráficos de la Nación, 1922.

García Bacca, Juan D. *"Comentarios a la Esencia de la Poesía de Heidegger," Revista Nacional de Cultura*, Nos. 112–13 (Sept.–Dec., 1955).

Genin, Auguste. *Légendes et Récits du Mexique ancien*. Paris, les Editions Ct. Crés et Cie, 1923.

Gillmor, Frances. *Flute of the Smoking Mirror, a portrait of Nezahualcóyotl, poet-king of the Aztecs*. Albuquerque, University of New Mexico Press, 1949.

Hernández, Francisco. *De Antiquitatibus Novae Hispaniae*. Facsimile ed. of the *Códice Matritense de la Real Academia de la*

Bibliography

Historia. Mexico City, 1926. Spanish tr. by L. Garcia Pimentel; Mexico City, Robredo, 1945.

Hernández Luna, Juan. "*El Iniciador de la historia de las ideas en Mexico,*" *Filosofía y Letras,* Nos. 51–52 (July–December, 1953), 55–80.

Huxley, Aldous. *Introduction to the Song of God, Bhagavad-Gita.* New York, New American Library, 1954.

Imbelloni, José. "*El Génesis de los pueblos proto-históricos de América.*" In *Boletín de la Academia Argentina de Ciencias Naturales,* VIII and following. Buenos Aires, 1942.

Jaeger, Werner. *Paideia, los ideales de la cultura griega.* 3 vols. Mexico City, Fondo de Cultura Económica, 1942–45.

Jiménez Moreno, Wigberto. "*Fr. Bernardino de Sahagún y su obra,*" in Sahagún, *Historia General de las Cosas de Nueva España,* I, pp. XIII–LXXXI. Mexico City, Robredo, 1938.

Katz, Friedrich. *Die Sozialökonomischen Verhältnisse bei den Azteken im 15. und 16. Jahrhundert.* In *Ethnographisch-archäologische Forschungen,* III, Pt. 2. Berlin, Veb Deutscher Velarg der Wissenschaften, 1956.

Kohler, J. *El derecho de los aztecas.* Mexico City, Revista Jurídica, 1924.

Kirckeberg, Walter von. *Altmexikanische Kulturen.* Berlin, Safari Verlag, 1956.

La Rosa, Agustín de. *Estudio de la Filosofía y Riqueza de la Lengua Mexicana.* Guadalajara, 1889. Appeared in part in *Et Caetera,* No. 1 (March, 1950).

Lehmann, Walter. "*Die Bedeutung der altamerikanischen Hochkulturen für allgemeine Geschichte der Menschheit,*" *Ibero-Amerikanisches Archiv,* April–July, 1943, pp. 65–71.

León-Portilla, Miguel, *Siete Ensayos sobre Cultura Náhuatl. Colección Facultad de Filosofía y Letras,* No. 31. Mexico City, National University of Mexico, 1958.

León y Gama, Antonio. *Descripción de dos misteriosas piedras que en el año de 1790 se desenterraron en la plaza mayor de México.* 2nd ed., Mexico City, 1832.

McAfee, Byron and Robert H. Barlow. *Diccionario de elementos fonéticos en escritura jeroglífica (Códice Mendocino).* Mexico City, Instituto de Historia, 1949.

Marquina, Ignacio. *"Estudio arquitectónico de la pirámide,"* in *Tenayuca,* an archaeological study of the pyramids of Tenayuca made for the Department of Monuments of the Secretariat of Public Education. Mexico City, 1935.

Martínez, Henrico. *Reportorio de los Tiempos e Historia Natural de Nueva España.* Mexico City, 1948.

Mendieta y Nuñez, Lucio. *"El derecho mexicano antes de la Conquista,"* *Ethnos,* Vol. I, Nos. 8–12 (1922), 168–86.

Monzón, Arturo. *El Calpulli en la Organización Social de los Tenochca.* Mexico City, Instituto de Historia, 1949.

Nicolau d'Olwer, Luis. *Fray Bernardino de Sahagún* (1499–1590). *Colección de Historiadores de America.* Mexico City, Instituto Panamericano de Geografía e Historia, 1952.

Noguera, Eduardo. *"Los altares de sacrificio de Tizatlán,"* in *Ruinas de Tizatlán,* Vol. XX, No. 20 (1929), *Publications* of the Secretariat of Education.

———. *"Bibliografía de los Códices precolombinos y documentos indígenas posteriores a la Conquista,"* in *Anales* (1933), National Museum.

Orozco y Berra, Manuel. *Historia Antigua y de la Conquista de México.* 4 vols. and atlas. Mexico, 1880; 2nd ed. (Garibay, ed.) Mexico City, Porrúa, 1960.

Ramos, Samuel. *Historia de la Filosofía en México.* Mexico City, Imprenta Universitaria, 1943.

Robelo, Cecilio A. *Diccionario de Mitología Náhuatl,* Mexico City, 1911.

Robertson, Donald. *Mexican Manuscript Painting of the Early Colonial Period.* New Haven, Yale University Press, 1959.

Séjourné, Laurette. *Burning Water; Thought and religion in ancient Mexico.* London, Thames and Hudson, 1957.

Simeón, Remi. *Dictionaire de la Langue Nahuatl.* Paris, 1885.

Soustelle, Jacques. *"Apuntes sobre la psicología colectiva y el sistema de valores en México antes de la Conquista,"* in *Estudios Antropológicos publicados en homenaje al doctor Manuel Gamio,* 497–502. Mexico City, Universidad Nacional de México, 1956.

———. *La Pensée Cosmologique des anciens mexicains.* Paris, Hermann et Cie, 1940.

Bibliography

————. *La Vie Quotidienne des Aztèques à la Veille de la Conquête Espagnole*. Paris, Librairie Hachtte, 1955.

Spence, Lewis, *The Civilization of Ancient Mexico*, Cambridge, 1912.

————. *The Gods of Mexico*. London, 1923.

————. *The Magic and Misteries of Mexcio*. London, n.d.

Spinden, Herbert J. *Ancient Civilizations of Mexico and Central America*. New York, 1943.

Toscano, Salvador. *Arte Pre-colombino de México y de la América Central*. 2nd ed. Mexico City, Instituto de Investigaciones Estéticas, 1952.

————. *Derecho y Organización social de los Aztecas*. Mexico City, 1937.

Vaillant, George C. *The Aztecs of Mexico*: Origin, Rise, and Fall of the Aztec Nation. New York, Doubleday, 1941.

Van Zantwijk, Rudolf A. M. "Aztec Hymns as the Expression of the Mexican Philosophy of Life," *Internationales Archiv für Etnographie*, Vol. XLVIII, No. 1 (1957), pp. 67–118.

Veytia, Mariano. *Historia Antigua de México*. 2 vols. Mexico City, Editorial Leyenda, 1944.

Walcot, E. Emmart. *The Badianus Manuscript*. Baltimore, Johns Hopkins Press, 1940.

Westheim, Paul. *Arte Antiguo de México*. Mexico City, Fondo de Cultura Económica, 1950.

Index

Index

Index

AZTEC THOUGHT AND CULTURE

has been set on the Linotype in eleven-point Caledonia, with
two points of spacing between lines. Caledonia was designed by
the late W. A. Dwiggins, the eminent American graphic artist,
who said of his creation that, while it resembles Scotch Modern,
which he admired, it also has something of Bulmer: in his own
words, "it touches both of them in spots." Caledonia has that
straightforward quality which has kept Scotch Modern in service
for so many years.

UNIVERSITY OF OKLAHOMA PRESS

NORMAN